Snow Babies, Santas and Elves

Collecting Christmas Bisque Figures

Mary Morrison

Mary Morrison

Photography by James Morrison

Schiffer Publishing Ltd

77 Lower Valley Road, Atglen, PA 19310

Published by Schiffer Publishing, Ltd.
77 Lower Valley Road
Atglen, PA 19310
Please write for a free catalog.
This book may be purchased from the publisher.
Please include $2.95 postage.
Try your bookstore first.

We are interested in hearing from authors
with book ideas on related subjects.

Printed in the United States of America.
ISBN: 0-88740-493-6

Table of Contents

Tables

Toward the back you will find two tables. Table 1 lists each piece with its "vital statistics." Included in this chart is a rarity scale and a price guide.

Table 2 includes only those pieces that have incised numbers; these are listed in numerical order. I have made many discoveries using this table. You might use it to find mates to your pieces or additional members of sets, or even to determine the manufacturer of a figure.

Acknowledgements

This research was begun by Mary Lou Edmiston, who built a collection of snow babies over a twenty year period. During that time she photographed each piece and kept careful records. Without her records I might not have undertaken this project. Her photographs are used for Figs 6.7, 6.12, 10.35, 10.78, 10.155, 13.50, 13.80, 15.16 and 15.17.

Beginning with this base, I studied and photographed forty collections on the East and West Coast and in the Midwest. Some of those collections are small; others contain hundreds of pieces. It seems astonishing, but in every collection, even small ones, there were "new" pieces to see and photograph. Some pieces did appear over and over, but many more were seen in only one or two collections.

It was the generosity of so many collectors that has allowed me to show such a broad assortment of pieces. Some collectors even brought or mailed pieces to be photographed! Along with my own collection and that of one anonymous collector, the pieces shown belong to:

Janet A. Banneck	Calvin and Kathy Levorson
Carola Bardwell	Jay B. Lewis
Bertha M. Bell	George & Elizabeth Mason
Denise Carpenter	Dianne Michels
Dorothy W. Cate	Cherie Wendelken Mortensen
Ron & Bobbie Cecil	Marie & John Myers
Ann Marie Coffel	June Nelson
Elaine Doran	Patti H. Peters
Ray Early	Mary Louise T. Peterson
David D. Eppelheimer	Bettie Petzoldt
Joyce Fuller	Margaret Schiffer
Marilyn Gunning	Carol Smith
Tim Hagerman	Nancy E. Smith
Marlene Hagerman	Elaine F. Spencer
Kate Hoffman	Mary E. Spencer
Gretchen Jackson	Marcie & Jayde Thueringer
Kathy Jackson	Terry Tiefenbrunn
Tracy Jackson	Charlotte Vizzier
Barbara Levitan	Evelyn Yoder

Many collectors and dealers have been generous with their own ideas, sharing theories, family history and personal research. Others pored over mountains of pictures to help me evaluate snow baby pieces for rarity and current market price. For these contributions I am grateful to:

Carola Bardwell	Janet Middleton
Elaine Doran	James Morrison (of Maryland)
Ray Early	Cherie Wendelken Mortensen
Mary Lou Edmiston	John Myers
Helen Forsythe	Marie Myers
Jean Crowley Goodman	Patti Peters
Tim Hagerman	Bettie Petzoldt
Kate Hoffman	Donald Pinegar
June King	Nancy Stewart
John Maxwell	Ann Wyatt

Jean Crowley Goodman's careful research on snow babies in the 1970s has formed the basis for almost everything written about them since. She reexamined her old notes and agreed to be frequently badgered about her sources of information.

Ray and Eileen Early produced the only previous book devoted to snow babies. Until now it has been the "snow baby bible". Ray invited me to photograph his collection. His help has been invaluable.

I am deeply indebted to Robert Peary Stafford, Marie Peary's grandson, and Edward Peary Stafford, her son. Each of them generously granted me interviews and allowed me to examine and photograph family pictures and heirlooms.

No one could have been favored with a better mate for this project than mine. My husband, James, shares my love of snow babies. His clear, careful photographs are certainly the high point of this book. He is also my friend, my sweetheart and often my inspiration.

Mary Morrison September, 1992

Introduction

When were snow babies first made, and why? What do they include? How many different ones were made? Why are they so hard to find? Collectors and dealers ask these and many other questions about snow babies. In this book I have tried to explore these questions, to examine what has been written about snow babies, to separate facts from assumptions and to locate information that would add substantially to what collectors already know.

Is It a Snow Baby?

The term "snow baby" can be defined broadly or narrowly. I have used it to refer only to grouted or ungrouted porcelain figures that include a baby or child. The broader term "snow baby piece" includes the other porcelain figures used in Christmas or winter snow baby scenes, or as table or mantel decorations. This term encompasses a wide range of fanciful figures, including babies, children, Santas, polar bears, snowmen, elves and dwarves.

The book focuses on snow baby pieces made before 1950, but chapter 19 shows some recently produced pieces. Also included are some related items sought by snow baby collectors, such as memorabilia related to the Peary family, post cards and a few valentines. And there are some displays of bisque-headed, cotton-bodied children. Collectors use them much like snow baby figures in Christmas scenes; some even call them snow babies.

Snow and No-Snow Pieces

Is the piece snow or no-snow? There has been confusion about the use of these terms. The distinction is easy if the figure wears a grout-covered suit. But the terms have been applied inconsistently to unsnowed figures on grouted bases, or pieces with glitter or coralene snow.

Here the terms "snow" and "snowed" refer to a snow baby piece that has coralene, glitter, crystal or grout of any color added to any part of the piece, including the base. The critical feature for defining a snowed piece is that some portion of it must have a snow-like finish that was applied after molding. All other figures will be called no-snow pieces. For example, a bisque figure without snow that stands on a snowed base is a snowed piece.

Nomenclature

If a piece is finished with a glaze over the paint, sometimes called a china finish, the picture caption will say so. If the finish is not stated in the caption, the piece is bisque.

The captions also indicate whether the piece (or another example of the piece) has been incised or stamped in any way. The majority of unmarked pieces pictured are German. If I suspect that an unmarked piece is not German, I say so in the caption. However, without seeing marked examples no one can be absolutely certain.

Measurement and Size

Each piece was measured to the nearest quarter-inch, vertically, from the surface on which it rests to its highest point. To be consistent, I have resisted the temptation to measure the length of a piece when the figure is lying down.

Many snow baby pieces are found in more than one size, probably because the process for making smaller sizes was so easy. First a mold was made from a fired piece. A figure cast from this new mold would shrink about 20% when it was fired. If a further reduction was desired, the new piece could serve as the model for yet another new mold. Pieces cast and fired from this second mold would shrink another 20%, and so on. The process was economically sound: when another mold was needed, no artist was needed to re-sculpt a figure.

Organization of Chapters

The two distinct periods of snow baby production were separated by World War I. This book generally presents the earlier pieces in the first chapters. But because the chapters themselves are organized by type of figure, some chapters show pieces from both periods. For example, the section on container pieces (chapter 7) appears early in the book because the most important of these were made before World War I. However, it also pictures tiny candleholders made in the 1920s and 1930s and a few pieces from as late as the 1940s. The Santa chapter appears later, because most Santas were produced in the 1920s, but a few may have been made before World War I.

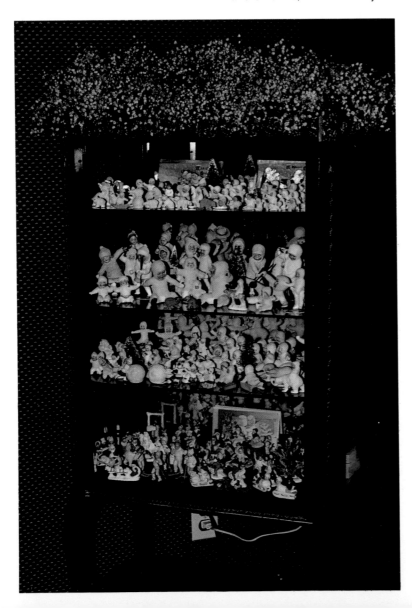

Chapter 1
Beginnings

SNOW BABY BEGINNINGS

Were the earliest snow baby figures made to commemorate the birth of Admiral Peary's daughter, Marie? Many collectors and writers have thought so, but this is an area where assumptions are difficult to tell from fact. There are two versions of the beginnings of the bisque snow babies. One is the American story of Marie Peary; the other places the origins of snow babies far earlier, in Germany.

Zuckerpuppen

Harry Wilson Shuart, in *Spinning Wheel* (1970), wrote that as long ago as the early 19th century, German candy toys in the shapes of igloos, polar bears and little sugar dolls, or *Zuckerpuppen,* were used to make scenes under Christmas trees. The original pieces were a mixture of flour, sugar and tragacanth (a gum that was used as a thickener). Later the pieces were made of marzipan.

June Fairchild, writing in the *Toy Trader* in 1970, stated that a confectioner, Gotthold Mueller, wished to use little marzipan figures in the displays he made for fairs. He and his wife, Lina, created prize-winning snow scenes using hundreds of figures made of white fondant, which they rolled in sugar to look like snow. Mueller also wanted to display brightly colored marzipan candies shaped like fruits and vegetables, so he sculpted a baby with outstretched arms to serve as a holder. A mold was made from the clay baby, so that it could be reproduced in bisque.

Mueller had never worked in porcelain, so he didn't know that when the castings were made and fired they would shrink by about 20%. When the first bisque babies were ready, the Muellers were bitterly disappointed. Only the eyes of the baby showed over the marzipan candy they placed in its arms. When they tried to sit it up without the candy, it tipped over backwards. (Could Fig 5.22a be this piece?)

Now return to Shuart's account. He stated that the firm of Johann Moll, a confectioner in Lubbeck, had commissioned Hertwig and Company to recreate the marzipan babies in bisque. Shuart contacted Herr Keil, the director of the Deutches Spielzeugmuseum [German Toy Museum] of Sonneberg, Germany. Herr Keil verified that Hertwig and Company produced the first snowbabies, and added that many other porcelain manufacturers in Thueringia made them, also.

How are the stories of Mueller and Moll related? Did Mueller work for Moll? Did each of them develop snow babies at about the same time? At present, no one knows the answer.

I also wrote to the Toy Museum in Sonneberg. Gudrun Volk, the curator, responded with information about some of the firms known to have made snow babies. But she also said that the museum didn't actually know very much about snow babies. I later wrote to

Fig 1.1 Two sizes of the famous Cook and Peary piece. Each is stamped "Made in Germany" in a donut. Every example I have seen has beautifully detailed faces, and each is stamped in the same aqua color. The numbers are incised by hand and difficult to read. **a.** This size is seldom seen. #9439; 4.37"
b. This size is more often seen, but it is by no means common. I have also seen an example stamped with the Heber and Company shield. #9447; 3.5"

Fig 1.2 Very rare no-snow version of the look and Peary pieces shown previously (Fig 1.1). The numbers are incised by hand and are difficult to read. Stamped with the Heber and Company shield (Fig 23.6). #9439; 3.5"

Marianne and Jürgen Cieslik, authors of the German Doll Encylopedia (1985), because they had also published an article on snow babies (1987). Marianne Cieslik wrote back, "There is no information in Germany about snow babies because they were only produced for the American market. We never found a correct German word for the figures!"

Marie Peary

The other, more popular account of the origin of porcelain snow babies is that they were made to honor Marie Peary, the daughter of Robert Peary, discoverer of the North Pole. This idea was first advanced in print by Jean Crowley Goodman (Crowley 1978). She believes that the piece showing Peary and Cook dressed as snow babies climbing the globe indicates that there was a close connection between the Peary family and snow babies. She reasons that it made no sense to commemorate such an important event by depicting these explorers as babies unless a connection already existed.

It is not necessary to choose the Peary or the Zuckerpuppen version; in a sense they may both be right. It is entirely believable that porcelain snow babies were being developed at a time when the world had focused its attention on polar exploration. Why wouldn't German novelty makers exploit that interest and, with inexpensive but charming bisque figures, encourage the Americans and the British to create fanciful little polar scenes of their own?

Polar Exploration

We live in an age when we can see films of the first moon walk and witness almost instant replays of war on our television sets. So it is difficult for us to comprehend how the idea of polar exploration must have seemed to the people of the United States and Europe at the end of the nineteenth century. Much has changed in the field of communications. In those pre-radio times, explorers far from civilization could spend months or years isolated from the outside world.

Even less was known about the North Pole at the turn of the century than is known about the surface of the moon today. For over 300 years explorers had been searching for a northern water route between the Atlantic and Pacific oceans. Often referred to as the Northwest Passage, such a route would provide safe journey for Europeans to the riches of the Far East. The alternative was a long and dangerous trip around the southern tip of South America. Fame and wealth awaited anyone who pioneered the shorter northern route.

Whaling, fur trade and the lure of discovery also drew brave men to the frigid Arctic, but these adventurers, too, faced many dangers. In the winter, temperatures fell as low as minus 85 degrees Fahrenheit. Blizzards could spring up at any time. Starvation was always a threat. Despite the danger many men made their way into the trackless arctic regions. Sometimes whole shiploads never reappeared.

The Snow Baby Arrives

In 1891 the nation was shocked to learn that a woman intended to spend the winter in Greenland. Josephine Peary, young wife of the explorer, would be the first white woman to winter over where so many men had lost their lives. Accompanying her husband and a

Fig 1.3 Container piece of uncertain function, possibly an ink well, that shows a caricature of Peary surmounting the globe and holding an American flag. The piece is hinged across the jaw, so that the top of Peary's head tips back to reveal the container. Incised "Germany". 3.0"

party of five other men, she proposed to spend long dark months in as desolate and forbidding a spot as most Americans could imagine.

Despite its dangers, her stay was such a success that two years later she decided to return with Peary, even though their first child was due that fall. And so in Greenland Marie Ahnighito Peary was born September 8, 1893. The story has been told time and again about the white baby whom dark-skinned natives came hundreds of miles to see and touch. They called her "Ah-poo-mick-ananny," Eskimo for snow baby. Her parents gave her the middle name "Ahnighito," after the woman who sewed her little fur suit. As an adult, Marie observed that this seemed an unlikely reason for choosing anyone's name. She said that she always suspected her parents simply found it amusing to give the initials "MAP" to the daughter of a famous explorer (Peary 1934).

After the Greenland trip when Marie was born, Peary spent much of the next 16 years seeking the North Pole. As an officer in the US Navy throughout this period, he needed leave to make his long journeys. He also needed to raise the money to fund these trips. As a consequence, when not exploring, his life was a constant struggle to keep the quest for the North Pole in the public eye. Peary and Josephine lectured and wrote books. The most enduring of these books—those that most interest snow baby collectors—are the children's books, two of which center around Marie and her life in the North.

Conquest of the North Pole

In July of 1908 Peary left on the expedition that would finally take him to the North Pole. Accompanied by Matthew Henson and several Eskimos, he reached his goal on April 6, 1909. It wasn't until August, when he returned to native villages in Greenland, that he heard the shocking news. His former companion, Dr. Frederick Cook, claimed to have reached the pole nearly a year earlier on April 21, 1908.

The controversy over who got to the North Pole first, or whether Cook ever got there at all, has never been entirely resolved. Much of the difficulty lies in the fact that the Pole is situated on ice in the Arctic Ocean. Because ice drifts at sea, a spot that at one time may have been at the North Pole would later have drifted south. If the Pole were on land,

Fig 1.4 Figural pitcher in the form of a head and torso of Admiral Peary, whose name appears in large letters across the lower front. He is dressed in a fur parka with the collar turned up. A pouch hangs from a strap across his shoulder. The porcelain is very thin and glazed, much like Schafer and Vater figural pitchers. I have seen a similar mug with the image of President Taft, who was president of the United States at the time Peary reached the North Pole. Incised "Germany". #5569; 4.37"

Fig 1.5 This and Fig 1.6 are taken from a small photo album of pictures of Marie Peary, assembled and hand-lettered by Admiral Peary himself. Marie would have been about five or six in this photo, which is labeled "First Schooldays".

Fig 1.6 From the same album as the above, this photo was taken at the time Marie graduated from high school in about 1911. She is standing behind her mother, Josephine, and her brother, Robert Peary, Jr., who would have been about eight years old.

physical traces might have remained to prove which explorer had actually been there. Recent photographic studies by the National Geographic Society have finally determined that Peary's photographs were actually taken at the Pole.

Like her adventuresome parents, Marie spent much of her life in the public eye. First she was the famous baby born in the Arctic. As a young woman she was identified as the daughter of (and later private secretary to) her father, who was by then Admiral Peary.

Marie was perfect in her role as the Snowbaby. (She spelled this term as one word, not two as we do today.) A bright, beautiful child, she became a witty and articulate woman who wrote several children's books of her own. Of these books, only *The Snowbaby's Own Story* has received recent mention, but she wrote four books for younger children: *The Red Caboose, Little Tooktoo, Muskox* and *Ootah and His Puppy.*

But No Snow Babies

Strangely enough, neither her son, Edward Stafford, nor her grandson, Robert Stafford, recalls ever seeing bisque snow babies. While gathering material for this book I interviewed each of them. Both are certain that Marie never owned bisque snow baby pieces. They had neither seen nor heard about the fanciful pieces that shows Peary and Dr. Cook hugging the globe.

Her son recalls that various manufacturers sent her knick-knacks reminiscent of the North Pole. Edward Stafford also remembers that on several occasions she was sent little penguin pieces. In response she wrote polite thank-you letters, gently pointing out that there were no penguins in the Arctic. It is astonishing to realize that she was never sent any little snow babies.

Her grandson remembered that in each room she kept some decoration that showed polar bears. The grandchildren would make a game of finding the polar bear item, room by room. But he had never seen a snow baby polar bear.

Photographs of the interior of her home show small porcelain figurines, but none that could be mistaken for snow babies. One Peary family album contains a faded photograph of a Christmas table centerpiece, very much like a snow baby scene. On it was constructed a North Pole that looked like a mound of ice and snow with a flag at the top. Although I searched carefully, I could see no snow baby pieces in that scene, either. If Marie was the sole inspiration for these little collectibles, she seems not to have known it.

However, there can be no doubt that polar exploration was celebrated in bisque snow baby figures. For years the Cook and Peary piece has fascinated collectors. The two explorers seem actually vying to be first to reach the North Pole. (Was the piece commissioned by a Peary partisan? It is his hand that rests on the pole itself.) Whatever its origins, it could not have been conceived before August of 1909: until then, according to Robert Stafford, the two explorers were not adversaries.

Other snow baby pieces feature related themes. In Fig 10.44 two babies try to plant a flag at the top of the world. Fig 10.159 shows a baby carrying a suitcase that says, "To North Pole." And pieces showing igloos and polar bears certainly represent something other than the usual winter sports!

Peary's Home Today

Collectors today can enjoy a visit to Eagle Island, where the Peary family summer home is open to the public. Eagle Island is in Maine's Casco Bay, a spectacular one-hour boat ride from downtown Portland. During the summer months you can tour the house that Admiral Peary designed, walk through the newly restored library, and picnic on the grounds. Snow baby collectors who prize the Peary books will take special pleasure in visiting the little bedroom that was Marie's.

Books and articles about the Peary explorations and the quest for the North Pole are as thrill-packed as any adventure novel! Your local library can probably provide you with books that tell the rest of the story. But even an encyclopedia account can supplement the fascinating story, barely outlined here, of the family that has become so closely linked to the origin of snow babies.

At least in part because the Pearys needed to maintain public interest in polar exploration, we know a great deal about the early life of the child who may have inspired the bisque snow babies. Whether or not she was that inspiration, it is certain that books and articles about her helped keep a focus on Marie Peary and on polar exploration from around the turn of the century until World War II. This in turn helped to create a demand for these small bisque pieces that are still used to make little polar scenes in homes, especially at Christmas time.

Fig 1.7 The summer house Peary built on Eagle Island, Casco Bay, Maine. The cylindrical stone structure was Peary's library, which was renovated in 1991. The house remained the family home until it was given to the State of Maine. It is now open for public tour. See text.

Part I: Early Snow Baby Production

The next 8 chapters will cover those pieces that were designed and produced largely in the first period of snow baby production, before World War I.

Chapter 2
Blue Snow Children

Among the rarest snow babies are these wonderful bisque children, dressed in blue winter clothing and called "blue snows." Although other snow babies have colored snow, these figures are so consistent in style and quality that they deserve treatment as a separate category. Unlike most other snow babies, these figurines were marketed as elegant mantel or china cabinet decorations rather than as knick-knacks.

Blue snow children show quality workmanship in every aspect of their design and production. Their poses are realistic and imaginative, evidence that the sculptors who created them were gifted artists. One child carries a bowl from which milk is spilling over. The falling liquid seems to arrest a moment in time. Children carrying books rush home from school; hair and jackets blow in the wind, and one boy seems about to lose his hat. Blue snows were decorated in a few soft colors. Highlighting the faces is color so subtly applied that it seems to give life to the bisque.

Dating Blue Snows

The exact period during which blue snows were manufactured has not been documented by catalog or by any other indisputable means. However, there are reasons to believe that they were produced by Galluba and Hoffman between 1900 and 1910.

Although snow babies are rarely found with a manufacturer's mark, a few blue snows have the factory mark still clearly visible (Fig 23.5). This is the mark of Galluba & Hoffman, who made dolls and figurines from 1890 to 1926. In his book about marks on porcelain, Robert Roentgen (1981) says that the use of this particular Galluba and Hoffman mark has not been verified earlier than 1905.

Each of the blue snows shown has a four-digit number beginning with "4" incised on the underside. Even the style and size of the numerals is the same on all the pieces. It is reasonable to assume that the incised numbers were assigned to pieces in numerical order. The smallest number I have seen on a blue snow is 4194, and the greatest is 4714. This concentration within a 500-number range seems to indicate a short period of manufacture beginning around 1905.

The painting of the face also helps to date them. The red dots accenting the nostrils and the red lines on the upper eyelids below the eyebrows are typical of some dolls made before 1910; these details were not used commonly after that time.

Fig 2.1 Two casually dressed children carry milk, probably to feed the animals (the girl is wearing a pinafore; she is clearly working). It is not drudgery: they seem happy. For such a small piece, this is carefully detailed (even the pitcher has a pattern). The rust color of the boy's stocking trim and the girls's bow is repeated in many of the other pieces shown here. The boy has "GH" printed on the bib of his overalls (it is not visible in the photograph). This probably denotes Galluba & Hoffman, the company that manufactured this piece. #4614; 4.87"

Fig 2.2 Three children wearing school clothes and carrying slates and bookbags on their way to or from school. They are mounted on a snowed, rectangular base. The boys' clothing is similar to that in Fig 2.1. #4603; 6.0"

Manufacture

Under a 30-power microscope, blue snow figures reveal some surprises. Each visible surface of every chunk of pale blue snow is uniform in color. The snow is actually blue porcelain that was crushed into small nuggets of grout. The color was mixed into the liquid porcelain before firing. However, the gray or dark blue color of the trim, which accents the edges or hems of the garments, was painted on. Under the microscope you can see this clearly: only the upper surfaces of the grout show the trim color. In some places it has worn off entirely.

I have seen one piece—not a blue snow figure—on which the more common white grout had been painted gray. Under a microscope this paint looks like a chalky coating which, when wet, filled in the spaces between the snow granules. The bits of grout are no longer sharp, discrete chunks, but look more like gravel over which a mud puddle has dried. Perhaps the intention was to create the illusion of a rarer and more valuable object. A similar method could produce a counterfeit "blue snow."

Other Pieces

This chapter includes photographs of other pieces that closely resemble the blue snows. They were probably all made by Galluba and Hoffman.

Fig 2.3 (five children in summer clothing) and Fig 2.13 (standing girl counting coins) were cast in the same molds as the blue snows, but finished differently. Both examples of the girl counting coins bear the same incised number. This figure also exists unpainted, with a soft yellow wash. The large piece showing five children in summer clothing was probably made earlier than the blue snow version showing three children; it has a lower number.

Fig 2.3 Five school children in summer clothing. Three are the same figures as Fig 2.2, but two chums have been added to the base. The molding is the same as in Fig 2.2, but without snow you can see the exquisite detail. These figures are very lightly snowed; the base is completely snowed. #4563; 7.0"

Fig 2.4 Back view of Fig 2.3. Note how skirts flow as children hurry along. This five-figure piece was also made with the blue snow finish.

The girl on the sled (Fig 2.22) and the boy with the lamb pull toy (Fig 2.21) are the only pieces in this chapter without an incised number. They are molded like the blue snows, but lack coloring except for a soft yellow wash. However, the girl sledder has been pictured with a painted face and blue snow (Leuzzi & Kershner 1975). The boy with the pull toy is so similar in coloring and molding to the girl on the sled that I suspect that he was also made as a blue snow.

Fig 2.5 There is a continuity in the children used as models for the blue snow pieces. In this one the boy is older, but he still waves his hat (compare Figs 2.2 through 2.4). The sled is unusual: are the handles for steering or braking? This example is stamped with the Galluba and Hoffman shield. #4714; 3.5"

Fig 2.6 An older girl pushes a younger boy on a simple sled. The girl wears a long coat; both are warmly dressed. The rust color is picked up in the girl's bow. #4705; 3.62"

Fig 2.7 A girl dressed up in a long coat, hat and muff. Her hat appears to be decorated with feather plumes. This is an early piece: it (and Fig 2.8) bear the lowest numbers of any blue snows shown. This piece was also made with a finish similar to Fig 2.22. #4194; 4.0"

Fig 2.8 Girl with a dulcimer (or umbrella). She is lightly snowed, but the base is completely snowed. She is the only character shown in this chapter with visible shoes that are not heavily snowed. She shares some characteristics with Fig 2.7, and the mold numbers are identical. Her nose was slightly misshapen in molding. #4194; 3.5″

Fig 2.11 This child (a girl?) sits on a bench counting coins. Like the face in a fine painting, her expression makes us wonder what she is thinking. Her basket may have been a pincushion. Stamped on the bottom with the Galluba and Hoffman shield. #4647; 3.5″

Fig 2.12 This standing girl counts the coins she holds in her left hand. Although some snow is missing from the front of her cap, her delicate fingers are undamaged. This is the tallest of the blue snow pieces. This piece was also made with a basket on the base next to the girl and a finish similar to Fig 2.22. #4584; 7.5″Chapter 2/13 6143.19

Fig 2.10 Bust of a boy wearing a hat and outer garment covered with blue snow. His white shirt collar shows at his neck. He seems to be holding back tears. His molding and expression are very much like Fig 2.9. Was there a girl to go with him? Many snow baby pieces were created in boy-girl pairs. Notice that all of the children are blonds. #4479; 4.0″

Fig 2.9 A girl and boy make a large snow roll. The boy looks unhappy (perhaps his hands are cold). Notice the similarity between this boy and the boy in Fig 2.10. The snow is blue and tan. #4653; 6.5″

Fig 2.15 Blue snow girl wearing a hooded cape skis down a slope. Note the single ski pole, as was usual before about 1910. #4656; 4.87"

Fig 2.13 Same as Fig 2.12 (it also bears the same incised number), but wearing summer clothes and lightly snowed. The shoes and base are heavily snowed. #4584; 7.5"

Fig 2.16 Blue snow boy skis down a slope. His cap is like the boy's in Fig 2.6, but here the ear flaps are up. This piece bears the same incised number as Fig 2.15. #4656; 5.0"

Fig 2.14 These two blue snow pieces bear the same number (4664). The two children wear outfits with similar short coats. The porcelain under the snow is tinted blue, so that if snow didn't adhere, there would be no bare white spot. **a.** Boy with pink umbrella. 3.75" **b.** Girl in fancy bonnet with pink umbrella. 3.62"

Fig 2.17 This is the same girl as Fig 2.15 but with red-painted snow. Her face may have never been painted. #4656; 4.87"

15

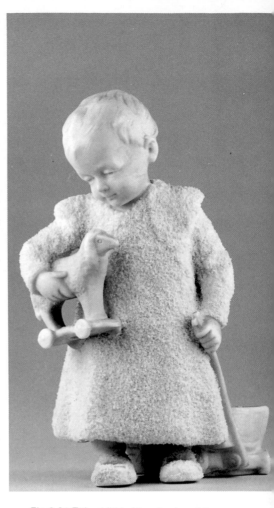

Fig 2.18 Boy carries a sled on his back. His snow has been painted rust and deep blue-green. His number is one digit higher than Fig 2.17. #4657; 5.25″

Fig 2.20 This boy, holding a beer stein, has the only bare, non-snowed feet of all the pieces in this chapter. The shape of the numerals on the base is identical to other Galluba and Hoffman pieces. #4645; 4.25″

Fig 2.21 This child holds a lamb pull-toy and pulls a small wagon. The texture of the snow is unusually fine. This piece bears no incised number, but it is included here because of heavily snowed shoes and creamy yellow finish. It bears the penciled inscription, "December 1907". 5.0″

Fig 2.22 Girl lies prone on a sled. She has heavily snowed shoes, creamy yellow paint and a beautifully molded skirt. There is a molded bow at the neck of her jacket. She has been pictured elsewhere with blue snow (see text). 2.5″

Fig 2.19 Girl in a long cape carries a puppy. She is numbered in the 4000 series, as are the Galluba and Hoffman blue snows. Her number is the highest of those pictured in this series. #4837; 4.25″

Chapter 3
Pink Snow Children

Previously, collectors divided these pieces into two groups. One group was called the "pink snows" because they have many features in common and some have pink snow. The other group was called the "sand children," possibly because some are shown with sand box toys and are dressed for summer play. Their grout represents sand, not snow. Pink snows and sand children are more alike than different. In this book they will all be called pink snow children, a term that accurately describes most of them.

There is general agreement that these pieces, like the blue snows, were part of the early development of snow babies. Though the evidence is not as strong as for the blues, the pink snows may all have been made by one factory.

Features in Common

In contrast to the snow on the blue snow children, the colored grout on these pieces is white bisque that was applied and fired, then painted and fired again. Here are some other features:

1. These figures are all roughly three to five inches high. The sole exception is the pair of swingers (Fig 3.13).

2. Six of these pink snow pieces are incised with two-digit numbers of similar size and shape. The other pieces are unnumbered. Other than the pink snows, only four pieces in this book are incised with two digits (see table 2).

3. Each child wears grouted clothing, highlighted with pastel colors. Shoes are smooth and painted, unlike the heavily snowed footwear of the blue snow pieces. Where the soles show, they are painted brown.

4. Although the faces of these children are very carefully rendered, none of them has the depth of character that makes the blue snow children so desirable. If hair is visible, it is almost always pale yellow, and it curls around the forehead. Even the style of the curls is similar. The children's faces are short and wide, with cheeks so chubby that their lips are pushed into a pucker. The highlighting or blush appears low on the cheeks, emphasizing this chubby look. Slightly protruding eyeballs and half-lowered eyelids make each child look drowsy. The eyebrows are painted close to the eyes. Like the blue snow children, each of the pink snow figures has red eyelid lines and nose dots.

The forty collections photographed for this book included only seventeen pink snows, only one of which was a duplicate. Perhaps some collectors, uncertain whether they belong with snow babies, pass them by. A more likely explanation is that they are very rare.

Fig 3.1 Matchbox girl wears a long coat with ermine collar. The chubby cheeks and drowsy eyes are typical of these children. The box (like all match boxes) has a striker surface. The snow is pink and white. #32; 3.12"

Fig 3.2 Matchbox girl seated, wears a knee-length coat and carries a muff. Her hat is tied on. Several of these children have shoes painted the way hers are. The snow is pink, blue and white. 3.87"

Fig 3.3 Seated matchbox girl wears a short coat and a long, pink skirt. She holds a small muff over her right hand and wears a fancy, feathered hat. 3.87"

Fig 3.4 Matchbox girl (no matchbox boys have been reported) with short coat and pink boots. Her rust-colored stockings are unusual and are about the same color frequently seen as trim on blue snow figures. She has a blue scarf at her neck. #52; 3.12"

Fig 3.5 This girl stands beside an urn that serves as a container. She wears a snowed, pink drape and blue-trimmed anklets. She is the only child in this chapter who wears no hat. She seems to be the companion piece to Fig 3.6. #42; 4.0"

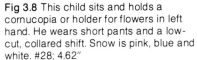

Fig 3.8 This child sits and holds a cornucopia or holder for flowers in left hand. He wears short pants and a low-cut, collared shift. Snow is pink, blue and white. #28; 4.62"

Fig 3.9 This child is seated with a rifle and holds a duck or rabbit in his left hand. The child is dressed in a kilt and wears a Scottish cap called a balmoral. The brown pouch on his lap, called a sporran, is also part of the traditional Scottish garb. The snow is in several colors. 4.75"

Fig 3.7 A child on his knees wears a large blue sash and a hat with ears, as if he is dressed for a school play. He holds a yellow ball between his knees. The snow is multicolored. 3.87"

Fig 3.6 This boy wears a top hat and a long, double-breasted coat. He stands in front of tree-stump container, which does not show in the picture. The snow is green, pink and white. Notice his polka-dot neck scarf. The bases of Fig 3.5 and this piece are unusual and similar, and their incised numbers are consecutive. #43; 5.25"

Fig 3.12 A boy dressed in a long coat holds what could be a broom or paddle, but he holds it like a shovel. An unsnowed scarf is knotted around his neck. 4.12"

Fig 3.14 A seated girl dressed in a cloak and scarf. She holds a drawstring purse over one arm. The snow is highlighted with pink and green. 3.62"

Fig 3.10 Girl balances on one knee and wears a long open "snowed" coat over a summer dress. She carries a brown bag (books?). Notice how similarly the hair was molded on these pieces. Pink, blue and white snow. 3.87"

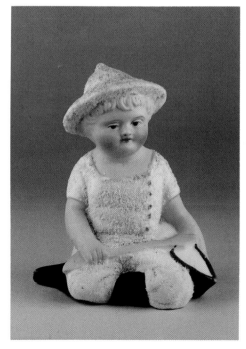

Fig 3.11 Boy in a sun suit and broad-brimmed sun hat sits with a toy boat and paddle. Pink and dark yellow colored snow (or sand). #10; 3.5"

Fig 3.13 This graceful boy and girl were made to swing, possibly from a gas ceiling fixture in a parlor. This was the only snowed example in a collection of 25 swingers. #67; 6.0"

Fig 3.15 This boy sits in a long coat and top hat. His hands are tucked into his sleeves. The snow is highlighted with pink. 4.12″

Fig 3.16 A girl sits in a long coat and fancy hat with her hands in a muff. She is the mate to Fig 3.15. Her snow is highlighted with pink. 4.0″

Chapter 4
Shoulder Head Dolls

Shoulder head snow babies serve as a link between snow babies and dolls. Of course, there are many other types of shoulder head dolls. The most abundant are the china shoulder heads that were made in great numbers in Germany beginning about 1840. It was not until the 1860s, however, that bisque shoulder head dolls began to appear (Borger 1983).

A shoulder head snow baby is a doll with a cloth body. The bisque head and shoulders portion is snowed except for the face. The lower arms and the lower legs are made of porcelain or a composition material; these are not snowed. The head is glued, or in some cases sewn, to the body. All of the examples of snow baby shoulder heads I have seen lack sew holes in the shoulder plates that would have allowed them to be sewn to bodies. These dolls were originally sold both as complete dolls and as porcelain parts that could be assembled into a doll on a homemade body.

Snow baby shoulder head dolls were played with, and many that survive have been damaged in some way. The bodies may be worn, and the arms and legs may be scuffed or even broken. But it is the shoulder head itself that is important. Even one without body, arms and legs is a good find. Because these dolls were often homemade it is appropriate to buy legs and arms and sew your own snow baby doll.

Complete shoulder head snow babies measure from about 4" to 13". The cloth body may be long or short, so the exact measurement of the overall height is not critical. All of the dolls shown in this chapter appear to have "original" bodies. However, some bodies may have been homemade, and others could have been replaced a long time ago.

There is some variation in the detailing, even among those dolls of similar size. Figs 4.1 through 4.3 are each about 11" tall. Notice that one has a molded bow at its neck, and another has its head turned slightly on its shoulders. The bonnets of a few of the smaller dolls are ruffled. These variations suggest that more than one manufacturer made these dolls.

Janet Johl (1950) showed a photograph of a large shoulder head snow baby. She quotes Emma Clear, a doll maker, who remembered such a "Christmas doll" from her childhood in the 1880s or 1890s. If this memory is accurate, it is the earliest date associated with any type of snow baby.

According to Jürgen and Marianne Cieslik (1985), Hertwig and Company produced shoulder head snow babies after 1910. This would mean that the shoulder head snow babies were made over a period of more than twenty years. In a later article the Ciesliks (1987) also credit Heubach with having made shoulder head snow babies, but they do not indicate any date of manufacture.

All shoulder heads are rare. Those that range from 7 to 9 inches in height are seen more often than the smaller or larger dolls. Babies with ruffled bonnets are much less common than are those with plain bonnets.

Doll collectors value dolls dressed in their original clothes. Doll dealers and collectors alike have told me that they have never seen a shoulder head snow baby with original clothes. Some believe that even when these snow babies were sold fully assembled, clothes were not provided.

Fig 4.2 Bisque head and shoulders measures 2.75." The lovely face resembles slightly the faces of the pink snow children. Notice the molded bow at the neck, under the snow. 11.0"

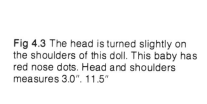

Fig 4.1 This shoulder head doll is elegantly dressed in a coat and long gown. Head and shoulder plate measures 2.5." 11.0"

Fig 4.3 The head is turned slightly on the shoulders of this doll. This baby has red nose dots. Head and shoulders measures 3.0". 11.5"

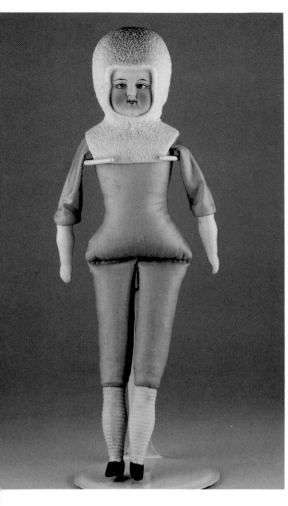

Fig 4.4 Here are the chubby cheeks again, as in Fig 4.2, but this piece has no molded bow. The fabric used for the body of this doll is not as shiny as it appears in this photo. Bisque head and shoulders portion measures 2.37". 9.0"

Fig 4.6 Shoulder head doll wearing white boots. The 1.87" bisque head is the size and type most commonly found. 6.75"

Fig 4.7 This small (1.37" shoulder plate) doll is uncommon in several ways. She has a ruffled bonnet and a furry body. The body is old and was probably meant to be a snowsuit. This doll wears unusual orange shoes. 4.25"

Fig 4.5 This doll has a rare ruffled bonnet and a 2.37" shoulder plate. Notice the unusual legs and shoes. 8.5"

Fig 4.8 Measuring only 0.87", this is the only shoulder plate this tiny I have seen or heard of.

Chapter 5
All-White Babies

Background

These babies, with their mittens and shoes as snowy white as their grouted suits, are sometimes snowed to the tips of their hands and feet. They have sometimes been called "babies with peaked hoods," but this title describes only a few of them. Furthermore, not every baby with a peaked hood has the other special features that characterize this group. The one attribute these pieces have in common is that neither their hands nor their feet have been painted.

Jean Crowley Goodman (1972) first called these babies "among the earliest." She told me that she suggested this because of the way the pieces look, and some sound reasons back up her assertion. But are these pieces really older than others manufactured before World War I?

Why They Might be Early

In addition to having brown eyebrows and black eyelid lines with attached eye dots, many have even more detailed eyes. Some faces have red eye lines and nose dots, like the blue snows and pink snows. These details required more time and effort than was usually devoted to such small pieces. Doll historians have documented that early dolls were produced with much more attention to detail than later ones. In general, as demand increased for dolls and figurines, quality fell. So the high quality of the all-white pieces is one good reason to believe that they were produced early.

The second reason is that these babies are much more difficult to find than pieces of a similar size with colored shoes. It could be argued that there has been more time for early pieces to be damaged and discarded. Of course, there are other possible explanations for their scarcity. Perhaps they were not made earlier than pieces with painted shoes, but were designed and produced in smaller quantities for more discriminating buyers. Could they have been experimental pieces?

All-white babies were pictured in Christmas displays in *Ladies' Home Journal* and *Good Housekeeping,* shown in chapter 21. But because pictures of babies with colored shoes were published at about the same time, documents do not provide support for the idea that the all-white babies were made earlier.

Chubby and Slender Babies

Perhaps it was their plump cheeks or their rounded stomachs that caused one group of these babies to be given the nickname "chubbies" (for example, Figs 5.3 and 5.5). Marie Johnson (1972) described them as babyish and lovable. Their charm and her praise have created a great demand for these babies.

Other all-white babies are so far from chubby that they might be called "slender babies" (such as Figs 5.18 and 5.20). Each is lean and angular. Many are poorly proportioned: their arms seem too short for the rest of their bodies. One baby (Fig 5.22a) tends to fall backwards unless it is propped up. These attributes invite speculation that slender babies were early experimental pieces, forerunners of the more popular snow baby shape. But they and the chubbies could have been created by porcelain factories striving for an individual look.

Snow Baby Angel

One of the most desirable all-white pieces is the snow baby angel (Fig 5.10). The face is sharply molded and delicately painted. It does not have red eye lines or nose dots. In fact, its face doesn't resemble the face of any other all-white baby. The thin wings, touched with pink, are so fragile that often they have been damaged. The molded loop between the wings, unique among all snow babies, allows it to be hung, possibly as a Christmas tree ornament.

The snow baby angel is rare, but not as rare as has been reported. At one time the collector whose two snow baby angels are pictured here owned four of them. In the forty collections represented here, five include this beautiful all-white baby.

Fig 5.2 Same style baby as Fig 5.1 (peaked hood, chubby cheeks, red eye lines). This is not its natural position; it is propped up on this sled to show the face better. 1.75"

Fig 5.3 This is a typical chubby snow baby. Neither the hands nor the feet are snowed, but the carefully painted face has eye lines and nose dots. It neither stands nor sits comfortably; it may have been made to be mounted on skis or to tumble in snow (or frosting). It was also made in a 2.25" size. 3.12"

Fig 5.1 This baby lies prone, on elbows, wearing a peaked, hooded suit. Even the soles of the shoes are snowed. This baby has red eye lines; the hands are not visible. 1.5"

Fig 5.6 Three all-white babies with snowy feet. The differences in face molding and painting shown here suggest that they were made by more than one company. **a.** 1.12″ **b.** 2.0″ **c.** 1.25″

Fig 5.4 Standing version of Fig 5.3, with the same facial characteristics. Although this example does have pale grey shoes, it is included in this chapter because this baby usually has white shoes. 3.25″

Fig 5.7 Three small babies with suits that are almost completely snowed. **a.** There are eye lines and nose dots, even on this very small piece. This baby wears an oversized hood. 1.75″ **b.** This piece was seen in pictures in the December 1916 *Good Housekeeping* (Fig 21.5), and in the December 1922 *Ladies' Home Journal* (Fig 21.6). 1.75″ **c.** Less attention to detail has been paid to the face of this tiny chubby. 1.0″

Fig 5.5 Slightly different from the previous all-whites, this baby has such chubby cheeks that the mouth seems to pucker, much like the pink snow pieces. This pose was also made in a 3.5″ size. The present owner made these skis, but this piece was shown on skis next to an igloo cake in the December 1922 *Ladies' Home Journal (Fig 21.6)*. 2.87″

Fig 5.8 **a.** This seated snow baby holds a snowball. It is one of the most common all-white pieces found, but it is still very desirable for its excellent detail. It has red eye lines and nose dots and a peak hood. Note the carefully molded flesh-colored hands. This piece was seen in articles in the December 1916 *Good Housekeeping* (Fig 21.5), and in the December 1922 *Ladies' Home Journal* (Fig 21.6). 2.5″ **b.** Tiny baby snowed to the tips of hands and feet. It lies prone, supported by one arm. 0.87″

Fig 5.9 Tiny baby in a position somewhat similar to that of Fig 5.8b. This piece was probably fired on a sled: a bit of broken porcelain still clings to the snow on the underside. 1.0″

Fig 5.12 These three tiny, chubby, all-white babies are arranged on a bisque sled in positions nearly identical to one of the Clapsaddle post cards (see Fig 21.7). 1.5″

Fig 5.13 This tiny, single, all-white baby sits with one knee tucked underneath it. The sled is unusual because it is snowed; it is incised "Germany" on one runner. 1.75″

Fig 5.10 This is the famous angel snow baby. The back of this piece seems as important as the front, so I photographed two together to show both. The face has been described repeatedly in articles, but it can be done justice only by a good picture—or the real thing! The back view shows the wings touched with pink on the outside only, and the molded loop that allows the piece to be suspended as an ornament. 1.62″

Fig 5.11 Two rather similarly styled chubby snow babies. They look as if they were intended to be girls. Notice the resemblance to Fig 5.5. These babies have chubby cheeks and stomachs. Red eye lines and nose dots accent their faces. Their feet are snowed, but their hands are left as smooth, white bisque. a. She reclines on her side and waves seductively. 2.0″ b. She stands on wooden skis and grasps a single ski pole with both hands. 3.5″

Fig 5.14 This beautiful, curvaceous sledder is clearly no baby! This piece and the next two were pictured in the table display in the December 1912 *Ladies' Home Journal* (Fig 21.4). Her sled is incised "Germany". Not apparent in the picture is the fact that the runners slant inward, bottom to top. Also notice the unusual shape of the head gear and the curls beneath it. I have also seen this piece with black shoes. Notice the incised decorative markings on the side of the sled. The number is incised on the runner. #8268; 2.37″

Fig 5.17 The body shape of this baby is typical of the "slender" all-white babies. Notice the long legs and short arms in proportion to the rest of the body. This baby does not stand without support, and may have been made to stand on skis. 3.5″

Fig 5.16 This baby is smaller than Figs 5.14 and 5.15 but they share some details, such as the shape of the sled and the curls (snow babies seldom have curls showing). The nose of this particular example was somewhat flattened during manufacture, prior to the time it was painted. But the piece was finished and sold, anyway; the quality standards of the era did not seem to demand that "seconds" be discarded. Pictured on the table display in the December 1912 *Ladies' Home Journal* (Fig 21.4). 2.12″

Fig 5.15 From the style and size this piece is clearly a mate to Fig 5.14. Even the sled is in the same style and bears the same decoration. Pictured in the table display in the December 1912 *Ladies' Home Journal* (Fig 21.4). #8263; 3.0″

Fig 5.18 Tiny slender baby with short arms. There is just a hint of curls visible around the face. Standing on a platform, it may have been a place card holder. #506N; 1.87″

Fig 5.21 These slender babies look almost rigid, especially as compared to some of the chubby babies shown in this chapter. Notice the stylized paint of the lips. **a.** This is a beautiful example, despite the repaired leg. 2.25″ **b.** Similar baby, but smaller in size. 1.87″ **c.** This piece has been shown in Fig 5.6a. Still only 1.12″

Fig 5.19 This small baby wears very long bisque skis that are grooved on their undersides. The ski pole seems too thick for such a small piece. The mismatch of such heavy equipment with such a beautiful baby suggests that these pieces may have been made early, before styles became more standardized. 1.62″

Fig 5.20 These babies resemble Fig 5.18 in their molding. Both have the curls, long legs and short arms typical of the slender all-white babies. **a.** Although this piece shows no evidence of having been removed from skis, it will not stand unsupported. It was probably made to stand on skis. 1.62″ **b.** This baby stands on bisque skis that are grooved on the bottom, identical to those of Fig 5.19. 1.62″

Fig 5.22 Two slender babies seem nearly identical, except for the degree to which they are bent at the waist. Both are angular and have short arms. **a.** This one leans backward at such an angle that to sit up it must be supported. Unless this baby was meant to be attached to a sled, it is hard to imagine why it was molded in such an awkward position. 1.5″ **b.** 1.5″

Chapter 6
Jointed Snow Babies

Fig 6.1 These two are the smallest and the largest jointed snow babies I know of. **a.** Incised with the number "2" inside the hip joint. 2.87" **b.** Incised with number "4" inside joint. 5.25"

Fig 6.2 These are both 4" babies, incised with number "2". **a.** Limbs are held to the body with elastic that runs through loops on the inside of the arms and legs. I believe this baby was made in this size only. **b.** The more common wire-strung baby. The ends of the wire are coiled.

Jointed babies are made entirely of bisque, but some parts of the baby—the arms, legs, or head—are formed separately and not fired onto the body. The separate parts are connected to the finished body with wire or an elastic cord. This arrangement permits some movement at the joint and results in a more doll-like snow baby.

Snowed Babies with Jointed Arms and Legs

The snowed, jointed babies in all-white snow suits were probably manufactured at about the same time as the other all-white babies. They are found in sizes ranging from just under 2.75 inches to about 5.25 inches. They have carefully painted and fired faces; the larger ones have red dots at the nostrils.

Most of these figures are held together with wires that extend through the body from shoulder to shoulder and from hip to hip. The looped ends of the wires are visible on the outside of the piece; they are usually double-looped at one end and single-looped at the other. A few of these dolls were designed instead with a molded loop on the inside of each limb, through which an elastic cord is strung (Fig 6.2a).

You can usually read a one-digit number incised on the inside of the arm or leg joint. This number is on the flat surface of the limb where it butts up against the shoulder or hip. Reading this number is easier in bright light, and should only be attempted if the joint is a bit loose, as they often are. On one baby missing some snow from the back of the hood I have seen a number that matches the number in the joints. Perhaps they are all numbered this way. If so, the snow usually hides the number on the head.

Notice that each baby wears a hood that comes to a peak just over the forehead and that separates slightly under the chin. No babies were found with stylistic differences (turned heads, ruffles, bows under the chin) as great as those found in the shoulder head snow babies. The similarities in style, which were observed on many more examples than are pictured here, could mean that all of the snowed babies with jointed arms and legs were made by the same manufacturer.

A jointed pincushion baby was shown in Plate 58 of Ray and Eileen Early's book (1983). Ray Early told me that this was not originally a pincushion, but had been home-made from a jointed baby.

No-Snow Children with Jointed Arms

Figs 6.4 through 6.6 show some no-snow jointed children. Doll collectors classify them as dolls with molded clothes. Their size and winter clothes help them fit right into a Christmas or winter scene. These babies were made in more than one size.

Jointed Polar Bears

The two larger jointed polar bears are called "Angione bears" because one was first pictured and described by Genevieve Angione (1981). These bears are so well-balanced that they can stand on their hind legs with no prop; they will also stand on all four legs and can even do an unsupported headstand! The smallest polar bear is the most common of the three. Perhaps it is simply a small Angione bear. It performs all of the above tricks reasonably well if its wires are not too loose.

Nodders

Nodders (Figs 6.11 through 6.15) are figures with separate heads. They are strung with a length of elastic that extends from the lower back to the top of the head and is knotted on the outside of the piece. Nodders do not usually have movable arms or legs. The children are so similar to each other in style, facial features, size and coloring that they seem almost certain to have been manufactured by the same firm. All snow baby nodders were probably made in the 1920s.

The Santa nodders are much more common than nodder snow children. The Santa in Fig 6.14b is shown in a reprint of Butler Brothers catalogs from 1928 through 1935, where he is described as having a "turning head." Fig 6.16 shows another type of nodder. The head of this Santa is supported by a rod across the body at the base of the neck. This type of nodder really does nod its head when it is nudged.

Fig 6.3 This baby has the number "3" inside the joint. There is a slightly different treatment of the hood. It is less peaked over the forehead, and cupped open more under the chin. 4.75"

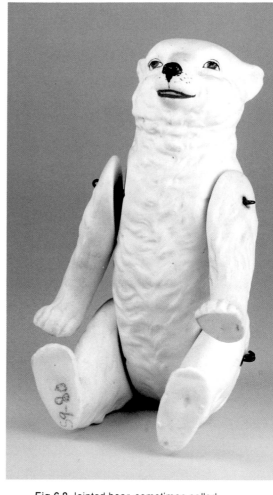

Fig 6.4 Unsnowed boy with jointed arms and legs, white sweater and cap. Dressed for winter, this type of figure is commonly used in snow baby scenes. This and the next several figures show children in molded clothes. 6.0″

Fig 6.6 Similar to 6.5a, but not marked Limbach. #1456; 5.37″

Fig 6.8 Jointed bear, sometimes called the Angione bear because it was first described by Genevieve Angione. It comes in several sizes. Incised with number "5" in joint. 6.0″

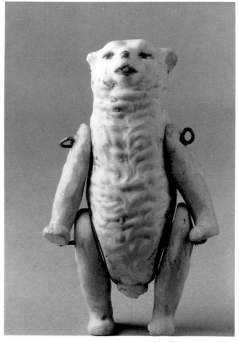

Fig 6.5 Jointed-arm boys dressed for winter sports. **a.** Incised with Limbach mark on his back; also incised "19". Shown in Butler Brothers 1908 catalog. 4.25″ **b.** Same as Fig 6.4, but without jointed legs. This example is 6.0″, but this figure was made in other sizes.

Fig 6.7 Pair of jointed-arm children with molded clothes and cotton batting hats. They are pegged to small, bisque sleds. **a.** This girl has a molded skirt. Her snowball is cotton batting. The trim around her neck is made of felt. 2.0″ **b.** Boy is 2.12″.

Fig 6.9 Smaller size Angione bear (see Fig 6.8). 3.37″

29

Fig 6.12 These and Fig 6.11 were obviously made by the same company. They are rather comic figures, and all four faces wear the same surprised look. A small amount of glitter snow remains.

a. Boy and girl wearing skis stand on a base. #1456; 3.5″ b. This standing boy might have been made to wear wooden skis. 3.0″

Fig 6.10 Small, jointed bear. This is the most common jointed bear. Incised "0" in joints. 3.25″

Fig 6.11 Boy nodder pegged to sled. Only a small amount of his glitter snow remains. This piece and 6.12a were mentioned in the *Favors* wholesale trade list of 1924-1925. 2.75″

Fig 6.13. No-snow angel nodders with elastic-strung heads. Each has a hole in its fist for a small sprig of feather tree. These are sometimes displayed with snow babies. a. 3.5″ b. 3.25″

Fig 6.14 Two elastic-strung nodder Santas. Each has a hole in his fist for a feather tree. **a.** This is among the most common of all bisque Santas. Incised "Germany". 2.5" **b.** Shown in a pre-World War II Butler Brothers catalog reprint (1928-1935). Incised "Germany". #748; 3.5"

Fig 6.16 This Santa's head bobs on a wire. Santa's aqua vest and yellow tie are unusual. 3.37"

Fig 6.15 One member of an elf nodder band sits on a square stool. This is a comic piece, with bulging eyes and large head. Incised "Germany". Head and base are both incised "741". Members of this set were purchased new between 1924 and 1934 2.62"

Chapter 7
Container Pieces

Each piece shown in this chapter has some type of container molded into or next to the figure. The container itself may be either smaller or larger than the attached figure. Collectors have called many of these pieces "planters." Some of them are quite small; others are among the largest shown in the book.

Collectors and dealers have suggested how these pieces may have been used. The largest containers may have held flowers or greenery, a plant or candy. Somewhat smaller containers are the right size for a large candle, matches, toothpicks or even cigarettes. Those definitely intended for matches have a rough striking surface, usually on the back of the container. Still smaller holders look like salts or individual nut and candy dishes. The tiniest are the candleholders that were used to decorate cakes. These opinions sound logical, but I have found no photographs or testimony to verify them.

Large Container Pieces

The sledders shown in Figs 7.1 through 7.3 are from a series made by Heubach. The snowed piece bears a strong resemblance to a marked Heubach sledder (Fig 8.19). The red trim and the type of snow on both pieces are typically Heubach. The snow is glossy, like china, although the unsnowed portion of the piece is bisque. The whistling boy (Fig 7.5) shows another unmarked Heubach figure that has many of the same characteristics. In her book about Heubach dolls, Jan Foulke shows this piece unsnowed and attributes it to Heubach (1980).

The snowmen in Figs 7.6 through 7.8 are also closely related. The largest of them is incised with the Heubach sunburst. Notice the typical Heubach dark red trim and glossy snow.

To determine the origin of an unmarked figure, Heubach dealers and collectors rely heavily on the look and character of the faces. The same faces show up again and again on marked and unmarked Heubach pieces; the same children were apparently used repeatedly as models for figurines and dolls. The skiing children shown in Figs 7.19 and 7.20 are marked only with numbers, but the faces have the look of Heubach children.

Googly-Eyed Babies

Figs 7.23 through 7.27 show babies with distinctive googly eyes. Each has an opening at the top of his head, and the entire body of the baby is hollow. The heads of these pieces are oversized, markedly out of proportion to the rest of the body. Although these pieces were made in at least three sizes, you probably won't realize it unless you see them side by side (Fig 7.23). So few are seen for sale that size doesn't seem to affect price.

Jean Crowley Goodman noticed a similarity of these figures to the children pictured in the ads for Clicquot Club ginger ale (Crowley 1978). She suggested that the babies might be linked to the soft drink company. To pursue a possible connection, she contacted the Clicquot Club Company. Its officials, she said, were cooperative, but they could find no information that would link the porcelain snow babies to their company. You might want to compare the snow baby pieces with a sample ginger ale ad (Fig 21.9). Even though no ties between the babies and the ginger ale have been established, these snow babies may never shake off the name Clicquot. However, it seems reasonable to call them by another name.

Carol Stanton showed a picture of one of these babies in her book (1978) and wrote, "It is my opinion that Heubach also produced some of the finest quality snow babies." Heubach made googly-eyed baby dolls and figurines, but so did many other manufacturers during the same period. These beautifully crafted pieces could have been made by Heubach, but we currently have no solid evidence of this.

Some googly-eyed babies have black faces. A possible explanation for the existence of black snow babies is that one of the first Arctic explorers was Matthew Henson, a black American who accompanied Admiral Peary on all but the first of his Arctic trips. Peary chose him, alone from the other non-Eskimos in his party, to make the final dash to the Pole.

Candleholders

The smallest container pieces are the tiny candle holders. How jolly they must have looked on cakes! Snow baby candleholders were made in many poses. Some look like the "tinies" in chapter 10, but with holders attached. Others (Figs 7.55 and 7.56) have no counterpart without containers. Even more variety is found in the dwarf candleholders. Most were bisque, but a few were made of china, which permitted fastidious cooks to wash off frosting without removing the paint. These tiny containers were made after World War I.

Fig 7.1 Heubach snowed planter has red and olive green trim typical of Heubach snowed pieces. The children's faces and the shiny, nearly translucent snow are also characteristic of Heubach. This piece shows very young children. Fig 7.2 and 7.3 seem to show some of the same children. 4.25"

Fig 7.2 Similar to Fig 7.1, but larger and no-snow. These children seem to be a little older. The entire hilltop is open to hold something. The faces are beautifully painted; the children wear old-fashioned stocking caps. #4628; 6.25"

Fig 7.3 Single Heubach boy on sled, obviously part of same series as Figs 7.1 and 7.2. #4612; 8.0″

Fig 7.6 Two Heubach children in snowman suits. In each case the backpack serves as the opening to a container. **a.** This example wears a Tyrolean hat with a feather in it. It has typical Heubach snow and trim color. "Made in Germany +" is stamped on the bottom in a double circle. #—38; 4.5″ **b.** Unsnowed, unsigned piece similar to 7.6a wears a stovepipe hat. He wears a hamper with the lid up for a backpack and leans on his silky umbrella. 4.37″

Fig 7.5 Whistling boy with his hands in his pockets. There is actually a hole between his lips. His clothing, snow and color all mark him as a Heubach piece. A non-snowed version of this piece was pictured in Jan Foulke's book, *Focusing on Gebrüder Heubach Dolls.* #6969; 6.0″

Fig 7.4 A smaller version of Fig 7.3, but was it made by Heubach? It lacks some of the usual carefully finished detail of Heubach pieces. 3.62″

Fig 7.7 Large, unsnowed version of 7.6a. Without his snow, the detailed molding is exposed. Notice that pink and soft yellow used like a wash are repeatedly used as trim colors for these pieces. 8.0″

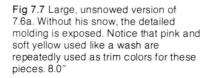

Fig 7.8 Here we see the child from Fig 7.6b in a slightly different pose with his container at the side. This is a much larger piece and is incised with a sunburst. #6627; 11.0″

Fig 7.12 Back view of Fig 7.11. Look for Limbach clover leaf at the base, and notice the stylized sled.

Fig 7.10 Girl in an egg on a sled. This piece is finished like Wedgwood Jasperware. Notice the girl's feet protruding from the end of the egg. The top half of the egg lifts off to reveal the container. Incised Heubach sunburst. 7.0″

Fig 7.9 Girl slides on an incline. She wears a hooded cape. The sled and hill resemble those of Fig 7.3. She is glazed and finished in just two colors, with a Heubach sunburst stamped in blue. #4013; 6.5″

Fig 7.11 Boy carrying a sled. A bud vase is built into the tree trunk of this fancy base. It is incised with a Limbach clover leaf. It and Fig 7.13 were probably made in about 1909, according to a dating method given in the Ciesliks' *German Doll Encyclopedia* (see text, chapter 21). #8535; 4.5″

Fig 7.13 Limbach girl on skis, on a fancy base with a bud vase in the tree trunk. The snow's color was not mixed into the porcelain as it was for the blue snows. Look at the similarity in molding and painting between this and Fig 7.11. Incised with Limbach clover leaf. #8550; 5.0″

Fig 7.14 Boy in snow suit skis down the side of a planter. Notice the intricate, raised decoration, some of which is touched with gilt. The boy wears yellow gloves. He and Figs 7.15 through 7.17 seem to be in the same series as Figs 8.1 and 8.2. #3204; 4.25″

Fig 7.15 Carefully molded, but unpainted, back of Fig 7.14.

Fig 7.17 Girl sits on a sled on the edge of a planter. This piece has evergreen boughs similar to the two previous planters. The girl wears pale yellow mittens and her dress, head gear and stockings also match Fig 7.16. #3200; 3.75″

Fig 7.18 This tiny baby on a sled seems to be a miniature version of 7.17. The face is not well-detailed on either of the examples I have seen, even taking into account its small size. But the container trim suggests that it was by the same company, or was intended to imitate the other pieces. The container is too small for anything but salt or tiny candies. Incised "Germany". 1.75″

Fig 7.16 Girl skis down the side of a detailed planter. Mate to 7.14. #3197; 4.75″

Fig 7.19 No-snow boy on short, beginner skis on a planter hill. This and its companion (Fig 7.20) are probably unmarked Heubach. Notice how life-like the children appear. #16; 5.75″

Fig 7.20 No-snow girl, companion to Fig 7.19. The wind blows her skirt as she glides down the slope. #16; 6.0"

Fig 7.21 Girl on skis next to an elaborate wood-pile container. She and her mate (Fig 7.22) are incised with the Karl Schneider mark. Their style is quite different from the Heubach pieces: the clothing doesn't flow as softly, and the positions of the arms seem stiffer. #11796; 7.75"

Fig 7.22 This boy is the mate to Fig 7.21, the previous girl. Both children carry uncommon ceramic ski poles. #11796; 7.75"

Fig 7.23 Two examples of googly-eyed container babies. They sit, wearing tiny bisque skis on their feet. Their large heads nearly rest on their stomachs. The pieces are open at the back of the head, and the entire body forms the container. The difference in complexion color is probably explained by conditions of firing. This pose has also been found in a 3.0" size. **a.** 3.75" **b.** 3.5"

Fig 7.24 Pair of googly babies of identical size (3.75″) wearing tiny ice skates and a look of surprise. None of these (Figs 7.23 through 7.28) have incised numbers or stamped marks. **a.** Caucasian baby. **b.** Rare, black-faced googly. His skin color is matte dark chocolate brown. He has a slight rub on his nose.

Above, and left:
Fig 7.26 a. Googly baby lies prone with feet up, smiling. 3.0″ **b.** Standing baby with short, squat body and very short legs. He carries what has been called a book, but on close inspection it is clearly a tiny sled. 4.0″

Fig 7.27 Black googly planter stands on skis. This baby carries no sled, and has a rose-bud mouth. All of the googly babies have very fine snow. 4.12″

Fig 7.25 Two googly babies of slightly different sizes. They have O-mouths and lie prone. Any of these large-headed container babies could have been used as spill vases, or to hold a large candle. **a.** Rare black-faced baby. 2.25″ **b.** Caucasian baby. 2.0″

Fig 7.28 Tiny googly baby, obviously related to Figs 7.23 to 7.27, but without a container body. In its hand it does have a tiny opening, just big enough to hold a tiny feather tree branch. 1.62"

Fig 7.29 Elegant no-snow planter, the largest I have encountered. It shows a boy and girl on a sled. These detailed figures were obviously applied after the planter was made. This piece is 8.0" tall and 10.0" wide. No factory logo. #2266

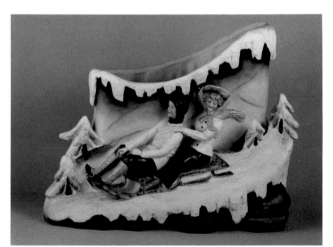

Fig 7.31 Father Christmas figure in a long hooded robe carries a container basket. He has red eye lines and nose dots. 5.0"

Fig 7.30 Close-up detail of Fig 7.29 sledding couple.

Fig 7.32 China Santa drives a sleigh that has log sides. Stamped "Made in Japan". 3.25"

Fig 7.33 Kitten peeks over the side of a cart. Perhaps not strictly a snow baby, it is made of bisque and fits in well with snow pieces. 1.62"

Fig 7.36 Girl rides a sled; an open basket sits on the sled behind her. This piece is commonly seen on the East Coast of the United States. Incised "C D Kenney", it was an advertising piece for a company that sold tea and coffee in Baltimore and 50 other cities. 2.25"

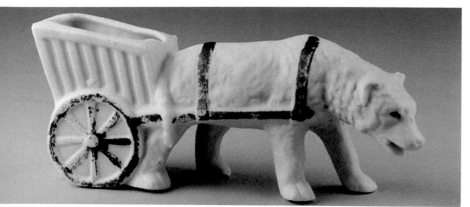

Fig 7.34 A polar bear pulls an open, two-wheel cart. The painted trim is gilt. Incised "Germany". #5855; 1.75"

Fig 7.35 Bunny pulls a fancy cart. Trim is gilt. 2.5"

Fig 7.37 Boy on skis. Notice the two ski poles, additional evidence that this is not an early piece (see text, chapter 12). Stamped "Japan". 5.0"

Fig 7.38 Boy on skis stamped "Made in Japan". I use this piece as a pencil holder on my desk. MK943; 5.0"

Fig 7.41 Candy container house (there is a plug in the bottom that can be removed to fill with candy). The entire piece is composition. The snow on the roof is coralene; glitter snow on white paint decorates other areas of the piece. Stamped "Germany US Zone". 3.5"

Fig 7.39 Tiny snow baby sits on a candy container box. Fired face. Overall height is 2.12"; baby is 1.12".

Fig 7.42 Glazed Santa carries his pack as he rides on a yellow scooter. Notice his blue mittens, typical of post-war Santas. The snowball container is covered with coralene; it separates in the middle and is lined with fancy paper. Marked "Germany US Zone". Container is 3.5"; Santa is 2.0".

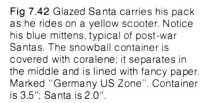

Fig 7.40 Tiny baby on cardboard skis stands on a candy box. Stamped "Germany" on the bottom of box. 2.5" overall.

Fig 7.43 Coralene-covered snowball candy container is decorated with tiny plaster birds on springs and a fence made of what appears to be actual twigs. Stamped "Germany". Overall height 5.0".

Fig 7.44 Dwarf drives a truck that is open to carry something small. Packages are molded around the upper edge of the truck bed. 1.87"

Fig 7.47 Two examples of the same tiny dwarf candle holder. It and Figs 7.48a through 7.48c are numbered consecutively. Incised "Germany". #3482; 1.0"

Fig 7.45 Two glazed container pieces. a. Dwarf stands by a tree stump container large enough to hold a candle slightly larger than birthday size. 1.75" b. Dwarf sits next to a small bud vase. 2.62"

Fig 7.48 The first three pieces are from a set of tiny dwarf candle holders that belong with Fig 7.47, but were photographed from a different collection. a. Crouches. #3483; 1.25" b. Stands. #3484; 1.37" c. Stands, hands clasped. #3485; 1.25" d. Single dwarf sits. The base of the candle holder is square. Stamped "Germany" in black. 1.25"

Fig 7.46 Pair of glazed, hence fully washable, dwarves next to a spotted mushroom. This sort of mushroom is described in chapter 14. a. Dwarf reclines under a mushroom. Stamped and incised "Germany". 1.25" b. Dwarf stands beside a mushroom. 1.37"

Fig 7.49 Set of tiny Japanese dwarf candle holders. Nicely executed, all are stamped "Japan" in black. Judging from the incised numbers, there were probably more than three to this set originally. **a.** Dwarf on one knee. #5803; 1.12″ **b.** Sits, legs apart. 1.12″ **c.** Lies prone. #5806; 0.75″

Fig 7.50 Unusual dwarf holds an urn candle holder. Notice the carefully molded fingers and beard. Curly hair is also uncommon. 1.75″

Fig 7.52 Two snow baby candle holders. These babies and the next three are similar to other babies made without candle holders (see tinies in chapter 10). **a.** Stands. 1.25″ **b.** Sits. 1.0″

Fig 7.53 Two tiny babies with candle holders. Both are stamped "Germany" in black. **a.** Lying on side. 1.12″ **b.** Sitting on one leg. 1.25″

Fig 7.51 Dwarf candle holder set. Somewhat stylized, these dwarves have long noses, long tasseled caps, long pointed shoes and white pants. The candle fits into the top of each head. All are stamped "Germany" in black. **a.** Sits. 1.37″ **b.** On hands and knees. 1.0″ **c.** Kneels. 1.25″

Fig 7.54 Identical to Fig 7.53b, but with red cap, mittens and shoes. 1.25″

Fig 7.55 Very unusual baby stands next to a candle holder. This piece and Fig 7.56 are unlike any babies without candle holders I know of. Stamped "Germany" in black. 1.75"

Fig 7.57 a. Santa sits in front of a candle holder. Notice that the holder itself is made to look like tiny bricks, very much like holders in Fig 7.48. I have seen several pieces identical to this, but none in other poses. Stamped "Germany" in purple. #657; 1.0" **b.** Snowman sits on one hip. A candle fits into his top hat. I have seen no other examples of this piece, but there are at least two other known poses, one standing. Stamped "Germany" in purple. #11963; 1.25"

Fig 7.56 Unsnowed baby holds a pair of skis. A candle fits into his head. 1.5"

Fig 7.58 Four no-snow angel candle holders, all incised "Germany". Judging by their incised numbers, there may be several additional poses. **a.** Stands and carries holder. #4640; 1.5" **b.** Sits with holder on lap. #4642; 1.0" **c.** Lies prone. #4646; 0.87" **d.** Sits next to holder. #4639; 1.12"

Chapter 8
Four Inches and More

By "four-inch snow baby" I mean the approximate height each would be, top to toe, if the figure were standing up. However, some of these figures are seated or lying down. This chapter also includes pieces that measure well over four inches; they are usually just referred to as large pieces. At least in part due to their size, extra attention was paid to the molding and painting of these large snow babies. Their beautiful faces give them such appeal that for some collectors these exquisite figures are the Cadillac of snow babies.

Although it is possible that some of these pieces were made after World War I, I have found no evidence to support this. The majority of these pieces share the traits that are characteristic of the pre-World War I period.

Fig 8.1 Boy on a mound holds his original metal sled. Notice the red nose dots and red lines over the eyes, signs that this was an early piece. #9224 (or 9227?); 4.25"

Fig 8.2 Girl on a mound holds a metal sled. This pair (with Fig 8.1) has much in common (ribbed socks, pale yellow gloves, type of clothing) with Figs 7.14 through 7.16. 4.0"

Store Decorations?

Harry Shuart suggested (1970) that the four-inch pieces might be store window decorations, and they are still called store display babies by some collectors. Although this suggestion seems reasonable, there are several reasons to doubt it.

I know of no pictures, catalogs or reminiscences confirming that these pieces were intended as store displays. If the four-inch babies were meant to be used by store owners, it is reasonable to assume they would have been sold or distributed separately. In fact, an article about snow babies in the German publication, *Puppenmagazin,* pictures a factory sample box containing a mixture of three-inch and four-inch snow baby pieces (Cieslik 1987).

An article about decorating for Christmas in the December 1912 issue of *Ladies' Home Journal* shows a table setting (Fig 21.4) that features four-inch babies. It seems unlikely that the magazine would suggest constructing a table display whose main elements were available only to store owners. A 1910 home photo of a Christmas cake (Fig 21.2) features four-inch as well as smaller babies.

Fig 8.5 Smaller version of Fig 8.4. The face is less detailed, and it was probably produced later. An example was shown on skis in the Hertwig and Company sample box (Cieslik 1987). 3.75"

Fig 8.4 This baby on skis may be deep in thought. He has an early, well-detailed face. Several examples of this piece are on a Christmas cake from 1910 (Fig 21.2). 4.25"

Fig 8.6 This baby lying on his side has just taken a tumble. He probably should hold a ski pole and wear skis. A splendid example. 2.5"

Fig 8.3 Often called "The Pouty," his expression is actually one of intense concentration, as if he was learning to ski. This example has an especially well-painted face. Note the wavy eyebrows, red nose dots and eye lines. He should be mounted on skis. He has been shown in a Hertwig and Company sample box (Cieslik 1987). 4.25"

Fig 8.7 a. Beautiful, early face of the baby shown in Fig 8.6. b. Face of a baby in same pose, painted with what I assume is a later face. An example of this piece on skis appears in the Hertwig and Company sample box (Cieslik 1987).

Fig 8.8 a. This baby sits holding both arms outstretched; the face is very early. His missing right hand hardly seems to mar his attractiveness. #9916; 3.12″ b. Also #9916, this baby sit with left arm up and right down. He has an early face. 3.12″

Fig 8.9 a. Same baby as Fig 8.8b. #9916; 3.12″ b. Same pose as Fig 8.9a., but the unfired face is losing paint. No red eye lines or nose dots. Unnumbered, this baby with a late face has also been seen with the incised number "9916". 3.12″

Store displays are much less common than the items they were intended to promote. Four-inch babies are rarer than smaller snow babies of this period, but the difference is not as great as for other areas of collecting. It is far more likely that the four-inch babies were not intended for special use.

Characteristics

Most four-inch pieces are not marked with numbers or factory insignia. Those that are marked are usually incised, rather than stamped. But even incised pieces show mysterious inconsistencies.

Fig 8.9 shows two examples of the same pose, one incised with the number 9916 and one not numbered. Fig 8.8 shows two different poses, each of which is incised 9916. Adding to the confusion is the fact that, upside down, this number could also be read 9166. Simple typography was used for the incised numbers, so no one knows which way is up. The correct reading remains a puzzle. For consistency I have used 9916 in this book.

A few four-inch pieces were made in at least two grades. Fig 8.9 contrasts one face, painted with great style and well-fired, with another piece that has more ordinary features and paint that is rubbing off. Fig 8.7 shows two identical four-inch babies; the first is painted with much more detail. Babies with better-detailed, fired faces were probably made earlier, but they could instead have been made at about the same time by different artists or factories.

Group Similarities

The two skiers in Fig 8.15, along with the sledders in Figs 5.14 through 5.16, were featured on the Christmas party table in the *Ladies' Home Journal* for December of 1912 (Fig 21.3). Examine their faces. The way the hair curls and the shape of the visor hoods suggest that all of these pieces were made by the same factory or artist.

The boy on the sled in Fig 8.19 is a rare, marked Heubach snow baby. Fig 23.1 shows the mark, a Heubach sunburst. Notice the color of the baby's stockings and the red trim around his neck and knees. The snow on the boy's clothing is shiny and nearly translucent. These features were used on several other marked and unmarked Heubach figures shown elsewhere in this book (especially chapter 7).

The child in a bear skin is also marked with a sunburst stamp. This piece was made by Heubach in at least one larger size and in two other slightly different positions. A variation (not pictured) shows these children in unsnowed brown bear suits.

One group of four-inch skater and skier babies (Figs 8.10 through 8.14) has companions in the three-inch size (Fig 9.12) and in the tiny pieces (Figs 10.168 and 10.169). Each boy wears a snowed sweater, cap, blue pants and pink scarf; each girl

Fig 8.10 Boy skater pegged to a ceramic base that represents a pond. Compare to Fig 8.13, boy skier; the two are versions of the same boy in different poses. Their pink scarves help collectors identify them. 4.0″

Fig 8.11 Girl skater, mate to Fig 8.10, glides along confidently. She is missing her ceramic base. Compare to Fig 8.12. 4.0″

wears a snowed sweater, cap and pink skirt. The face paint used for the three- and four-inch pieces is quite distinctive. The lip color is a bright and shiny crimson, a feature not common among snow babies. One of these babies, Fig 8.12, has been shown in a photograph of a Hertwig and Company sample card (Cieslik 1987). It seems likely that the six larger babies, and perhaps even the tinies, were made by Hertwig.

Similarities may also link the boy and girl with metal sleds (Figs 8.1 and 8.2) to the children on planters (Figs 7.14 through 7.17). All the girls are dressed in strikingly similar outfits and headgear, and all five children wear pale yellow gloves.

Three examples of skiers with striped cuffs are shown in this chapter (Fig 8.21 and 8.22). These pieces were made in at least four sizes. I have seen two poses in each size. The smaller sizes are shown in chapter 10. Unlike most snow baby pairs, it is difficult to tell boys from girls. The striped cuff snow babies all wear pants (pink, blue or green), and most seem to have blonde hair about the length of a short bob.

Today there is such a demand for these large pieces that they are seldom seen for sale. Because so few poses were made, collectors who have two alike often keep both rather than selling one. It may seem as if all four-inch pieces are rare, but some are much more common than others (see rarity scale in table 1).

Fig 8.12 Girl skier, similar to Fig 8.11. She looks as if she is better at skating than skiing. Note her bright lip color, often found on the children of this group (Figs 8.10 through 8.14 and Fig 9.12). An example of this figure was shown in the Hertwig and Company sample box (Cieslik 1987). One example has been seen with "Chamonix" printed in red on the skirt. Chamonix is a ski resort in France. The piece may have been intended as a souvenir. 4.0"

Fig 8.13 Mate to Fig 8.12, this boy skier also wears a pink scarf that blows in the wind. His mouth is open and we can see his red painted tongue. This piece often has a pale, almost shiny complexion. One example was seen with "Chamonix" printed in red on the pants. See Fig 8.12. 4.5"

Fig 8.14 Boy skier with pink scarf. This is the same boy as Fig 8.13, unsnowed but with flocked clothing. The scarf is not flocked. This piece has also been seen with a blue scarf and different colored flocking. 4.12"

Fig 8.15 Children featured in a Christmas table centerpiece in *Ladies' Home Journal* for December 1912 (Fig 21.4). They do not have red eye lines or nose dots, although they are early pieces. Both have curls showing under their hoods, which is uncommon, and both wear heavy shoes and very short bisque skis. **a.** Girl skier. Notice the unusual snowed leggings beneath her skirt. 4.25″ **b.** The boy's suit is snowed all over, like many large pieces, but his stance and the features mentioned above set him apart. 4.12″

Fig 8.17 Chubby cheeked girl on roller skates holds a rabbit skin muff. Notice the rabbit's face in bas-relief on the front of her muff. She has a molded bow on the back of her hooded jacket. She has been pictured wearing ice skates with long, curved blades (Cieslik 1987). 4.75″

Fig 8.18 Girl carries a basket and fur muff, and wears a hooded cape over a floor-length white dress. (The tree in the basket is not original.) She has red eye lines and nose dots. A close-up view shows dimples and the outlines of individual teeth. 3.87″

Fig 8.16 Both the snowed and unsnowed portions of these two figures have a china finish, unusual in snow babies. Both children have visible hair. The sleds are bisque. This pair has also been seen on dark brown sleds. **a.** Girl wears long hooded coat. 3.25″ **b.** Snowed portion of boy's suit is knee length, which is unconventional. His sled has been broken and repaired. 3.5″

Fig 8.19 Heubach boy lies prone on a sled. Notice the olive green stockings and typical Heubach features of red trim around neck and legs. The sled is unusual and stylized. The Heubach sunburst logo is stamped in green on the underside of the sled. 2.62″

Fig 8.20 Child wearing a polar bear skin scratches one ear with his foot. Or is this a polar bear with a child's face? The snow consists of shiny, distinct particles that are almost translucent, typical of Heubach snowed pieces. Stamped with Heubach sunburst in green. I have also seen this piece in a 3.75" size. 3.0"

Fig 8.21 Pair of striped cuff skiers. At 5.5" each, this is the largest pair I have seen. Smaller sizes of this pair are shown in Chapter 10. **a.** All sizes of this girl wear pink pants. She should carry a ski pole in her right hand. **b.** Boy (or girl?) usually wears blue pants.

Fig 8.22 Same as Fig 8.21b, but 1" shorter. Pants color is closer to green than to blue. 4.5"

Fig 8.23 Graceful boy slides on a slope. Snow on the slope is crystalline clear, not bisque. The boy himself is 6" long. The piece is incised with mark of Fritz Pfeffer, the only snow baby example I have seen with this mark. #3978; 3.62"

Fig 8.24 No-snow boy with an all-white ribbed sweater and leggings. The face paint is pale with no red eye lines and nose dots. The wooden sled is a replacement; the style of the original sled is not known. 3.25"

Fig 8.25 Two children in polar bear skins, unsnowed. Their bodies are more like bears than children. Compare to Fig 8.20. It is unclear who made these pieces, but it seems doubtful that they are Heubach (the incised numbers are in a different style, and the faces are not typical of Heubach). **a.** Crouching baby. #4925; 4.12" **b.** Standing boy holds a stick across his body. #4924; 7.0"

Fig 8.26 Girl skis down a slope; a molded tree stands behind her. Judging from the style of the base, molded tree and girl's coloring, this is probably a late Heubach piece. #8912; 5.75″

Fig 8.28 Bare-foot boy piano baby wears a snowed night shirt and holds a flower pot. He has red nose dots. 2.5″

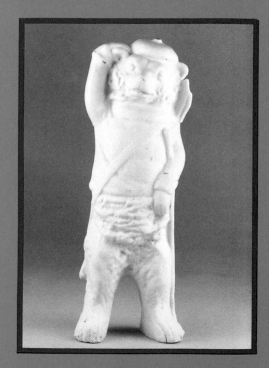

Fig 8.27 Comic bear dressed in sweater and tam. He carries skis across his back. Traces of the original gold paint cling to cap and cuff. I do not know whether this piece had any other paint. #9885; 7.75″

Fig 8.29 Girl piano baby, mate to Fig 8.28. She wears a snowed night shirt and snowed cap with ribbons. 2.75″

Chapter 9
Three Inch Babies

If they could stretch to their full height, the babies discussed in this chapter would be roughly three inches tall. Some were manufactured before, others after World War I, so they span the two major time periods during which "old" snow babies were produced.

Tumblers

Among the three-inch babies are five seen more frequently than the rest. Collectors sometime refer to these as "the tumblers." Jean Crowley Goodman first used that term casually to designate two of them. These solitary babies can be found sitting or standing alone, pegged to sleds or glued to wooden skis. Figs 9.1 through 9.10 show the tumblers in various positions.

Perhaps because of their intaglio eyes and nicely detailed faces, the tumblers are sometimes attributed to Heubach, but there is no evidence to confirm this origin. In fact, two (Figs 9.1a and 9.3a) have been found on a Hertwig and Company sample card (Cieslik 1987). Both of these appear on that card wearing skis, although they are seldom found in the United States on skis.

There is evidence that some tumblers were made as early as 1909, and some as late as 1928. The paper label on Fig 21.1 tells us that it was produced in 1909 or earlier. Of all the pieces in this book that can be dated precisely, this is the oldest. The Alaska Yukon Pacific Exhibition, in addition to selling little snow babies, exhibited real Eskimos in an Eskimo village. The souvenir bisque "Eskimo baby," as the tag reads, makes sense in this context. Some old catalogs used this term rather than "snow baby" to describe snow-covered bisque pieces. Line drawings in catalog reprints show that some of these same tumblers (Figs 9.2b, 9.3a and 9.4) were being produced as late as the early 1930s.

Marie Johnson (1972) stated that the earlier examples had muted colors and carefully painted features, whereas those made later had more "orangey" complexions and hastily painted features. This interpretation mirrors the changes that took place in doll and figurine production during the same period.

All the tumblers except Fig 9.3b are sometimes seen pegged to sleds as singles, pairs and even triples. The combination of babies shown in Fig 9.7b is the one most frequently seen on a sled together. Other combinations occur, supporting the theory that these pieces were made by the same company at roughly the same time.

Fig 9.9 features two tumblers and an unusual baby in a matte black suit. The object extending from his lap is probably a brush: chimney sweeps were popular symbols of luck in Edwardian times. The Cieslik's article (1987) shows this baby in black on a similar, snow-covered sled with one tumbler, and in a smaller version with an Alaska tot (Fig 10.168b) on a sled.

Fig 9.2 Two examples of the tumbler who sits leaning forward. a. An early example with a fired face. Notice the molded creases in his snow suit. 2.12" b. This nearly identical baby was probably made in the late 1920s: the face is slightly orange-colored, the pose is less naturalistic and there is no evidence of the careful molding of clothing creases. An example of this piece was purchased new in the 1930s. 2.25"

Fig 9.3 a. This is the tumbler who lies on his side. He was not meant to stand; his drain hole is in his side. This is a carefully done, early fired face with nicely shaded cheeks. An example of this piece is shown on a 1910 Christmas cake (Fig 21.2). 2.0" b. An early example of the tumbler who stands, crouching slightly. This baby looks like he is just learning to walk. An example on skis is shown in a Hertwig and Company sample box (Cieslik 1987). 2.75"

Fig 9.1 Two examples of a tumbler who is usually seen on a sled. This tumbler leans back. Unsupported and unpegged, he does not sit up well. Both are early examples with fired faces. a. Finding this tumbler on skis in the United States is unusual. However, an example on skis is shown in a Hertwig and Company sample box (Cieslik 1987). This particular example was never pegged to a sled: his drain-hole is too small for a peg. 2.75" b. This baby is often found without his sled, but with the peg still in place. 2.5"

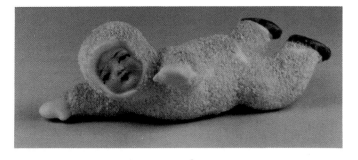

Fig 9.4 The tumbler who lies prone. His feet and his left hand are raised. Notice the nose dots and curved eyebrows; this is a carefully made, early example. I have seen a later example of this baby dressed in a mustard yellow suit. This baby was also finished in a red-flocked suit, with a slit in his back to hold a place card! 1.12"

Other Three-Inch Babies

The Christmas 1911 issue of *Ladies' Home Journal* (Fig 21.3) pictured a Christmas cake decorated with three-inch snow babies. The standing baby on the cake (Fig 9.11b) is less common than the tumblers. I have not seen it pictured in a catalog from the twenties, nor have I seen it with a "later" face. It may have been produced only briefly.

Another pair found fairly often are Figs 9.12a and 9.12b. These are surely younger versions of the four-inch children molded as skiers and skaters (Figs 8.12 and 8.13). Their clothing is like that of the older figures. The faces are similarly drawn, using an especially vivid red for the mouths. The little girl is also shown on the Hertwig sample card mentioned above.

Several children in this chapter are unquestionably unsigned Heubach figures. The boy skater (Fig 9.15b) is a variation on the famous little Dutch boy, who sits in a similar position, made and signed by Heubach. Also unmarked, the pair of girls in black (Fig 9.16) were sold in 1982 at auction by Theriault's, who attributed them to Heubach.

Fig 9.5 Two more examples of the prone tumbler, both probably made later. **a.** This baby's face, although nicely painted, is probably not fired on. 1.25″ **b.** This one has an enameled face, and the molding is slightly different; he was made with less care. 1.12″

Fig 9.6 Prone tumbler with an early face. He is pegged to a bisque sled that is incised "Germany" on one runner. 1.75″

Fig 9.8 Three tumblers on a sled. The front one leans back, the other two lean forward. These babies have early fired faces. A variation of this piece is shown on a 1910 Christmas cake (Fig 21.2). Sled is incised "Germany". 3.0″

Fig 9.7 These are early pieces with fired faces. Both sleds are incised "Germany". **a.** The tumbler who sits leaning back (Fig 9.1) pegged to a sled. If you find a solitary tumbler on a sled, it is usually this one. (Identical to Fig 21.1). 2.87″ **b.** Two tumblers pegged to a sled. The front tumbler leans back, the rear one leans forward. This is the two-tumbler combination most likely to be found pegged to a sled. Shown in 1911 on a cake (Fig 21.3). 3.0″

Fig 9.9 The three babies on this sled are facing the wrong direction. Probably at some time they were incorrectly re-pegged. From left to right: The first is the tumbler on his side; the last is the tumbler who leans forward. The middle one is dressed in a matte black suit. He could be a chimney sweep baby, with a small broom tied to his waist. Sweeps were considered good luck in Victorian times. The sled is snowed, which is quite unusual. See text for more information. 3.0″

Fig 9.10 The tumbler who sits leaning back, dressed in a gold suit. At one time it probably had a gold glitter finish; now it looks like tarnished brass. The sled is probably not original. Baby is 2.5".

Fig 9.12 These two young children are dressed and painted much like Figs 8.12 and 8.13. Although they look as if they have been fired, I have seen examples with no paint. They are sometimes found pegged. **a.** The girl was shown on wooden skis on a Hertwig sample card (Cieslik 1987). 2.0" **b.** Boy. 2.0"

Fig 9.11 **a.** Baby with an unfired face in a tassel cap, sparsely snowed. He is meant to lie on his side in this position. It is likely that this was a late piece. 2.12"
b. Examples of this standing baby were pictured around a cake in the December 1911 *Ladies' Home Journal* shown in Fig 21.3. Another is shown on a 1910 Christmas cake in Fig 21.2. Notice the way his pants legs hang down around his shoes, nearly covering them. This style is quite different from the clothing of the tumblers. This baby has an early, fired face. 2.87"

Fig 9.13 An unusual piece, carefully painted and fired. His sweater and hat have been covered with a very fine-textured grout, which was necessarily fine because the lettering on the cap was simply painted onto the snow. This was probably an advertising or souvenir piece for some European town: the lettering ends in -berg. I sent the picture to a family in Germany, who were unable to determine what town it might be. The scarf around the boy's neck is clearly visible under the snow. The sled is unique in my experience: the post that sticks up in front of the boy is threaded. Could this have been a steering device? #8195; 2.25"

Fig 9.14 This child in carefully molded clothing has a snowed hat. He lies on his back with his head tilted forward. Could he have been on a sled at one time? 1.12"

Fig 9.15 These two skaters, although not marked with a factory logo, were made by Heubach. The face and pose of the boy closely resemble other Heubach figures. Both figures have snowed caps, sweaters and skates; snow is also sprinkled on other parts. I have seen pictures of two other "fallen skaters" in similar colors and poses that must have been a part of this set. a. Girl appears to have just fallen. She wears a brown skirt; her hat is tied on with a long scarf. #8516; 1.25" b. Boy leans back, propped up by his arms. The lining of the ear flaps of his cap matches the girl's scarf. 1.75"

Fig 9.18 Two children wearing real mohair wigs slide down a wedge. They don't appear to be dressed for snowy weather. It is unlike any other piece I have seen. #457-I; 3.0"

Fig 9.16 These girls closely resemble a child who appears on post cards from Munich, which means "the home of the monks." The two were advertised by Theriault's as Heubach. Gold paint highlights the sleds. a. This girl probably held a cord in her left hand that passed through the hole in the crossbar of her sled. In her right hand she holds a stick. 2.87" b. This sled is also drilled for a cord, but there is no provision for the girl lying on the sled to hold it. 2.5"

Fig 9.19 Little girl in a cap who seems to have taken a tumble from her skis. She is not dressed warmly. A smaller snowed version of this piece is shown in Fig 10.141a. 1.25"

Fig 9.17 This baby has obviously just taken a fall. His head and shoulders haven't even hit the ground! The snow on this piece is translucent and shiny— the type usually associated with Heubach pieces. 1.37"

Fig 9.20 Two skaters on pedestal bases, each marked "Occupied Japan" in red. The figures have been carefully molded and painted. a. Child in green shirt. 3.5" b. Child in blue shirt losing his balance. 3.25"

Part II: Later Snow Baby Production

The next chapters are devoted to the snow baby pieces that predominated during the years following the war.

Chapter 10
Later Babies

This chapter shows the types of snow baby made between the world wars. These figures are smaller than the three-inch babies, and they make up the bulk of most snow baby collections. Indeed, many collectors are interested only in these smaller pieces.

Quality and Age

It is firing at the correct temperature that gives ceramic paint its permanence. Most snow baby pieces made after World War I were not fired after painting, or were fired at a temperature too low to bond paint to porcelain. Consequently, these later pieces must be handled carefully and protected from dust and dirt.

Over the entire period that snow babies were produced, there was a general decrease in the attention given to the details of face paint. In the later pieces, eyebrows became a hastily applied dash of paint or were omitted altogether. Eyes were often indicated with a round black dot instead of an eyelid line with pupil underneath. Even the mouth was sometimes reduced to a red dot. It is not possible, however, to determine the age of a snow baby simply by noting how elaborately the face is painted. Some factories continued to produce more detailed faces, whereas others probably never did spend much time on such decorations. In general, as demand and production increased, quality declined.

A few of the babies made during this period, especially the small solitary babies, resemble earlier pieces. There are babies lying prone, reclining on their sides or sitting with their legs apart. But these later pieces usually lack the detailed face painting of the earlier ones. Solitary babies were now cast in many new poses and painted with more and brighter colors. Some were provided imaginative props that add novelty and interest.

During the twenties and thirties a number of group pieces were made. These often incorporate several figures, including children, animals and snowmen. Some pieces create tiny scenes on molded bisque bases. Often the base is the only part of the scene that is grouted, but sometimes the figures themselves are snowed. Other pieces were made with no base. If you are trying to identify a piece from a verbal description, the question "Does it have a base?" can sometimes help.

Tinies

Small babies measuring about one inch, sometimes referred to as "tinies," appeared during this time in far more poses and with sketchier faces that those manufactured before World War I. Even within this category there are several sizes. The difference in scale between a piece ¾ inch high and one that is an inch high is considerable—33%, in fact. The faces of these tinies range from carefully molded and painted to poorly detailed. Some faces were fired after painting, an indication that they may have been made somewhat earlier.

Fig 10.2 Baby hugs a brown bear cub. They look like the same baby and bear as in Fig 10.1. Stamped "Germany" in blue. 2.0"

Fig 10.3 Between them, two babies carry a brown bear, lashed upside down to a pole. #1649; 1.87"

Fig 10.1 Baby climbs cautiously onto a snow cave or small house of ice. Does he know that a brown bear cub is sleeping inside? Stamped "Germany" in blue. #2702; 2.0"

Fig 10.4 a. This baby carries an object that could be an Olympic torch with a blue flame. It has also been suggested that this could be a very short bag of golf clubs. The baby strolls along with a snowed, pink-nosed polar bear. Stamped "Germany" in blue. 2.0" b. This one carries a pair of tiny skis over his shoulder; a small dog or bear cub nips at the seat of his trousers. In some examples the animal is also snowed. Stamped "Made in France", but it looks just like German pieces. #1180; 1.75"

Fig 10.5 This baby has taken refuge under a ledge from a very friendly looking snowed polar bear. It has been found with "50¢" pencilled on it. #378; 1.87"

Fig 10.6 Snow baby carrying a lantern leads a bridled polar bear. The bear hauls a pack of toys from which dolls overflow. 1.5"

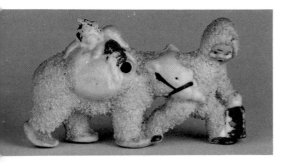

The very smallest of the solitary tinies (Fig 10.175) were probably made late. They almost always have a blue "Germany" stamped on the underside; as a group they are unusually free from dirt. Several collectors have told me that many of these tiny snow babies were sold in the 1970s as leftover store stock for $3.00 each! Even so, they are difficult to find.

No-Snows

Even before World War I, some snow babies were made in both snowed and unsnowed versions. This happened more frequently after the war. Babies without grout were sometimes coated with either coralene or glitter snow. Some were left completely unsnowed, their suits either white or painted red.

The inspiration for the red-suited babies has not been determined, but from about 1916 until at least the mid-1920s, the Whitney Company published Christmas post cards showing little babies dressed in red (Fig 21.9). These "Nimble Nicks," as they were called, are pictured both at play and hard at work making toys. Could they be a link between the babies and Santa's elves? Nimble Nicks engaged in more varied activities than the sledding babies Ellen Clapsaddle drew years earlier (Fig 21.7), just as the snow babies of the 1920s were created in far more poses than those of a decade before. Maybe the post cards inspired the bisque babies, or vice versa.

Bands and Other Sets

Most of the babies that make up sets were also produced during this time. The best-known of the sets are the two snow baby bands. In one band each baby marches on his own base. In the other band each figure is stationary and has no base.

The marching band babies (Figs 10.64 and 10.65) are thinner and wear pants that expose their red-orange shoes. They stride along in unison. The fife player and the drummer are slightly more difficult to find than the other members.

There is considerable disagreement over whether the marching band has five or six members. The piece in dispute (Fig 10.64a) could be either the conductor or a baby playing stick ball. In his left hand this baby holds either a baton or a bat. The baby's feet are positioned just like those of the band members, but stuck to his backside is a red sphere. This is difficult to explain unless he is playing baseball, and the sphere is the ball he has just missed. The incised numbers on these figures should resolve the dispute, but they don't. The rest of this band is numbered 1181 through 1185, but the number on the piece in question is not easy to read. It could be 1180, 1780, or 1880 —depending on who reads which sample.

The stationary band (Fig 10.67 and 10.68) is slightly more common. These stout babies have baggy trousers, and only the toes of their black shoes show. In this six-piece band the drummer is more difficult to find. This is probably because, with the cymbal raised high in the air and the baby standing on one foot and the other heel, this piece is more vulnerable to breakage.

The hunting party (Figs 10.62 and 10.63) is an uncommon set. Tall and thin, these babies have the proportions of older children. They wear bell-bottomed pants and carry unusual items such as a rope and a collar or noose. Two carry clubs, and two hold guns! The guns are especially rare. Among over 1000 different snow baby pieces, I have seen only 3 firearms: these 2 figures plus the pink snow child in the Scottish kilt (Fig 3.9). The whole party seems to be outfitted for hunting, probably polar bears or walruses.

Fig 10.7 Igloo with a snow baby standing inside and a polar bear standing on top. This piece is stamped "Germany" in black, but I have seen what appears to be an identical piece stamped "Japan". 2.37"

Fig 10.8 Two consecutively numbered pieces show babies in red with attentive polar bear nannies. a. Polar bear on his hind feet strolls along hand in hand with two tiny babies on a snowed base. #371; 1.62" b. Upright polar bear gives a baby a ride on a sled. #370; 1.62"

Fig 10.9 With rope and ice ax, this baby is ready for ice climbing. A tiny bear nuzzles his leg. Stamped "Germany" in blue on a no-snow base. 2.0"

Series

Several snow babies (for example, Figs 10.85, 10.88 and 10.128) with similar facial features have four-digit incised numbers in the 5100 series. Although collectors don't think of them as a set, they do have some features in common. These babies have facial features and stout body shapes similar to the stationary band members, and they often have heavy black eyebrows. All of these babies are sledders, skiers or skaters. It is likely that they were all made by the same manufacturer, along with other babies that have these same features but no incised numbers.

Snow Dome Inserts

Several Japanese pieces have been called bottle stoppers, but they are probably all snow dome inserts. No collector reported seeing a snow baby piece actually used as a bottle stopper. Furthermore, disassembled snow domes, such as Fig 17.13, contain inserts with bases exactly like those of the "bottle stoppers." Additionally, many of these pieces have been seen in intact snow domes.

Original Pricing

Several pieces have been found still bearing their original store tags. The prices typically range from 10¢ to 25¢. Other pieces are found with prices as high as 50¢ pencilled onto their undersides. The pencilled prices are less reliable, of course, unless the piece has remained with the original owners who can vouch for its authenticity. To put these prices into perspective, in the late 1920s 10 cents would buy a can of spaghetti, and 25 cents would buy a women's magazine. The snow baby pieces made during this period were inexpensive novelty items not intended to be treasured the way they are today.

Fig 10.12 The molded dress of this little girl shows clearly under her applied snow. The well-defined, muscular bear ambles along. Examples of this piece were purchased new between 1924 and 1934. 2.25"

Fig 10.10 This snowed baby rests his head in one hand and waves with the other as he sits atop a pink-nosed polar bear. Stamped "Germany" in purple. 2.0"

Fig 10.13 a. This no-snow piece shows two babies riding a pink-nosed polar bear. The rear baby holds a bit of holly in his hand. The material used to make this piece is not high quality porcelain; it has a chalkier feel than that used for most snow babies. Stamped faintly on the bottom is a word that could be either "Germany" or "England". 1.75" b. Tiny baby rides a tiny pink-nosed polar bear. Stamped "Germany" in blue. 1.5"

Fig 10.11 a. This baby has the remnants of glitter snow clinging to his suit. Holding a banjo, he sits on a polar bear. Stamped "Germany" in black on the opposite side of the polar bear. 2.25" b. This baby sits with both arms in the air on a grinning polar bear. 2.25"

Fig 10.14 These no-snow pieces show children in nearly mirror-image positions. They wear Eskimo-type snow suits and ride carefully detailed polar bears. Each incised #2938; each is 4.12" high. a. Waves left hand. b. Waves right hand.

Fig 10.15 This baby is not marked, but it is not German. Although it is carefully molded and painted, the snow is coarse and was probably glued on. 2.75"

Fig 10.16 Three babies in red ride on the back of a snowed polar bear. From the front it is difficult telling whether these are babies or elves, but they have no wings and their hoods are attached to their little suits. Stamped "Germany" in purple. #367; 1.75"

Fig 10.17 Seeming to call out, a baby leans back and waves as he rides on the back of a large reindeer. Stamped "Germany" in red. #347; 2.62"

Fig 10.18 Baby on a reindeer. In this example the base is snowed, but the piece can also be found on an unsnowed base. 2.25"

Fig 10.19 A red baby sits on the back of a walrus. The baby holds a violin and brandishes a bow. This is the only walrus piece I know of, although walruses received much attention in the Peary books about the Arctic. 2.0"

Fig 10.20 A dog jumps up onto this reluctant snow baby for a lick. Stamped "Germany" in black. #2865; 2.0"

Fig 10.21 Snow baby feeds a seal from a baby bottle. Stamped "Germany". #2364; 2.0"

Fig 10.22 Two examples of the baby who holds a ball over a seal's nose. a. Stamped "Germany". #2366; 2.0" b. Probably a snow dome insert. Unmarked, but probably not German. 2.5"

Fig 10.23 This baby with the seal and ball is not German, and is a late-production piece. The snow is coarse and appears to be glued on. 2.0"

Fig 10.24 Another baby with seal and ball. In this example the snow is crystalline. Although unmarked, this piece is probably not German. 1.5"

Fig 10.25 Two examples of a baby hugging a penguin. a. Stamped "Germany". #2365; 2.0" b. Plaster. 1.87"

Fig 10.26 This baby pulls a sled carrying the famous single-file penguins. This is the same baby who appears in the hunting party, Figs 10.62 and 10.63. Are these penguins the "catch?" Stamped "Germany" in black. 1.37"

Fig 10.27 Penguin nanny pushes two snow babies strapped to a sled. This does not appear to be original paint. #515; 1.62"

Fig 10.28 Two huskies pull a baby in a sleigh. This piece is numbered "7153" on the back of the sleigh, but it can also be found with "8512 Germany" on the base. 1.37"

Fig 10.29 Japanese version of Fig 10.28. Stamped "Japan". 1.25"

Fig 10.30 Chubby snow baby sits on a sled pulled by a single grey dog. 1.75"

Fig 10.31 Baby in a sleigh sits with both arms raised. The reindeer is meant to pull the sleigh, but there are no reins. 1.5"

Fig 10.32 This baby sits in a cradle-shaped sleigh that is definitely being pulled by the reindeer. 1.37"

Fig 10.33 a. A snow baby soccer player guides the ball with his foot. Stamped "Germany" in black. 1.75" b. This baby plays hockey. A small brown dog nips at his cuff. #1188; 1.87"

Fig 10.34 a. This baby holds a large ball on his shoulder. It could be a basketball, but he holds it more like a medicine ball. Medicine ball was an exercise popularized during the Hoover administration, 1929-1933. Stamped "Germany" in black. #2718; 1.62" b. One foot in the air, a baby kicks a ball. A small dog seems to be interfering. Stamped "Germany" in black. #2293; 2.25"

Fig 10.37 a. Baby carries a pair of skis, which he holds at a slant across his body, cradled in his arm. 1.62" b. This baby holds either a hockey stick or a golf club. 1.87"

Fig 10.35 Four seafaring snow babies. a. Tiny baby paddles an orange kayak. 1.12" b. Baby paddles a yellow kayak. 1.37" c. This baby steps from a canoe. He holds a double-bladed paddle. #2867; 2.0" d. Baby stands on a raft. The wind seems to be blowing hard. There are waves in the water, and the baby clutches at the sail and mast. A black dog or seal lies at his feet. Stamped "Germany" in black. #1636; 2.5"

Fig 10.38 Undaunted by his snowsuit, this baby brandishes a tennis racket. Stamped "Germany" in blue. 1.62"

Fig 10.36 Two tiny boating babies. a. Baby sits in a boat and holds a fishing pole. The line drifts into the pale blue water. Stamped "Germany" in black. 1.12" b. This baby carries a kayak at an angle and waves with his right hand. Stamped "Germany" in black. (There is also another piece—not pictured—that is nearly a mirror image of this one, but with the kayak held more upright; that baby waves his left hand.) 1.25"

Fig 10.39 Each of these pieces is stamped "Germany" in blue. a. Two babies dance together. This piece has been crudely reproduced; one version uses fluorescent paint. #2714; 2.0" b. Two babies in a tug of war over a nursing bottle. Notice that even the fingers are carefully molded. 1.5"

Fig 10.40 One baby visits another (his sweetheart?) at the window of an igloo. Of course, real igloos do not have windows. 2.25″

Fig 10.41 This is clearly a companion piece to Fig 10.40. One baby sits atop the igloo and holds a snowball. The other seems to be sliding in (or out) of the low entrance. Perhaps they are having a snowball fight (lovers' tiff?) 3.25″

Fig 10.42 Two babies climb an elaborate ice ledge. One signals that he has made it to the top. 3.12″

Fig 10.43 This is a companion piece to Fig 10.42. Notice that the orientation of the top ice ledge has been reversed. In this piece a single baby tumbles down the ledge near the bottom, perhaps frightened by the bear on top. Stamped "Germany" in red inside a donut. 2.75″

Fig 10.44 Two babies plant an American flag atop what must be a world globe. The globe has an opening at the back, but it doesn't look as if it was meant to be used as a container. I have been told that there is a snowed version of this piece. Incised "Germany". #5617; 3.25″

Fig 10.45 Baby stands on the bottom rung of a bisque ladder. 2.62″

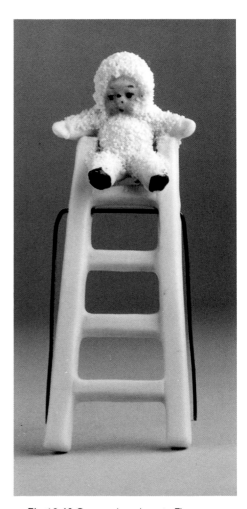

Fig 10.46 Companion piece to Fig 10.45, this baby sits on the top rung of the same bisque ladder. In each case the uprights of the ladder have been punctured for a thin wire that serves as a stand. 3.5″

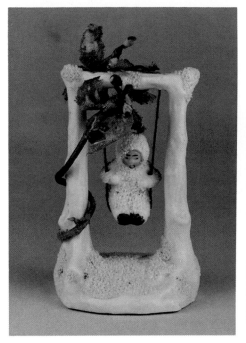

Fig 10.47 A baby on a string swing in a bisque arch. A similar piece is shown with a Santa in Fig 13.9. 3.12″

Fig 10.50 Two babies slide down a snowed stone wedge. The lead baby sits, the one behind is on its stomach. #6602; 1.5″

Fig 10.52 Two babies slide down an unsnowed brick wedge. The first sits, the second seems to have belly-flopped. 2.25″

Fig 10.48 The snow baby air force. **a.** Baby sits on top of a silver plane. A similar piece with a Santa is shown in Fig 13.74. Although not common, this is the easiest to find of the baby-in-airplane pieces. Sometimes the plane is red. An example on a red airplane was purchased new between 1924 and 1935. #1699; 1.75″ **b.** Tiny red baby sits atop a biplane. 1.5″ **c.** Baby sits in the cockpit of a plump red airplane. This piece is quite heavy, and though it is stamped "Germany" in block letters, it is possible that it isn't German. 1.5″

Fig 10.53 Two children slide down a no-snow brick wedge. The girl is in front and wears a blue skirt; the boy wears black pants. This is a commonly found piece. This example is glittered; the piece can be found unsnowed or with grouted snow. It was also done in a composition material. An example of this piece with grouted snow was purchased new in the 1930s. Stamped "Germany" in black. 2.25″

Fig 10.51 Similar to Fig 10.50, this piece is harder to find. These two identical babies are both sliding down a snowy wedge on their stomachs. Stamped "Germany" in black. 1.5″

Fig 10.49 Two tiny babies look quite out of place on a World War I tank that is rumbling over rough ground. #514; 2.25″

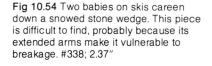

Fig 10.54 Two babies on skis careen down a snowed stone wedge. This piece is difficult to find, probably because its extended arms make it vulnerable to breakage. #338; 2.37″

Fig 10.55 a. Single baby slides down a snowed wedge. The incised number appears on the front of this piece. An example was purchased new as a party favor in about 1934. Stamped "Germany" in blue. #1221; 1.62" b. One baby runs along pushing a smaller baby on a sled. 1.25"

Fig 10.56 Japanese version of Fig 10.55a. Incised "Japan" and stamped "Japan" in purple. 2.12"

Fig 10.58 Three children stand proudly around their snowman. One child adjusts the hat. Stamped "Germany" in purple. 2.25"

Fig 10.59 The back view of Fig 10.58 shows the beautiful detail, even on the side that was not normally viewed. It also shows how each child, touching the snowman, feels pride in their creation.

Fig 10.60 Two babies on either side of an igloo. A small snowman squats behind one baby. There are enamelled trees in the background. This piece was once coated with coralene. The substance used is of a low quality similar to Fig 10.13a. I cannot say where or when these pieces were made. 2.0"

Fig 10.57 Two non-German, late-production pieces. The snow on each is coarse, and appears to be glued on rather than fired on. a. Baby slides down a wedge on his stomach. 1.5" b. Baby stands on a wedge. 1.87"

Fig 10.61 A piece made of material similar to Fig 10.60. This girl strides along in a winter coat, hat and fur-trimmed boots. She carries a tree that is so thin it looks more like a leaf. It was purchased in England, but I don't know where it was made. 2.37"

Fig 10.62 The pieces shown in Figs 10.62 and 10.63 form a six-person hunting party. All of the members but Fig 10.62b are stamped "Germany" in black; all are 1.5" tall. **a.** Runs along with a gold club. **b.** Holds a club or harpoon. **c.** Carries a noose or collar.

Fig 10.63 The remainder of the hunting party. All stamped "Germany" in black; all are 1.5". To see what they caught, turn back to Fig 10.26. **a.** Holds a rifle across his body. **b.** Carries a rifle upright under his arm. **c.** Carries a coiled rope across his shoulder.

Fig 10.64 This and Fig 10.65 show the marching snow baby band. Each of these pieces has been found stamped "Germany" in one collection or another. Each is 2.0" tall. **a.** This is the band conductor or baseball player. (See text.) His number has been read as 1180, 1780 and 1880—take your pick. **b.** Plays the fife. #1182 **c.** Plays the drum and cymbals. #1181

Fig 10.65 Marching snow baby band, continued. **a.** Plays the sousaphone. #1184 **b.** Plays the concertina. #1185 **c.** Plays the saxophone. #1183

Fig 10.66 Two members of the marching band (Figs 10.64c and 10.64a), made of composition material. They have a glazed finish, and their suits are covered with coralene. They were probably brought into the United States after World War II. Each is 1.62" **a.** Plays the drum and cymbals. **b.** Holds the baton (or bat), but has no red sphere on his backside.

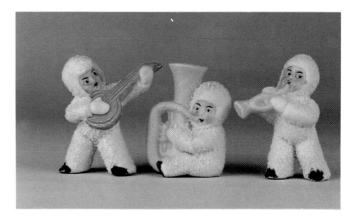

Fig 10.67 This and Fig 10.68 show the stationary snow baby band. Compared to the marching band, these babies are stouter; only the tips of their shoes show under their long, wide pants. This band has no leader. Examples of these pieces were purchased new in the 1930s. Each player has been found stamped "Germany" in black. **a.** Plays the banjo. 1.75" **b.** Sits to play the tuba. 1.62" **c.** Plays the trumpet. 1.75"

Fig 10.68 See Fig 10.67. **a.** Plays the saxophone. 1.75" **b.** Plays the concertina. 1.75" **c.** Plays the drum and cymbals. 2.0"

Fig 10.72 Two children dressed in matching clothes push large snowballs. Each is 2.0" **a.** This appears to be the same girl shown sitting on a snowball in Fig 10.71. **b.** Boy, mate to Fig 10.72a.

Fig 10.70 Stationary band drum and cymbals player with a coralene finish. This piece is bisque and not the composition material used for Fig 10.66. This baby is stamped "Germany US Zone" in black. 2.0"

Fig 10.69 China-finished version of the stationary band. These pieces are very similar, but not identical, in molding to the bisque version. Two are stamped "Foreign", indicating that they were probably imported into England in the late 1930s or 1940s. Examples of these pieces were purchased new in the 1930s or 1940s. Notice the blue mittens on several pieces. Glazed Santas from the 1940s (Figs 13.89 through 13.97) wear mittens like these. Top row. **a.** Baby plays concertina. Stamped "Germany" in purple. 1.75" **b.** Baby plays saxophone. Stamped "Germany" in purple. 2.0" **c.** Baby plays banjo. Stamped "Foreign" in purple. 1.87" **d.** Baby plays trumpet. Stamped "Foreign". 2.12" **e.** Baby plays drum and cymbals. 2.37" **f.** Seated baby plays tuba. 1.87"

Fig 10.73 Snow baby pushes a large snowball. There is also a baby sitting on a snowball (unpictured). 1.87"

Fig 10.71 Unsnowed girl in a red skirt sits on a snowed snowball. See her on a sled with Santa in Fig 13.87. 2.5"

Fig 10.74 Plaster baby pushes a snowball. 1.87"

Fig 10.75 Plaster girl pushes an enormous snowball. Stamped "Made in England" in a circle. 1.5"

Fig 10.78 A pyramid of three babies. A tiny baby in yellow sits on a red baby on his hands and knees, who in turn rests on a snowed baby, all on a base. #2773; 2.0"

Fig 10.81 This is a tiny no-snow boy with his hat tied on. He sits on a sled on a very tall base. This piece was purchased attached to the black snow dome base shown in the picture. 1.75"

Fig 10.76 Snowed mother or nursemaid pushes two babies in a buggy. In some examples the mother's shoes are snowed; the babies' hoods can be found unsnowed. An example was purchased new between 1924 and 1934. Stamped "Germany" in black. #7156; 2.5"

Fig 10.79 Two snow baby figures made of composition material. They stand on thick bases, and are probably snow dome inserts. **a.** Pyramid of babies similar to Fig 10.78. 2.25" **b.** Girl skater. 2.87"

Fig 10.82 Boy carries a sled on a snow dome insert base. This piece has been seen in a snow dome. Stamped "Japan" in black. 2.62"

Fig 10.77 Snow baby crawls along giving a ride to a baby in red. 2.62"

Fig 10.80 Tiny no-snow boy skier on a tall base. This was meant to be attached to something through the holes low on the base. It could have been in a snow dome, or sewed to something decorative such as a pincushion. It is unmarked, but definitely German. Height, including base, is 1.5".

Fig 10.83 Two snow dome insert skaters. **a.** Boy in a snowed sweater and hat. It has been seen in a snow dome. Stamped "Japan" in black. 2.62" **b.** Girl dressed in warm clothes carries a muff. This piece is not German. 2.62"

67

Fig 10.84 Three tiny babies on a long tan sled. Stamped "Germany" in purple. 1.5"

Fig 10.87 Two babies with fired faces sit unattached on a snowed bisque sled. 1.62"

Fig 10.85 Two sets of babies on bisque sleds. They are identical except that the second is snowed and slightly larger. **a.** Three no-snow babies on a sled. #5106; 1.62" **b.** Same, with snow. 1.75"

Fig 10.88 Two babies on a sled, similar in style and position to those in Fig 10.85. They are numbered in sequence with Fig 10.85a. Stamped "Germany" in red. #5107; 1.75"

Fig 10.86 These pieces, composition material with a china finish, were probably made after World War II, but I don't know where they were made. **a.** Baby lies on his side. Most of his coralene finish is gone. 1.5" **b.** Three coralene babies on a crude sled. 2.0"

Fig 10.89 Two examples, German and Japanese, of one baby pulling another on a sled. Each is 1.62". **a.** An example of this piece was purchased new in the 1930s. Stamped "Germany" in purple. #5299 **b.** This less carefully molded piece is stamped "Japan" in purple.

Fig 10.90 One baby pushes a much tinier baby on a simple, boxy sled. An example of this piece was purchased between 1924 and 1934. Stamped "Germany" in black. #5010; 2.25"

Fig 10.93 a. Two children in old-fashioned clothes on a toboggan. An example of this piece was purchased new in the 1930s. Stamped "Germany" in black. 1.62" **b.** Three children on a sled. Incised "Germany". 1.5"

Fig 10.91 Identical to Fig 10.90, except that the children's snowed clothing has been painted. Stamped "Germany" in black. #5010; 2.25"

Fig 10.94 Two examples of the same pose, showing a girl riding behind a boy on a sled. The first example is made of German bisque; the second is made of a composition material. **a.** The children have applied snow on their hats, and snow sprinkled on the horizontal surfaces of their clothing. Stamped "Germany" in purple. #2236; 1.62" **b.** No applied snow, but there is molded snow on the caps. 1.5"

Fig 10.96 Tiny baby in a snowed suit that has been gilded. 1.25"

Fig 10.92 a. A baby sits on another baby who lies prone on a red sled. Stamped "Germany" in black. 1.87" **b.** Baby kicks a soccer ball with his right foot. 1.37"

Fig 10.95 Tiny, uncommon baby on a boxy sled. His snow is coarse, even when viewed from a greater distance. 1.75"

Fig 10.97 The first three of these pieces are German babies on red sleds. The last is from the 1979 Shackman set, made in Taiwan and shown for contrast. **a.** Baby rests on left hip and hand. 1.37" **b.** Baby sits with right foot and arm raised. Stamped "Germany" in black. 1.37" **c.** Baby stands, both arms outstretched. Stamped "Germany" in black. 1.62" **d.** Baby from 1979 Shackman boxed set. 1.62"

Fig 10.98 Baby on a sled. The baby is made of a composition material and has coralene snow; it is probably not German. 1.5"

Fig 10.99 Baby leans back on one elbow and waves from a sled. These are two examples of the same German piece in different sizes and finishes. **a.** Snowed piece. #5130; 2.0" **b.** Baby in red. 1.5"

Fig 10.100 Two non-German examples of the piece shown in Fig 10.99. Each is 1.62" **a.** Coarse snow that is probably glued on. **b.** Red-suited baby.

Fig 10.101 Pair of children in matching clothes astride bisque sleds. Each is incised "Germany 8721", and each is 2.25". **a.** Girl. **b.** Boy.

Fig 10.102 Tiny versions of the children in Fig 10.101, painted in a different combination of colors. **a.** Girl in an orange skirt astride a sled. 1.5" **b.** Boy in orange pants on a sled. Stamped "Germany" in black. 1.62"

Fig 10.103 Girl in a lavender skirt lies on a bisque sled, propped up on her elbows. She wears a snowed sweater and cap. This is a common piece. She has a near mirror-image boy mate, not photographed. Stamped "Germany" in black. 1.5"

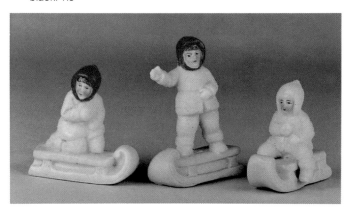

Fig 10.104 Three girls wear molded winter clothes snowed with coralene. On their undersides the first two pieces still have their original price stickers: 15¢. a. Girl kneels on a bisque sled. This and the next piece have no coralene on their red hoods. #4882; 1.75" b. Girl stands on a bisque sled. #4883; 2.25" c. Very like the other two, this girl has been seen with a red hood covered with coralene. Stamped "Germany" in black. #7; 1.5"

Fig 10.105 A boy wearing a sweater, cap and knee-length pants sits on a bisque sled. He has a fired face, and he has been molded with careful attention to detail. His snow and sled have been dusted lightly with snow. #8113; 1.87"

Fig 10.106 Boy and girl in bright-colored clothing sit on oversized sleds. Each has fired paint. Each is incised #5891 and is 2.5" tall. a. Girl holds something in her hand, but what is it? b. The boy also appears as a skier in Fig 10.133.

Fig 10.107 This child pulls a tiny sled up a low wedge. Notice the similarity to the children in Fig 10.106. Incised "Germany". #5714/6/0; 2.37"

Fig 10.108 Pair of children wearing snowed sweaters and caps. They recline on bisque sleds. Both pieces are incised "Germany", and they are numbered consecutively. a. Boy wearing orange knickers and high-button leggings lolls on his sled. #4642; 1.62" b. Girl wearing a collared blouse and a suit jacket over her orange skirt lies on her side and holds something to her ear. It looks like a fish! (What is it really?) #4641; 1.75" (She is slightly taller than her mate, due to the fish.)

Fig 10.109 Three consecutively numbered babies on sleds. Each of them wears a snowed suit and separate cap. The sleds are all similarly molded. Each is incised "Germany". a. This baby looks as if he has just crawled onto the sled and is pushing off. #5119; 1.5" b. Baby sits with one leg on the sled, one dangling. #5121; 1.75" c. This baby sits with both feet on the sled and waves. #5120; 1.75"

Fig 10.112 This is the same baby as Fig 10.111b, but the snow has been painted red and highlighted with gold. 1.87"

Fig 10.110 Three snow babies on sleds. a. Similar to Fig 10.109c, but in a smaller size. Stamped "Germany" in red. 1.37" b. Tiny baby stands on a bisque sled. 1.62" c. Baby lies on his left hip and arm on a bisque sled. 1.62"

Fig 10.113 Baby lies prone on a boxy sled, his head and shoulders raised. This same baby and sled are seen in other poses: see Figs 10.114 and 10.90. Usually, little attention was paid to the detail of these faces. An example was purchased new between 1924 and 1934. 1.75"

Fig 10.114 Similar to Fig 10.113, this one sits erect on a boxy bisque sled. An example was purchased new between 1924 and 1934. Stamped "Germany" in black. 2.25"

Fig 10.111 Two versions of a classic snow baby pulling a sled. a. Beautifully painted red baby. These pieces have not been carefully fired, so they are seldom found with their paint in such pristine condition. 2.25" b. This slightly smaller snowed version can also be found in the 2.25" size. An example was purchased new between 1924 and 1934. Stamped "Germany" in purple. 1.87"

Fig 10.115 These three pieces are numbered consecutively. a. Commonly found girl in a short violet skirt, snowed sweater and cap. She lies on a bisque sled and kicks her legs. Stamped "Germany". #8447; 1.62" b. This girl sits, reclining on one elbow, one leg on the sled. She wears a snowed sweater and cap. Stamped "Germany" in blue. #8446; 1.25" c. No-snow girl, nearly a mirror image of Fig 10.115a. Stamped "Germany" in blue. #8448; 1.62"

Fig 10.116 Two Japanese babies recline on bisque sleds. The black paint on the sleds was probably meant to simulate cut-outs of a more elaborate sled. Examples of these two pieces were purchased new in the 1930s. **a.** This child has snow on his cap only. Incised "Japan". 1.75" **b.** This girl reclines seductively and flaunts her lavender shoes. Stamped "Japan". 1.5"

Fig 10.117 This baby is coated with crystalline snow. It is unmarked, nicely painted and probably Japanese. 1.5"

Fig 10.118 Two Japanese babies. **a.** No-snow version of Fig 10.117. It is incised "Japan". 1.75" **b.** Small baby in suit and hat, waving. 2.37"

Fig 10.119 No-snow girl in textured snowsuit and hat. She sits with both arms outstretched on a bisque sled. You can see the cord that prevents her from losing her mittens. I have not seen this piece with good face paint. Compare to the Santa on a sled (Fig 13.15). Faintly stamped "Germany". 3.0"

Fig 10.120 Three snowed skaters in motion on bases. Each wears gold skates, and each is stamped "Germany" in black. These are more commonly found as no-snow pieces. **a.** Boy balances on left foot. 2.0" **b.** Boy races, right foot touching the base. 1.87" **c.** Girl glides with both feet on her base, leaning forward. 2.0"

Fig 10.121 **a.** No-snow version of Fig 10.120c. Stamped "Germany" in black. 2.0" **b.** No-snow relaxed girl skater on a pedestal base. #11905; 2.25" **c.** No-snow boy similar in design and decoration to Fig 10.121a. He sits on a wooden sled stamped "Germany". 1.75"

Fig 10.122 Three little no-snow children who seem similar in design and execution to those in the previous two pictures. **a.** Boy seems about to throw a snowball. 2.37″ **b.** Girl stands on tiny wooden skis, each of which is stamped "Germany" in purple. 2.25″ **c.** Girl holds a snowball. 2.25″

Fig 10.125 **a.** Girl snowed skater carries a muff; both feet are firmly planted on the ice. She is probably the intended mate for Fig 10.123a. Stamped "Germany" in blue. #461; 2.0″ **b.** Boy and girl skaters on a single elaborate base with molded trees. #2711; 2.12″ **c.** No-snow boy in short pants, jacket and cap throws snowballs. Stamped "Germany" in blue. #5012; 1.87″

Fig 10.123 Pair of children skate on pedestal bases. They wear gold skates and are partly snowed. These are two of the four skaters found snowed and unsnowed that are mixed and matched as pairs. **a.** Boy with both feet on the base. Stamped "Germany" in purple. #461; 2.12″ **b.** Girl skates on one leg. Stamped "Germany" in purple. #460; 2.0″

Fig 10.126 Non-porcelain copy of the girl in Fig 10.123b. 2.0″

Fig 10.127 China-finished boy skater on a pedestal base. Stamped "Japan" in red. 2.87″

Fig 10.124 Pair of no-snow skaters, wearing gold skates. The girl is the same as Fig 10.123b; this time she is out with a different boy. Each glides along on one foot and each is incised #460 and is 2.0″. **a.** Boy skater. **b.** Notice the pompon ties on the girls coat. Girl is stamped "Germany" in purple.

Fig 10.128 Baby with silver skates who has just taken a spill. He is set on a little ice base which has the remnant of a blue line running around it. Incised "Germany". #5117; 1.25″

Fig 10.129 These two babies are in the 5100 series (see text). **a.** Baby on silver skates was probably meant as a mate to Fig 10.128. Stamped "Germany" in red. #5115; 1.62" **b.** Baby standing with his arms down, on long bisque skis. Incised "Germany". #5114; 1.75"

Fig 10.130 Although it is not numbered, this skiing baby with both arms up is an obvious mate to Fig 10.129b. Stamped "Germany" in black. 1.62"

Fig 10.132 Set of three cheery, no-snow babies wearing textured snowsuits. They sit or stand on low, hilly bases. Each baby wears shiny red mittens and shoes, and each costume is slightly different. Each piece is stamped "Germany" in black in a donut. **a.** Sits on a tiny sled, careening down a slope. 2.75" **b.** Stands on skis and waves. #3488; 2.87" **c.** Small tufts of hair show around his cap; his position is nearly a mirror image of Fig 10.132a. #3516; 3.0"

Left:
Fig 10.133 Boy wearing bright clothing skis up (!) a slight incline. Notice the similarity between this boy and Fig 10.106a. His incised number is in the same series as that of Fig 10.107. Incised "Germany". #5714/4/0; 2.25"

Fig 10.131 Two skiers with coralene snow. **a.** Boy in hooded sweater and orange pants. Although the coralene itself looks orange, it is really the orange paint under the coralene that lends color to these clear, glass beads. Both skis are incised "Germany". 2.12" **b.** Tiny boy wearing skis and carefully molded clothing stands on a mound. He is numbered in sequence with the coralene sledders shown in Fig 10.104. Incised "Germany". #4881; 1.75"

Fig 10.134 Two skiers wearing bright colors are numbered sequentially. **a.** Boy skis down a mound, using two ski poles. This piece bears a gold sticker of the McLellan Company of San Francisco. The EW McLellan Company was a wholesale florist that flourished from the early 1900s until 1933. In 1934 they disappeared from the city directory. Stamped "Germany" in red. #12056; 2.75" **b.** Girl skier wears long braids, a dress and cap. Stamped "Germany" in red. #12057; 2.87"

Fig 10.135 a. Boy on skis in a sweater and a snowed cap of unusual shape. He carries one ski pole. 1.87" b. Tiny baby on skis with crystalline snow, waving. Stamped "Germany" in red. 1.37"

Fig 10.139 Slightly larger version of the striped cuff skiers. Each is 2.75". a. #9470 b. Stamped "Germany" in black on the skis. #9469

Fig 10.136 Two Japanese skiers. a. Baby waves and carries a pole. 2.0" b. Tiny skier with green shoes. Stamped "Japan" in black. 1.5"

Fig 10.138 Two skiers with striped cuffs. Each is incised "763"; each is 2.5" tall. a. Child with blue pants. b. Child with pink pants.

Fig 10.140 Two boys made of composition material. They have glitter snow on their caps and sweaters. a. This skater has fallen. The skates are silver. 1.5" b. This boy holds a pair of skis upright in the crook of one arm. 2.75"

Fig 10.137 One snow baby skier gives a piggy-back ride to a smaller snow baby. Stamped "Germany" in purple. 2.62"

Fig 10.141 Pair of young children wearing snowed winter clothing and wooden skis. I saw examples of these babies only in New England. a. A baby who has just fallen. Her chin rests on her hands. A larger no-snow version of this piece is shown in Fig 9.19. 0.87" b. This child stands, knees bent slightly, gazing timidly down. 2.25"

Fig 10.142 These are the snow baby singers. These babies huddle together, reading and singing from the same sheet of music. #6712; 1.75"

Fig 10.143 Three babies, dressed in red, frolic around a white bisque sled. I have not seen a snowed version of this piece. An example was purchased new between 1924 and 1934. 1.75"

Fig 10.144 Three snowed babies walk hand in hand. There is a no-snow version with babies in red. That piece was stamped "Germany", but this one is not marked. 1.87"

Fig 10.145 Baby and a teddy bear walk along with their arms around each other. The teddy bear wears a blue bow at his neck. I have heard, but not verified, that the cloth flower was a trademark of the Hertwig Company. Stamped "Germany" in purple. 2.25"

Fig 10.146 No-snow version of Fig 10.145 has the baby in red. Stamped "Germany" in black. 2.25"

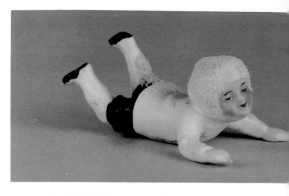

Fig 10.147 Two sets of the snow baby huggers. Both are German. **a.** Smaller, snowed huggers. An example was purchased new between 1924 and 1934. It has been nicely reproduced recently. This piece also exists in a 2.12″ version. Stamped "Germany" in black. 1.75″ **b.** Red-suited, no-snow version of the snow baby huggers. A similar piece is currently being made and sold; it is shown in Fig 19.6. 1.75″

Fig 10.152 The expression on this child's face doesn't reflect the fact that he has obviously just fallen down. There is snow on his helmet-type cap; the rest of him is lightly dusted with snow. #8187; 1.12″

Fig 10.150 Baby with a round, fat face and an O-mouth. Another example has been seen on skis. 2.25″

Fig 10.148 Has this baby taken a bigger step than he can manage? 2.5″

Fig 10.153 **a.** Unusual baby wears a pointed cap, ice skates and a look of anguish on his face. He has obviously just fallen. His snow is very finely textured. He comes close to qualifying as an all-white piece, but the expression on his face and the skates seem to set him apart from babies in that category. 1.5″ **b.** By contrast, this seated baby looks serene. Stamped "Germany" in blue. 1.37″

Fig 10.149 This baby seems to be hugging himself. 2.25″

Fig 10.151 This baby appears rather stiff. He is quite uncommon. Stamped "Germany" in blue. 2.0″

Fig 10.154 This baby with the slightly peaked hood appears in several poses. Usually his suit is white; less frequently he has an unsnowed red hood. In any pose the stomach protrudes and he has bell-bottomed pants. **a.** Smiling baby in red hood, mittens and shoes sits with arms waving. Stamped "Germany" in purple. 2.0″ **b.** Commonly found standing version of this baby. An example of this piece was purchased new in the 1930s. Stamped "Germany" in purple. 2.5″

Fig 10.155 This is the same baby as in Fig 10.154, molded to lie on its side. 1.5"

Fig 10.156 Same baby again, carrying snowballs. 2.0"

Fig 10.157 a. This baby is similar to the stationary band babies (Figs 10.67 and 10.68), but what is he carrying? It is painted gold—is it an oversized ring? A tire? (A gold tire?) 1.5" b. This one seems surprised to have taken a tumble. He leans back, resting on both arms. 1.0"

Fig 10.158 This baby resembles the stationary band members, but he carries an umbrella with a gold handle. Stamped "Germany" in black. 1.75"

Fig 10.159 This baby is on his way. His suitcase announces his destination: To North Pole. 1.75"

Fig 10.160 Three boys with very round heads and features that seem almost caricatured. The boys seem almost a cross between humans and snowmen. a. This standing boy might be a good quality reproduction of a German piece. His features are good, but not as fine as the other two shown here. There also exists a poor quality reproduction of this piece with very coarse snow. 2.75" b. This baby must be propped to sit. Perhaps he belongs on skis or a sled. An example was purchased new between 1924 and 1934. He was also made in a slightly different sitting position. 1.5" c. No-snow and better detailed version of the first piece. Marked "Germany" in black. #9774; 2.5"

Fig 10.161 Two babies in bunny suits. They do not stand well without skis. The baby in red shows the carefully molded ears that become indistinct when the piece is snowed. a. Snowed baby. Stamped "Germany" in purple. 2.5" b. Baby in red. 2.62"

Fig 10.162 Three snow babies in bunny suits. a. This baby kneels and could hold a feather tree in the hole in his fist. Stamped "Germany" in black. 2.37" b. This one lies on his side, with his ears back. You can see his tail. Stamped "Germany" in black. 1.87" c. This baby kneels on one knee; perhaps he is trying to stand. 2.12"

Fig 10.163 Two babies with stubby pompon caps and O-mouths. They are similar in style to Fig 10.150. These faces are not the original paint. a. Baby crawls. 1.0" b. Baby sits, knees and hands up. 1.12"

Fig 10.164 Baby who sits and leans on one hand. He has very coarse snow. 1.62"

Fig 10.165 This small sitting snow baby has very fine snow. Stamped "Japan" in black. 1.25"

Fig 10.166 Three snow babies on snowballs. The first is pre-World War II Japanese; the others are from the 1979 Shackman box, marked "Made in Taiwan". a. Baby stands on a snowball. It is covered in very fine snow. Stamped "Made in Japan" in black. 2.0" b. The pose is similar to 10.166a. 2.25" c. Baby sits on a snowball. 2.12"

Fig 10.167 This baby is similar in pose to Fig 10.166a,b, but it is finished with crystalline snow. Unmarked, but probably Japanese. 1.75"

Fig 10.168 Two examples of the baby described in the 1914 Marshall Field catalog as an "Alaska Tot". There she was sketched on tiny bisque skis. She has a tiny blue molded bow at the back of her neck. Each is 1.12" tall. a. Very unusual example of this baby, with deep red detailing. b. More usual Alaska Tot, photographed from an oblique perspective to show how far back she leans.

Fig 10.169 This tiny baby is the mate to Fig 10.168. He is more often found without his bisque sled. He measures 1.62″ with the sled, 1.12″ without.

Fig 10.170 Two similar babies. a. Common baby holds an upright pair of skis. Examples were purchased new between 1924 and 1934. Stamped "Germany" in black. 1.62″ b. Small baby kneels on one knee. 1.5″

Fig 10.171 Four babies, sometimes called "tinies." All of these babies have fired faces; for that reason they may be somewhat earlier than other tinies. a. Sits. 1.12″ b. Stands, legs apart. 1.37″ c. Stands, legs together. 1.25″ d. Tumbles onto right side. 1.0″

Fig 10.172 Tiny baby lies prone. An example of this piece was purchased new in the 1930s. 0.75″

Fig 10.173 The faces of these tiny babies are painted simply; the paint is probably unfired. a. Sits on one foot. Stamped "Germany" in blue. 1.12″ b. Stands with legs apart. 1.12″ c. Lies on left side. Stamped "Germany" in blue. 1.0″

Fig 10.174 Three tiny babies with fine snow, made in Japan. a. Stands, legs together. 1.37″ b. Sits, one leg under him. Stamped "Japan" in black. 1.12″ c. Stands, legs apart. 1.37″

Fig 10.175 Four babies of the tiniest size. Examples of the first two were purchased new in the 1930s. All are stamped "Germany" in blue except the first, which is stamped in purple. a. Sits. 0.87″ b. Sits, one leg underneath. 0.87″ c. Stands, legs together. 1.0″ d. Lies on its left side. 0.87″

Fig 10.176 Four very tiny babies in red caps, mittens and shoes. All but the last are the tiniest size. All are stamped "Germany" in purple. **a.** Lies on left side. 0.87" **b.** Sits, one leg tucked underneath. 0.87" **c.** Sits. 0.87" **d.** Stands, legs apart. 1.12"

Fig 10.178 Figs 10.178 through 10.180 show tiny no-snow children. In this piece a boy looks out from a window in an igloo while a girl tries to reach the penguin standing on top. Each is 1.75" **a.** Stamped "Germany" in black. This piece can also be found with snow applied only to the igloo. **b.** Unmarked, this is probably of good quality composition material. It is heavy and solid, with no drain-hole.

Fig 10.177 Two examples of the same tiny baby on wooden skis. The skis are stamped "Germany" in black on the bottom. An example of this piece was shown in the *Favors* wholesale trade list (L-W Book Sales, 1985) for 1924-25. Each baby is 1.5" tall.

Fig 10.179 Two examples of children posed beside a brick bell arch. The girl blows a golden horn while the boy pulls the bell rope. The bell is also golden. Each is 2.0" tall, and each is stamped "Germany" in black. **a.** Snowed. **b.** Unsnowed. An example of this piece was purchased new in the 1930s.

Fig 10.180 From top. **a.** Tiny child stands beside a smiling snowman and throws snowballs. The snowman was built behind a fence. An example of this piece was purchased new in the 1930s. Stamped "Germany" in black. 1.5" **b.** Three children on a molded snow hill. The two at the top throw snowballs while a third slides downhill on a sled. Stamped "Germany" in black. 2.0" **c.** Two children climb on a grouted snow hill. One has reached the top; the other has just begun his climb. 2.0"

Fig 10.181 **a.** Glass Christmas ornament contains a composition baby on a tiny wooden sled. 2.0" (measured up to the pike of the ornament). **b.** Tiny snow baby made of celluloid. Incised "Japan". 1.37"

Fig 10.182 Set of five tiny bisque Eskimo figures and their bisque summer home. All pieces are carefully executed and incised "Germany". Father, mother and summer home incised 17682. **a.** Father in a fur-trimmed, hooded parka. He carries a long bow. 1.87" **b.** Girl stands with her arm around a seated husky dog. 1.25" **c.** Boy carries a hatchet. 1.37" **d.** Mother carries a baby on her back. 1.75" **e.** Summer home appears to be made of skins. 2.87"

Chapter 11
Carolers

Caroling has been a tradition throughout Europe for several centuries. Carolers must have been a common sight in the cities and the countryside, because they were pictured frequently in late 19th century British and American periodicals at Christmas time. Groups comprising all children, all adults and a mixture of both were pictured in publications such as the *Illustrated London News, The Graphic* and *Harpers*. It is not surprising that German snow baby manufacturers created sets of Christmas carolers in addition to other winter snow figures.

What is surprising is that every bisque piece, with the exception of one solitary figure (Fig 11.3a), consists of exactly three figures. Snow babies, dwarves and elves come in pairs as well as trios, but carolers seem to have been made only in groups of three. The one group of caroling babies (Fig 10.142) is also a trio.

Some of these caroling groups, namely Figs 11.3b and 11.5b, and their Japanese counterparts, Figs 11.4 and 11.6, are among the most commonly found snow baby pieces. For that reason they tend to remain unsold in dealers' cases, and the mention of carolers for sale excites little interest from collectors. However, none of the other carolers is easy to find. All are charming and well-executed pieces that display especially well with snow baby or dwarf bands.

One caroling group has been shown here front and back (Figs 11.8 and 11.9) because these cheerful singers seem to be wearing only hats, shirts and shoes. You can judge for yourself. Surely the backsides of this endearing group were molded this way intentionally, but collectors may never know why.

Fig 11.1 Two uncommon trios of caroling children. Both sets are dressed in winter coats and hats. **a.** Three children with a song book wait their turn to sing. Incised "Germany". #7476; 2.25″ **b.** Three children sing enthusiastically. The carol book is marked "Xmas". 2.12″

Fig 11.4 This china-finished Japanese piece with crystalline snow is an apparent copy of Fig 11.3b. Stamped "Japan" in black. 25¢ is pencilled on the bottom. 2.0″

Fig 11.2 Two sets of no-snow adult street musicians, all male. **a.** These three men in wide-brimmed hats wearing capes over their clothing appear to be Italian carolers. The center musician plays a mandolin. #8461; 2.0″ **b.** Three Germanic instrumentalists, each in a red jacket, bow tie and bowler hat. Stamped "Germany" in black. 1.75″

Fig 11.3 a. Enthusiastic girl singer wears galoshes, coat and hat. The only solitary singer I have found, she may not have been intended as a snow baby piece. 2.5″ **b.** This commonly found set of children carolers, 2 boys and a girl, has snow on hats and base. It should have a lantern like Fig 11.5b. Stamped "Germany" in black. #9700; 2.25″

Fig 11.5 Both of these pieces have snowed hats and base. **a.** Three colonial men carolers, two with instruments. The base has a hole to attach a lantern. #9699; 1.87" **b.** Very common piece shows 2 men and one boy in red. This piece is more often found without its original lantern. #381; 2.25"

Fig 11.6 This is a Japanese version of Fig 11.5b. Hats and base are snowed with a crystalline grout. An example of this piece was purchased new in the 1930s or 1940s. 2.25"

Fig 11.8 Three children dressed in Dickensian clothing, all singing enthusiastically. Stamped "Germany" in blue. 1.75"

Fig 11.7 Three men musicians with a lantern molded onto the base. The lantern and base are each dusted with snow. Stamped "Germany" in black. 2.25"

Fig 11.9 Rear view of Fig 11.8. Notice the detailed molding of fingers, and the fact that the two boys seem to be wearing no pants! To save time, many snow baby figures were painted only on the front, but this unique piece carries production efficiency one step further.

Chapter 12
Adult Snow Figures

Red Skiers

Many of the figures in this chapter are variations on a single couple, the commonly found red skiers. These variations are sometimes called the red skiers even when they are neither skiing nor wearing red. When they are skating and dressed in glitter tops, they are referred to as the "red skiers in glitter tops, skating." Collectors have probably fallen into this habit because so many of them have seen this girl, dressed in a blazer and skirt, and boy, dressed in a pullover sweater and trousers.

In most cases these pieces still have "Germany" stamped in black on the underside. This suggests that these pieces are new enough that careful housekeepers have not had time to wash away the stamps, or that the pieces were not used as cake decorations. The marks could also mean that these pieces were largely made for import into the United States. Unlike the United States, England apparently did not require imported goods to have a country of origin stamp.

Of the figures in this group, the red skiers are the most common, followed by the red skaters and glitter skiers. Extra time and effort went into the finishing work on the glitter pieces. Notice that Fig 12.5 has more elaborate eye treatment, contrasting eyebrow color, multi-colored clothing and applied glitter snow. Compare these features with the pieces finished in red which, other than flesh-colored faces and occasionally brown ski equipment or silver skates, were painted only in red and black. Even their black eyes were applied as simple dots.

Art Deco Pieces

All the Erphila pieces (Figs 12.9 through 12.11) are young women dressed in 1920s clothing. Each piece is glazed (china), and bears the distinctive Erphila mark in orange on the underside. No men skiers or sledders have surfaced to accompany these women, but it seems logical that they should exist.

Similar in style are the German and Japanese art deco sledders and skiers (Figs 12.12 through 12.14). In these examples the Japanese pieces, although not quite as refined as the German ones, are well proportioned and pleasing.

Sonja Henie

In 1923, at the age of 10, Sonja Henie became the figure skating champion of Norway. She went on to win the women's world figure skating championship ten times. Surely she inspired the lovely figure skater (Fig 12.20) and its Japanese counterpart (Fig 12.21), and she may also have been the model for other pieces shown here.

Fig 12.1 These commonly found red skier pieces are almost always marked "Germany" in black ink. They wear bisque skis and carry two ski poles. a. Woman skier in typical white pants, red jacket and cap. This example has been too vigorously cleaned. Stamped "Germany" in black. 2.25" b. Man skier, companion to Fig 12.1a, dressed in red cap, turtleneck and pants. "Germany" stamped in black. 2.25" c. Smaller version of Fig 12.1b. An example of this piece was purchased new in the 1930s. There is also a woman skier in this size. "Germany" stamped in black. 1.87"

Fig 12.2 These adult skiers are molded like Figs 12.1a and 12.1b, but wear tops and caps decorated with applied glitter snow. The blue, white and black color combination is typical of these figures. a. Woman skier stamped "Made in Germany" in red. 2.25" b. Man skier stamped "Germany" in black. 2.25"

Fig 12.3 Woman carries a pair of skis. She is dressed in a blue skirt, black leggings and white jacket with blue lapels, like the companion woman ice skater (Fig 12.5b). Her glitter snow has almost disappeared. Stamped "Germany" in black. 2.5"

Fig 12.6 These are the same figures as shown in Figs 12.4 and 12.5, but with a china finish. The faces are less well-defined than in the previous pieces. Both are stamped "Germany" in purple. Each is 2.5" tall. a. Glazed man skater. b. Glazed woman skater.

Fig 12.7 The same woman has now taken up sledding, and races down a wedge. Her lapels are rust-colored, uncommon among these pieces. Her coat and hat still show traces of glitter snow. "Germany" stamped in black. 2.12"

Fig 12.4 Basic man and woman skaters in red. Without the long skis for a base, the skaters have instead been given graceful pedestals for support. They wear silver skates. The woman has changed from her ski pants to a skirt for this new sport. Each piece is stamped "Germany" in black; each is 2.5" tall. a. Man skater in red sweater. An example of this piece was purchased new in the 1930s. b. Woman skater in red jacket.

Fig 12.8 Composition version of the woman skier shown in Fig 12.1a. Her skis are mounted on a thick base. Painted with fluorescent paint, she glows brightly in the semi-dark. She was probably made by the Shackman Company to replace those snow babies it had been importing from Germany just prior to World War II. 2.87"

Fig 12.5 These are the same skaters as Figs 12.4, but with glitter tops and hats. Both are stamped "Germany" in black. a. Man. 2.62" b. Woman. 2.5"

Fig 12.9 Four women skiers, all china-finished. All are stamped in red with the Erphila logo, which includes the word "Germany". The style of their clothing and two ski poles suggest that these pieces were made in the 1920s. All of the Erphila pieces are also incised "Germany". a. Skier appears ready to jump. #K95; 3.25" b. Stands on a base, holding ski poles in one hand, skis in the other. #K93; 3.5" c. Kneels to put on her skis. #K94; 2.0" d. Stands on skis, with a pole in each hand. This piece is incised, but the number is illegible. 3.0"

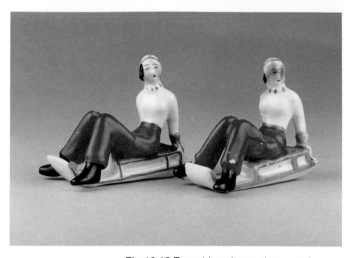

Fig 12.12 Two china pieces show nearly identical women on sleds. They are dressed in sweaters, tiny caps and bell-bottom slacks. Each woman is winking; each is 1.75" high. a. An example of this piece was purchased new in the 1930s. Stamped "Germany" in black. b. Stamped "Japan" in black. The molding on this piece is not quite as deep, and the face painting has been done with a bit less care.

Fig 12.10 Two Erphila pieces show women on sleds. These graceful women wear short, nicely draped skirts; their scarves flutter behind them. Both pieces are stamped "Erphila" in red. a. Two women ride a sled down a wedge. #K92; 3.0" b. One woman slides down a wedge. Incised "Germany". #K89; 2.75"

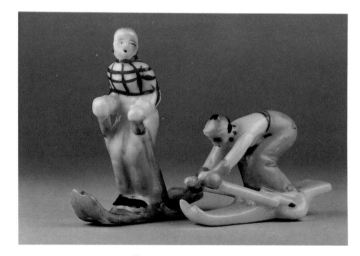

Fig 12.13 Two attractive, glazed Japanese skiers wear much the same style dress as the sledders in Fig 12.12. Examples of these two pieces were purchased new in the 1930s. Both are stamped "Japan" in purple. a. Red-checked shirt is distinctive. 3.0" b. This one can also be found finished in all-white china with gold trim. 1.75"

Fig 12.11 Young woman kneels, about to push off on a downhill sled run. Stamped with Erphila logo. #K90; 2.87"

Fig 12.14 Art deco woman skier wears a blue-checked shirt. This German version is more carefully molded and painted than the Japanese example (Fig 12.13a). Stamped "Germany" in black. #F0656; 3.25"

Fig 12.15 Sonia Henie-type skater, gracefully posed and beautifully detailed. Unusual use of flesh-colored paint on legs. Known to have been purchased new in late 1920s or early 1930s. Stamped "Germany" in red. 2.87"

Fig 12.16 This is another ice skater probably inspired by Sonia Henie. Stamped "Germany" in black. 2.12"

Fig 12.17 These skaters on long-bladed, silver skates are rather stylized and wear tight-fitting stocking caps. Each is 2.12" tall, incised "5866" and stamped "Germany" in blue. a. Woman skater in white dress. b. Man skater.

Fig 12.18 Man and woman on a sled with a steering device, sliding down a wedge. Incised "Made in Germany", but I have seen a nearly identical piece marked "Japan". #14824; 2.0"

Fig 12.19 Competition ski jumper wears the number "12" on his chest. His skis are mounted on a small, steep incline, and he carries no poles. This is the only snow baby piece that I have seen showing an athlete in competition. Stamped "Germany" in red. #8607; 2.75"

Fig 12.20 Graceful Sonia Henie-type ice skater. Her face and clothing are beautifully detailed. Her tall pedestal suggests that this piece was probably intended for use in a snow dome. Incised "Germany". 2.5″

Fig 12.21 This Japanese skater snow dome insert is similar to Fig 12.20, even to the use of color. Stamped "Made in Occupied Japan" in red. 2.5″

Fig 12.22 Highly unusual man (or boy) and woman who have been caught in a runaway snow ball. Arms and legs protrude in various directions. She doesn't look a bit unhappy, but he looks miserable; there must be a story to this. The piece is superbly detailed and painted; you can even see quilting on the man's hat. 3.5″

Fig 12.23 Covered wagon pulled by a horse; the owner stands with his left arm on the flank of the horse. The man may be a workman: he wears an apron under his coat. Note the penny-farthing wheels. The piece is nicely detailed, but what the man is up to is a mystery. Stamped "Germany" in black. 1.75″

Chapter 13
Santa

What a variety of Santas were created in bisque! Most Santa pieces date from the 1920s and early 1930s, though a few may have been done earlier. They have many of the same characteristics as the babies of this period: bright colors, grouping of figures on bases, poorly fired or unfired paint and, in some cases, whimsy.

Painting and Decoration

Early Santas made as blown glass ornaments, papier mâché figures or chromolithographed post cards and scraps wear coats of various colors—sometimes white, blue, brown or lavender. Unusual coloring makes the piece more desirable because it reflects an earlier style, before red became established as Santa's color. But snow baby Santas almost always appear dressed in red. An occasional Santa has a dusting of snow on his cap, but only three are clothed in garments completely covered with snow.

Fig 13.1 is the only Santa who carries a muff. This snowed piece is unusual in many other ways. Santa's beard is grey instead of white. He is slightly stooped, and his eyes are downcast, almost sad. Although the face painting is not detailed, the artist conveyed deep emotion with an economy of brush strokes. The soft colors and fired face, in addition to its rarity, suggest that it was probably made before World War I.

In bisque, Santa usually wears a full-length coat. It is often assumed that shorter coat versions came later, but all of the US Zone and Western Germany bisque Santas pictured here wear long coats. And whereas contemporary American Santas usually do have waist-length coats, the English Father Christmas still wears a long coat. Santa's coat length does not reliably indicate the age of these pieces.

Snow baby Santas usually sport a mustache and beard, but an occasional individual wears only the beard. Some Santas are cheery, others look apprehensive or stern. Some faces reappear again and again and must have been created by the same artist or group of artists.

Some of the Santa pieces are painted only on the front side. Although Santa's robe may be completely painted, the rear walls of houses, the backs of bushes and wagons are left stark white. This practice was by no means limited to Santa pieces. It saved time and money in the production of many pieces that were sold essentially as disposable novelties.

Poses

Most collectors are less interested in figures of Santa that stand alone and have no companion figures or other props, even though some of these are skillfully painted and have beautiful faces. With a few exceptions, even these solitary Santas are becoming difficult to find for sale.

Santas are more desirable when they are shown making their rounds by exotic means. For the child who wonders how Santa manages in the desert, here he is on a camel. How are toys distributed in Africa? Here's Santa on an elephant. He also travels by polar bear, dog sled, donkey cart, sailboat, motorboat and racing car (his number is "1," of course). It must have been reassuring to think that no home, however remote, would be inaccessible to Santa.

Figs 13.66 and 13.67 show Santa and an elf together. However, I know of no examples of Santa with a bearded dwarf. Perhaps this is because dwarves were meant to be the Scandinavian equivalent of Santa himself (see chapter 14). Although many pieces show Santa with no-snow children, only three feature Santa and snowed babies together. Of the three, Santa and the baby on the see-saw is the rarest.

The glazed Santas pictured near the end of this section were among the last of the "old" Santas to be made. They have similar faces, paint color and style of dress. In particular, they all wear blue gloves. Some are unmarked, but others are stamped "Germany", "Germany US Zone", or "Germany Western". Perhaps they were all made before the war and marked "Germany" at that time; the designations "US Zone" and "Western" could have been added later, when they were actually exported.

Because old snow baby pieces are rare and valuable, they are being copied and sold by contemporary artists. I know of two such artists working in California. Pieces that are well-executed and artist-signed may provide a new generation of collectible bisque Santas. Unsigned pieces signal the need for caution among collectors.

Fig 13.1 Santa in a long, snowed, hooded garment carries a pale yellow muff. His beard is grey and he stands on wooden skis. This Santa is an exception to most of the pieces seen in this chapter in that he was almost certainly made before the first world war. 3.5"

Fig 13.2 Unusual Santa with an extraordinarily long beard. He is styled differently from most bisque Santas— notice his hat. He is very slender, and he is the only one holding a signboard. #89; 3.75"

Fig 13.3 Here are two Santas, each in two sizes. They are typical of solitary Santas. Each one should be carrying a feather tree. **a.** 3.25" **b.** 2.25" **c.** #6080; 2.25" **d.** #4284; 1.5"

Fig 13/7 Four examples of very similar Santas with lanterns. **a.** This one is slightly different from the others in that his feet are placed together. 1.87" **b.** In this size, this is one of most common Santas found. 2.12" **c.** One of only 3 snowed Santas I have seen. 2.5" **d.** #8433; 3.0"

Fig 13.4 Four solitary Santas in various poses. **a.** Carries tiny bisque tree. Incised "Germany". #5136; 2.0" **b.** Santa with pack; a cane is in his left hand. Incised "Germany". #8434; 2.37" **c.** Santa bent over, cane in his right hand. 2.5" **d.** This Santa is unusual for the short coat and blue pants. An example of this piece that measures 2.25" was purchased new in the 1930s, and an even smaller size has been reported. Stamped "Germany" in black. 2.75"

Fig 13.6 Another example of Fig 13.5b, but finished with coralene. This is the only Santa I know of covered in coralene. His coat shimmers in the light. It is not usual to find examples of the same piece painted differently. Notice that the shoes, cane, bag and doll of these two examples are painted different colors; perhaps the two were produced a significant time apart. 2.75"

Fig 13.5 **a.** With dolls and toys hanging from his belt, Santa carries a toy-filled wicker basket on his back. #LH376; 2.5" **b.** At his waist Santa carries a pouch that contains a doll. He carries a pack on his back. "Germany" stamped in purple. 2.75"

Fig 13.8 Santa with beautifully molded face and beard. He walks with the aid of a stick and carries a basket of toys that includes a teddy bear. 2.5"

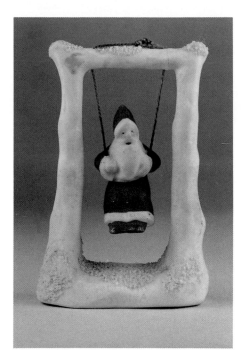

Fig 13.9 Tiny Santa sits on a rope swing in an arch. There is snow on the top and floor of the structure. This same piece is shown with a baby in Fig 10.47. It has also been reported with a dwarf or elf. Incised "Germany". #5401; 3.0"

Fig 13.13 Set of 5 tiny Santas. All are stamped "Germany" in black, and all are 1.5" tall. Several of them look anxious. a. Santa rides a sled on a slope. b. Santa on skis. c. Santa with a cane at a fence. d. Santa pulls a sled over a bridge. e. Santa with a stick and green pack.

Fig 13.11 Santa talks on a telephone mounted on a tree trunk. The tree trunk has a tiny opening at the top, but it does not appear to be a candle holder. Both the phone and bell are painted gold. Stamped "Germany" in black. 1.5"

Fig 13.12 This Santa climbs over a fence. The base is snowed, and there is a dusting of snow on Santa's pack. An example of this piece was purchased new in the 1930s. Stamped "Germany" in black. 1.75"

Fig 13.10 Santa stands beside a bell arch. A bird perches on top of the arch. There is snow on the arch and on the ground. #379; 2.37"

Fig 13.14 Four small Santas. a. Common Japanese Santa on skis has a nicely painted face. Stamped "Japan". 1.87" b. Tiny, common Santa on ice skates. An example of this piece was purchased new in the 1930s. Incised "Japan". 1.5" c. Santa sits on a sled and waves. Notice the similarity to Fig 13.15. The bisque has a slight sheen. 1.75" d. Tiny Santa skis down a minuscule wedge. 1.75"

Fig 13.15 Santa on a sled in a long, white coat that is belted at the back. The coat and hat are completely snowed. This is one of only three Santas dressed all in white. 2.25"

Fig 13.20 Two tiny Santa figures, both stamped "Germany" in black. **a.** In a sleigh pulled by a reindeer. An example of this piece was purchased new in the 1930s. 1.25" **b.** On a sled, sliding down a wedge. The snow is molded, not applied. 1.5"

Fig 13.18 Santa sits on a sled on a snowed wedge. Unmarked, but German. #6698 on front; 2.25"

Fig 13.16 Three Japanese Santas. **a.** Santa's face and coat are painted with enamel. His coat has a braid closure. Stamped "Japan" in black. #S/095; 3.5" **b.** Santa carries a green sack over his right shoulder. Incised "Japan". 4.0" **c.** Santa on base with a green sack over his left shoulder. Incised "Japan". 2.5"

Fig 13.19 Nicely executed Santa rides a yellow sled on a snowed wedge. Similar to Fig 13.18, but incised "Made in Japan". 2.5"

Fig 13.21 Santa in a gold-trimmed sleigh pulled by a reindeer. He holds one package; the sleigh holds other packages painted blue. No-snow piece stamped "Made in Germany" in purple. #8266; 2.25"

Fig 13.17 Santa walks down a trail on an unusual ice mountain. Snowed piece stamped "Germany" in black. 2.37"

Fig 13.22 Two examples of Santa in a sleigh pulled by reindeer. **a.** China piece is unusual for the shape of reindeer and antlers and for Santa's very long beard. The sleigh could serve as a container. "Germany" stamped in red and incised. 2.0" **b.** Deeply molded tiny Santa is snug under a yellow lap robe. This sleigh, pulled by a galloping reindeer, is loaded with packages and a large bag. 1.25"

Fig 13.23 Two Santas in sleighs on snowed bases are probably waiting to be pulled by reindeer, but there are no harnesses. **a.** Santa carries a pack over his shoulder. This is the more common of the two. Stamped "Germany" in black. #6699; 1.75" **b.** Santa carries a package on his lap. He has no pack and no mustache, and grins broadly. Incised "Germany". #8395; 2.25"

Fig 13.26 Similar to Fig 13.25, but Santa is a molded part of the piece. Stamped "Germany" in purple. 1.5"

Fig 13.24 Santa carries packages in a sleigh pulled by reindeer. I am not certain that this piece is German. 1.87"

Fig 13.27 Santa sits on a low sleigh and carries a Scottie dog. The sleigh is pulled by a doe that seems to be looking back at Santa. Snowed piece, stamped "Germany" in black. #730; 2.5"

Fig 13.25 In this version Santa carries a feather tree and can be lifted out of the sleigh. This sleigh is sometimes found without its Santa. 2.0"

Fig 13.28 Santa sits in a cart, but the donkey isn't pulling. A duck, rabbit and toy can be seen. Snow dusts Santa's hat, the donkey's head and the cart. #9696; 1.75"

Fig 13.29 Santa rides in a small sled pulled by huskies. These seem to be the same two huskies that pull the snow baby in Fig 10.28. The Santa version is less common. #7154; 1.62"

Fig 13.30 Santa on skis pulled by a galloping horse. No-snow piece. Santa wears no mustache, and has what looks like a puppy in his pack. #508; 1.87"

Fig 13.31 Santa drives a giant Christmas cracker that is tied to a toboggan. He has an elephant, doll and Scottie dog in his pack. He does not wear a mustache. No-snow piece. #7155; 1.75"

Fig 13.32 Santa steers a toboggan, with a clown and Scottie in his pack. (Scotties were popular in the 1920s.) Stamped "Germany" in purple. 1.5"

Fig 13.33 This Santa rides a sled on his belly. A teddy bear sticks out of the pack on his back. No-snow. #2294; 1.37"

Fig 13.34 This common-looking Santa is unusual because he is pegged to a sled. He came from a Portland, Oregon, collection (see text, chapter 21). Stamped "Germany" in black. #4513; 2.0"

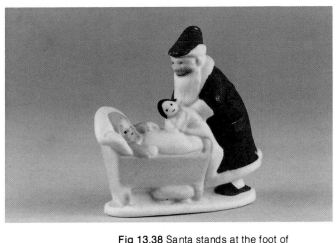

Fig 13.35 There are only three pieces that show Santa with a snow baby. Here are two of them. **a.** Santa is on the roof of a snowed igloo, custom-made for him with a chimney. A tiny, snowed baby waits inside. The baby is an add-on, so its exact position inside the igloo may vary. An example of this piece was purchased new between 1924 and 1934. There is also a Japanese version of this piece that is less carefully detailed. The piece shown is stamped "Germany" in black. 2.37" **b.** Santa walks with a snow baby holding each hand. Santa has no mustache. His hands are occupied, so he has a pouch at his waist, presumably for toys. Stamped "Germany" in black. #2724; 2.0"

Fig 13.37 Santa stands at the foot of a cradle or small bed. The little girl holds a doll. Incised "Germany". 3.0"

Fig 13.38 Santa stands at the foot of another cradle, giving a doll to the baby. Santa wears ear flaps on his cap and has no mustache. Is he wearing slippers? Stamped "Germany" in purple. #507; 2.12"

Fig 13.39 Santa stands beside a sleeping child. Stockings are hung on the bedstead. There is a teddy bear in Santa's pack. Stamped "Germany" in purple. #758; 2.12"

Fig 13.36 Santa shares a teeter-totter with a snow baby, who is able to balance the presumably heavier Santa. There is a hole in the base to hold a bit of feather tree or other decoration. Incised and stamped "Germany" in purple. When this piece was purchased it was very dirty. It has had many hours of careful cleaning by the method described in chapter 22. 2.0"

Fig 13.40 Both of these are no-snow pieces. **a.** A little girl chooses an elephant from Santa's pack. The two stand on a mound with the toy pack between them. Santa has no mustache, and looks remarkably like the Santa in Fig 13.38. Stamped "Germany" in purple. #511; 2.25" **b.** Santa gives a doll to a little girl in bed. He carries his toys in a basket. Stamped "Germany" in black. 1.67"

Fig 13.41 Apprehensive Santa and a little girl with a bag of toys between them. Stamped "Germany" in black. 1.87"

Fig 13.46 Two Santas with carts. Each is stamped "Germany" in black. **a.** He pushes a sack full of toys in a two-wheeled luggage cart. The wheels are gilt. 1.5" **b.** Apprehensive Santa pulls a toy-filled cart that has two large wheels. 1.75"

Fig 13.42 Santa with a lantern next to two sleepy children. "Germany" stamped in purple. #869; 2.25"

Fig 13.47 Each Santa is stamped "Germany" in black. **a.** Santa pulls a wagon full of toys. 1.25" **b.** Santa pulls a sleigh full of toys, with an angel sitting in the sleigh. This is one of the commonest Santa pieces to be found. 1.25"

Fig 13.43 Apparently resting, Santa leans against his huge pack of toys, which contains several stuffed animals. Stamped in purple and incised "Germany". #365; 2.12"

Fig 13.45 This Santa pulls a low buggy with a baby inside. No-snow and no mustache. There is a clown in Santa's pack. 2.25"

Fig 13.48 These two pieces feature Santa and an angel. **a.** Santa and the angel carry a basket of toys between them. 1.87" **b.** Walking together, the angel carries a small basket, and Santa has an unusual yellow and black pack. What could it represent? An example of this piece was purchased new in the 1930s. Stamped "Germany" in black. 1.87"

Fig 13.44 In a hurry, Santa pushes a baby buggy. He is frowning and seems pretty unhappy. This is a no-snow piece. #5959; 1.75"

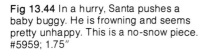

Fig 13.49 Santa carries a small tree and pulls a sled across a base. The sled contains a girl (or doll), clown and dog. Stamped "Foreign"; presumably it was made for the English market. 2.12"

Fig 13.50 a. Santa with a pack on his back rides on a camel. There is snow on Santa's hat and on the base. This camel's head is a replacement, molded by its owner. #9650; 2.62" b. Santa rides on an elephant. There is snow on the elephant's head and tail, and on Santa's hat. Across the elephant's back is a pack that contains a doll. #9692; 2.37"

Fig 13.51 Santa stands in front of an elephant, holding the reins. The elephant is laden with toys, including a teddy bear and a gold-painted horn. Stamped "Germany" in black. 1.62"

Fig 13.52 Santa on a bucking donkey. He is reaching back to keep his pack from sliding off the donkey's back. The donkey has a gold bridle. 1.87"

Fig 13.53 Santa rides a polar bear. He wears a pack in which small animals are visible. "Germany" stamped in purple. 2.37"

Fig 13.54 This small piece showing Santa on a polar bear is much less common than the larger Fig 13.53. 1.5"

Fig 13.55 Three Santas on reindeer. a. Stern Santa on a reindeer with detailed molding. The Santa should be carrying a feather tree. Stamped "Germany" in black. 2.75″ b. In this, the more common piece, there is snow on the base and Santa smiles and carries a bag. A similar piece features a baby instead of Santa (Fig 10.18). 2.25″ c. This Santa and reindeer are a close copy of Fig 13.55b, only smaller. They are being chased by a comic bear cub, much like those in Fig 16.47. The base has a hole for a feather tree. 2.0″

Fig 13.59 Santa stands next to a duck or goose that appears to have a tooth ache. Santa carries a bag. What's the joke here? Is the duck pretending to be too sick to be put into Santa's bag? "Germany" stamped in black. 1.5″

Fig 13.58 Santa similar to Figs 13.56 and 13.57 sits on a small wedge holding a teddy bear in the air. #6141; 3.0″

Fig 13.60 Apprehensive Santa huddles over the wheel of his own racing car. 1.37″

Fig 13.56 This is the first of three no-snow Santas with consecutive numbers and similar faces. All are larger than the usual Santa piece, and all are incised "Germany". This Santa rides a reindeer (or moose) and waves his left hand. #6142; 3.12″

Fig 13.57 Beautifully detailed Santa walks a West Highland Terrier (Westie) and carries his sack over his shoulder. This is the classic, sweet-faced Santa, but he has the dog on a very short leash. The dog is looking up at him. Santa's coat flares from the waist, another unusual feature. #6140; 3.25″

Fig 13.61 Santa carries his bag and waves as he sits on the hood of a silver car. Stamped "Germany" in black. 1.5″

Fig 13.62 Santa drives a red roadster trimmed in silver. There are packages and a Christmas tree in back. This is a tiny piece with a lot of detail. It also comes in at least one larger size (2.62"). This piece is just 1.12".

Fig 13.63 Santa drives a yellow car, with his bag full of toys (and a teddy bear) in the rumble seat. There are patches of snow on Santa's hat and on the car. #4696; 1.62"

Fig 13.64 These two, small, no-snow pieces feature Santas and silver cars. a. Santa drives his car up a wedge. A teddy and packages are in the rumble seat. 1.37" b. Apprehensive Santa, with raised eyebrows, drives this car down a slight incline. Stamped "Germany" in black. 1.5"

Fig 13.65 Santa rides on a motorcycle with a large headlight. He carries a pack on his back and bends over, perhaps for speed. There is a small package on the luggage carrier. #9056; 2.12"

Fig 13.66 Santa and a small elf ride this motorcycle. A dog peeks out from Santa's pack, which is in front of him. Santa has no mustache on this no-snow piece. This is one of only two German pieces showing Santa with an elf. #877; 2.12"

Fig 13.67 Engineer Santa with an elf and small (or stuffed) animals behind him. There is snow on Santa's hat and on the front of the train. Stamped "Germany" in purple. #9695; 1.62"

Fig. 13.67 Engineer Santa with an elf and small (or stuffed) animals behind him. There is snow on Santa's hat and on the front of the train. Stamped "Germany" in purple. #9695; 1.62".

Fig 13.68 Nicely executed Japanese example of Santa and elf in train locomotive. There are some slight molding differences between this piece and Fig 13.67—the door of the engine is narrower and taller in this piece, and Santa's elbow is therefore bent more sharply. This piece is not numbered. Stamped "Japan" in black. 1.75"

Fig 13.69 Santa is in a train engine with a golliwog; a doll and a toy monkey ride behind. Santa seems to be calling out. The train has a small amount of snow. This is a well-detailed piece; notice the molded smoke coming from stack. #731; 1.87"

Fig 13.70 Santa sails a boat with a doll, teddy bear and Scottie dog as passengers. Santa's left arm reaches back to hold the tiller. He wears a big grin and no mustache. #506; 2.0"

Fig 13.71 Japanese version of Santa in a sailboat. Santa is in about the same position, but a bit squatter. This version has no incised number. Stamped "Japan" in black. 2.25"

Fig 13.72 Santa steers a motorboat that carries a doll, clown and rabbit. #7152; 1.62"

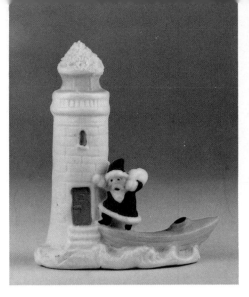

Fig 13.73 Tiny Santa disembarks from his kayak at a lighthouse. Notice the molded waves. There is snow on the top of the lighthouse. Stamped "Germany" in black. 2.5"

Fig 13.76 Santa waves from the driver's seat of a stagecoach pulled by a pair of white horses. A teddy, clown and packages ride behind him. The wheels of the coach are painted gold. I have also seen this piece with a glazed finish, typical of the 1940s. A slightly different version of this piece is shown in the box shown in Fig 13.104. 1.5"

Fig 13.74 Cheery Santa sits atop a silver monoplane. Santa has no mustache. His pack is slung over his left shoulder. One collector told me that he bought eight examples of this piece, each with a wire hook in Santa's head for hanging! I know of no other bisque snow baby pieces fitted with wire hangers. Stamped "Germany" in black. A similar piece features a baby instead of Santa (Fig 10.48a). #6697; 1.5"

Fig 13.77 This Santa drives a stagecoach pulled by two prancing horses. The coach is loaded with toys, including a clown and a black doll or child. Stamped "Germany" in black. 1.62"

Fig 13.75 An apprehensive Santa sits at the controls of an open-cockpit airplane that bears the insignia of the British Royal Air Corps. The back seat contains well-defined articles: elephant, teddy bear, clown and several packages. Stamped "Germany" in black. 1.25"

Fig 13.78 Solemn Santa rides on an old-fashioned coach, pulled by two slender horses. This piece is unusually shallow, measured from one side of the coach to the other. Note the relative wheel sizes on this and figure 13.77. A teddy bear rides on back, a doll on top. #377; 1.75"

Fig 13.79 Santa drives a stagecoach sleigh pulled by two polar bears. The bears and base are snowed; a panda and several toys peek from windows. #510; 1.62″

Fig 13.82 Two nearly identical snowed pieces, German and Japanese. Both show Santa climbing into (or out of) the chimney of a white house. a. Santa's hands are together and his fingers are nicely molded. Windows and doors are painted blue or red and are trimmed in gold. This piece is also found 1.75″ tall. Stamped "Germany" in black. #6695; 2.25″ b. Santa's hands are separated on the chimney lip; the chimney itself is not snowed. There is no red coloring at the windows. The detail is not as fine. Stamped "Japan". 2.37″

Fig 13.80 a. Tiny bisque Santa stands on a ledge and peeks into the window of a no-snow house. 2.12″ b. Santa climbs into (or from) the chimney of a two-story snowed house. 3.0″

Fig 13.83 These two no-snow pieces show Santas on housetops. a. Tiny Santa climbs from or into a chimney. Stamped "Germany" in black. 1.62″ b. Santa dumps toys from his bag down a chimney. This piece is nicely detailed, showing a doll, clown and a teddy bear. Stamped "Germany" in black. 2.0″

Fig 13.81 Santa on the roof of a house, where his airplane has just landed. He seems to be climbing into the chimney. The no-snow piece is stamped "Germany" in black. 2.0″

Fig 13.84 Santa stands at the door of a house that looks like it is made of ice. He has toys, including balloons, two teddy bears and a doll. Two robins perch on the roof. This piece lacks depth from front to back. Stamped "Germany" in black. 1.75″

Fig 13.85 Santa takes a break to read the newspaper. Two animals peek from the bag beside his chair. The thin porcelain newspaper is quite vulnerable. No wonder few examples of this piece have survived. #9688; 2.37"

Fig 13.86 Santa stands at the mantlepiece, putting a teddy bear into a stocking. A fire burns in the grate. His bag contains molded, unpainted toys. Like Fig 13.84, the piece is quite shallow. "Germany" stamped in black. 1.5"

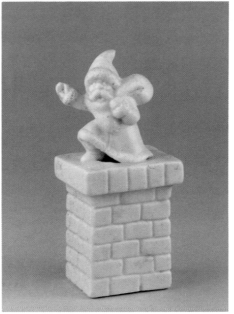

Fig 13.88 Santa waves as he climbs out of a free-standing chimney. The piece has no paint. It is still stamped "Germany" in purple, so it may have been sold unpainted. 3.0"

Fig 13.89 Glazed, bent Santa carries a large lantern in his right hand and steadies his pack with the left. Notice the aqua blue mittens, typical of the Santas of the post-war period. This piece is unmarked, but many like it are stamped "Germany US Zone" or "Germany Western". 2.5"

Fig 13.87 a. Remarkably short Santa stands on a sled behind a little girl. She looks like the girl who sits on a snowball in Fig 10.71. 2.25" b. Stern Santa with a walking stick stands near a lamp post. 2.25" c. Apprehensive Santa balances on a very large chimney. He is either tugging his bag out of the chimney or is about to push it in. Stamped "Germany" in black. 3.0"

Fig 13.90 Glazed Santa stands beside a sign post. He carries a grey pack over his shoulder. None of these glazed pieces has incised numbers. "Germany US Zone" in purple. 1.87"

Fig 13.93 Two glazed pieces. a. Santa dumps toys from his pack onto the ground. A crude doll lies on the ground. 1.62" b. Santa is on vacation with a bag of gilded golf clubs on his back. He carries one club in his left hand. Stamped "Germany US Zone". 2.0"

Fig 13.91 Three glazed Santas. a. Santa carries a glazed porcelain tree and a grey sack over his shoulder. Notice his fur-trimmed coat and hood. The long coat drags on the ground. 1.87" b. Santa carries a lantern in his outstretched right hand. Notice the similarity to Fig 13.91a. This piece was also made with the same Santa holding a walking stick in his outstretch right hand. 1.87" c. Glazed Santa carries a lantern that hangs from a ring. A large gilt key is also attached to the ring. Under his left arm he carries a sack of oranges. He wears an unusual fur hat that looks Russian. I have seen this piece in a slightly smaller version (2.5") marked "Germany" in purple. Both sizes were also made molded next to tiny candle holders. 3.0"

Fig 13.94 Tiny glazed Santa seems to be reaching into his pouch to find something for a young deer. Stamped "Germany Western" in purple. 1.37"

Fig 13.92 Two glazed pieces. a. Santa and a little girl stand at opposite corners of a tiny house. 1.12" b. Santa climbs a ladder to the roof of a small house. The brown walls are bisque finished; this was also made with grey glazed walls. 1.25"

Fig 13.95 Four tiny glazed Santas that look surprised. All but the second are marked "39¢" in pencil, and all are owned by the family of the original purchasers. a. Santa skis on a tiny wedge, carrying his pack on his back. Stamped "Germany US Zone" in purple. 1.62" b. Santa rides a running giraffe that has a bell around its neck. Marked "49¢" in pencil and "Germany" in purple. 1.5" c. Santa carries a walking stick and stands next to a seated dog with a red scarf wrapped around its neck. "Germany Western" in purple. 1.37" d. Santa and a teddy bear walk hand in paw. Santa carries a brown walking stick. Stamped "Germany Western" in purple. 1.37"

Fig 13.96 Glazed Santa walks beside a donkey bearing packages. 1.75″

Fig 13.97 Two glazed Santas. **a.** Tiny Santa pushes a two-wheeled cart full of toys and packages. 1.12″ **b.** Santa holds his pack, which rests on the ground, and waves the other hand. 2.25″

Fig 13.98 Glazed piece shows Santa outside a building. The incised, unpainted sign reads, "TOY SHOP". Some toys show in window. Stamped "Made in Occupied Japan" in red. 1.37″

Fig 13.99 Santa carries a tree, a pouch and a basket containing a teddy bear. 2.87″

Fig 13.100 This Santa, carefully detailed and dressed in brown, was purchased in a snow dome. It is unusual to find bisque Santas in colors other than red, and they are not commonly found in snow domes. His face is reminiscent of Fig 10.83a, a skating boy snow dome insert that is stamped "Japan". This piece is unmarked. 2.5″

Fig 13.101 Two English plaster Santas, often called cake decorations. a. Santa rows across a blue lake. The front of his rowboat is incised "Santa". Stamped "Made in England" in a circle. 1.0" b. Santa rides a rocket, which has a fuse made of wood. 1.75"

Fig 13.103 Two Santas of a composition material similar to papier mâché. a. Santa stands on a mound with his hands on his belt. Is he singing or laughing? Stamped "Japan" in black. 3.0" b. Along a snow-colored base Santa pulls a sled that carries his pack of toys. Stamped "Made in Japan" in black. 2.0"

Fig 13.102 Two plaster Santas. a. Santa posts letters at an English mail box. 1.5" b. Santa drives a touring car, which holds a Christmas tree and packages. Note the similarity to Fig 13.62. 1.12"

Fig 13.104 This intact sample box shows a variety of pieces that may have been made by the same factory. The box is not marked with a factory name, but Margaret Schiffer, who first showed this box in her book *Christmas Ornaments,* attributed it to the German firm of Carl Schneider. Many of these pieces have been individually displayed elsewhere in this book, except the witches (which are not snow baby pieces), this particular Santa on the coach, Santa pushing a wheel barrow and Santa in the fireplace. The numbers on the labels under the pieces do not always correspond to the incised numbers I have found on those pieces.

Chapter 14
Dwarves

Not all collectors distinguish between dwarves and elves; in children's literature the terms are sometimes used interchangeably. Snow baby dwarves and elves usually dress in red, and sometimes they are similarly posed. However, they are different enough to consider separately.

Characteristics

Bisque dwarves always wear full beards and seldom have mustaches. Their faces may appear smooth and youthful or craggy and aged. Although a few are snowed, their typical wardrobe is red and consists of pants, hat and a loose, waist-length pullover top. They occasionally wear long coats.

Sometimes snow baby dwarves are mistakenly labeled Santas by dealers or collectors. However, dwarves don't carry sacks of toys, and their garments don't have Santa's white fur trim.

In contrast to the energetic motion of elves, dwarf behavior is restrained. They stand, sit and recline; they gesture, grin or grimace. Almost all of their activity, other than resting (they are often seen resting), is some form of work. They drive trucks (Fig 7.44), shovel snow and paint mushrooms. Others carry papers, valises or baskets. Except for the musicians, only a few engage in any form of recreation.

Fig 14.3 Two dwarves in the same pose, one knee bent, one leg straight. Each holds a snowball. **a.** Snowed. 1.0″ **b.** #2769; 1.75″

Fig 14.1 All the dwarves shown in Figs 14.1 through 14.6 are of this same design. These two Christmas dwarves were made in at least two sizes. **a.** Dwarf stands and waves. 2.87″ **b.** Dwarf plays leap-frog. An example was purchased new between 1924 and 1934. Incised "Germany". 2.62

Fig 14.4 **a.** Dwarf waves as he sits on a stump or rock. 1.75″ **b.** Dwarf carries a carpet bag that bears the incised letter "H". I wonder what the "H" stands for? 2.12″

Fig 14.2 Larger, snowed version of Figs 14.1a and 14.1b. Careful attention has been paid to both the molding and face-painting. **a.** 3.5″ **b.** 3.37″

Fig 14.5 Dwarf lies on his left side with his right hand and leg in the air. This is a large piece. Stamped "Germany" in black. #2757; 2.0″

A red mushroom with white spots appears on several dwarf pieces; it is also seen on some of the elf pieces (see chapter 15). This is fly agaric, the mushroom or toadstool so often pictured in fairy tales. In large amounts it is poisonous, but it was used as an hallucinogen or intoxicant until about four hundred years ago. Its intoxicating effects could certainly account for dwarves dancing or painting mushrooms! In fact, the whole idea of dwarves and elves could have originated in the use of fly agaric as a hallucinogen.

Origins of Dwarves

Dwarves appear in legends and folk culture all around the globe. In almost every culture they delight in mischief, have extraordinary powers and dress in earth-colored clothing. Some myths hold that these little people attach themselves to households, where they might either create mischief or make themselves useful. At times they have been blamed for broken furniture, crumbled crockery and lost children. But they have been given credit for making bread dough rise, producing butter from cream, protecting the master of the house against deception and performing other beneficial acts. It is said that they come and go by way of the chimney and that they will remain friendly and helpful if treated kindly. They appreciate an occasional bowl of milk and rice pudding.

How did dwarves come to be dressed in red and to have ties to Christmas tradition? The answer probably lies in the Scandinavian celebration of Christmas. One account

Fig 14.6 a. Dwarf lies prone, left arm and leg raised. Stamped "Germany" in purple. #2755; 1.5" b. Dwarf carries papers under one arm and waves his hand. An example was purchased new between 1924 and 1934. Stamped "Germany" in black. #2766; 2.5"

Fig 14.8 Relatively common, 6-piece dwarf band. All are stamped "Germany" in black. Each is 2.25". From the top: a. Sousaphone. b. Saxophone. c. Banjo. d. Conductor. e. Possibly a krummhorn, or bass clarinet. f. String bass.

Fig 14.7 Unusual pair of snowed dwarves. They have long broad noses, beards that are short (for a dwarf) and long coats. They also have little holes in their caps, probably for some decoration that has been lost. Both are stamped "Germany" in black. a. Sits and gives a "thumbs up" sign. 2.25" b. This dwarf looks like he is quite surprised at having just tumbled. 1.62"

Fig 14.9 Members of other dwarf bands. They stand with the aid of pedestals. The first three seem to belong together; the last is a smaller version of the third. a. Violin. 2.25" b. Drum and cymbals. 2.0" c. Sousaphone. Stamped "Germany" in purple. 2.25" d. Sousaphone player from an even smaller band. 1.87"

(Crichton 1987) holds that the original inhabitants of Norway and Sweden were nomadic people, small of stature. Gradually these countries were settled by tall Norse farmers who fenced what had been open lands. As the newcomers moved in, the original inhabitants were forced to take shelter in forests and caves, where, as the story goes, they hid themselves and survived for a long time.

They did not give up their lands without a struggle. At night they would sneak from their hiding places to harass the farmers. When crops failed or cows went dry, the farmers blamed these little men, who later came to be called Nisse in Norway and Tomtar in Sweden. Long after these little people died out, they were blamed for problems that couldn't otherwise be explained. The Norse farmers began leaving peace offerings—often a gift of food—that would placate the Nisse and encourage them to use their powers to make good things happen.

Fig 14.12 Four tiny dwarves that may not all be part of one set. They are similar in size and style. Examples of all but Fig 14.12b are known to have been purchased new between 1924 and 1934. a. Stretches, on knees. #6119; 1.25″ b. Lies prone, with right arm outstretched. Stamped "Germany" in black. 0.75″ c. Sits. #6118; 1.12″ d. Stands with hands on his beard. #2635; 1.87″

Fig 14.13 Tiny snowed version of Fig 14.12d. 1.62″

Fig 14.10 This and Fig 14.11 show an uncommon, carefully detailed dwarf band. All the members wear long red coats and have cheerful, child-like expressions. Five of them were purchased together; they are incised with consecutive numbers and stamped "Germany" in black. These pieces had the store stock numbers pencilled onto the bases, and were part of an extensive estate in Portland, Oregon (see text, chapter 21). Original price: 10¢ each. a. Guitar player, purchased separately, is unnumbered and unstamped. It was obtained from a dealer who bought it in Germany. 2.37″ b. String bass. #6023; 1.87″ c. Cymbals. #6022; 2.37″

Fig 14.11 Note that these six band members (with Fig 14.10) have eyebrows that are not only raised, but painted white. a. Seated saxophone player. #6020; 1.5″ b. Concertina player, also seated. #6019; 1.62″ c. Conductor, with a tiny, wooden baton. His cap is decorated with gold scallops. #6021; 2.37″

Fig 14.14 Unusual, well-molded dwarf in a snowed suit and no-snow boots. He holds a shovel and stands next to a mound of molded snow. This individual has a molded mustache, but the artist apparently forgot to paint it white. A tuft of hair shows under the hood of his cap, and he has a luxuriant, curly beard. #13667; 2.25″

As Christianity spread throughout the civilized world, missionaries incorporated local traditions into religious practices by giving them a Christian interpretation. This made the conversion of the local people to Christianity easier. In Scandinavia this process is seen in the role of the Nisse and Tomtar in the observation of Christmas. For more than a century Julenisse in Norway (Jultomte in Sweden) has been pictured dressed in red. He decorates the house for Christmas, and in certain areas of Scandinavia he even brings presents to the children. The children leave him a dish of rice gruel, which they always find empty on Christmas morning.

Fig 14.15 Two members of a snowed dwarf band. a. Snare drum (all other drummers among snow baby pieces have played the bass drum). Incised "Germany". #5129; 1.87" b. Bugler. 2.0"

Fig 14.16 Snowed dwarf in an unusual, broad-brimmed hat. He sits hugging his knees and has a short beard and a big smile. He is numbered, but the snow obscures part of the number so that only a "6" can be read. 2.0"

Fig 14.18 Two cheerful dwarves dance on a fly agaric mushroom. See text. 2.12"

Fig 14.20 Dwarf sits on a bisque swing. This piece was made to be suspended, but has no arch from which to hang. The dwarf is much larger than the swinging baby (Fig 10.47) and swinging Santa (Fig 13.9). 1.25"

Fig 14.19 Two dwarves slide down a molded, snowed brick wedge. Two babies in a similar pose are shown in Fig 10.52. 4.0"

Fig 14.17 Almost identical in molding to Fig 14.16, this dwarf's hat is attached with an elastic cord in the manner of nodder heads. #7658; 2.0"

Fig 14.21 Set of deeply molded, rather severe-looking dwarves. a. Prone, with left arm and leg raised. 1.37" b. Sits with left hand touching his cap in a sort of salute—or perhaps he is just trying to adjust it. 1.75" c. Reclines on his left hip and hand. 1.62"

Fig 14.22 Dwarf sits with arms up and both legs to one side. Because the top of his suit blouses out, he looks as if he is wearing a short skirt and tights. "Germany" stamped in black. 1.62"

Fig 14.23 Two identical dwarf pieces, the first mounted on a sled. Both sit with their hands raised and their legs spread. They wear long tops. **a.** Molded separately and glued or fired to a narrow bisque sled that is identical to the sleds in Fig 10.102. 1.5" **b.** Same dwarf without the sled. He is more commonly found this way. This example has lost much of his face paint. 1.25"

Fig 14.24 Dwarf with very long feet and an arched back. One hand is raised in the air. There is a hole through his raised fist to hold something, perhaps a flower or flag. 2.25"

Fig 14.25 Two dwarves with exceptionally long noses and feet and large googly eyes. **a.** Squats with his hands on his thighs. An example was purchased new between 1924 and 1934. 2.12" **b.** Stands with his hands tucked up his sleeves. 2.5"

Fig 14.26 Dwarf lies on one side and balances an egg on his knee. A bird has perched atop the egg. (There must be more to this story than meets the eye.) His legs are crossed at the ankles. The back of the egg is stamped "Germany". #4787; 1.5"

Fig 14.27 Tiny dwarf and a black cat on either side of an English letter box. The box and the base are snowed. The fabric greenery is part of the piece. 1.87"

Fig 14.28 Carefully molded set of dwarves: you can see their individual fingers, and even the buttons on their shirts. Their style and delicacy sets them apart from all other dwarves shown in this chapter. They are numbered differently from almost all other snow baby pieces, with each number ending in a capital letter. (The final digit of the fourth dwarf's number is obscured but looks most like a "G", suggesting that there may be at least one additional figure to this set.) **a.** Lies on right elbow. #6006C; 1.37" **b.** Sits holding a bouquet. #6006E; 1.62 **c.** Stands, arms outstretched. #6006A; 2.37" **d.** Sits, hand to cap. #6006-; 1.75 **e.** Stands on one foot. #6006B; 2.37"

Fig 14.31 Dwarf carries a baby dwarf on his back. The baby dwarf also has a beard! The larger dwarf's arms, nicely detailed, encircle the baby dwarf for support. The dwarves stand against a short pillar, which helps to steady them. 2.37"

Fig 14.29 **a.** Dwarf with urn, previously pictured (Fig 7.50). 1.75" **b.** Dwarf stretches on one knee. An example was purchased new between 1924 and 1934. 1.75" **c.** Curly haired dwarf sits on something green. He carries a small basket over his arm. 2.0"

Fig 14.30 **a.** Curly bearded dwarf plays a string bass. Incised "Germany". #18378; 2.12" **b.** Tiny china dwarf works at an anvil with a gold hammer. Stamped "Germany Western" in purple. 1.5"

Fig 14.32 Dwarf stands on a short ladder to reach the top of a smiling-faced mushroom. A pot of orange paint sits at the base of the mushroom. Is the dwarf trying to paint over the spots of this fly agaric mushroom to disguise it? Because he is not dressed in red, he is not strictly speaking a Christmas dwarf. #1638; 2.25"

Fig 14.33 The woman who brought this tiny china dwarf to the Unites States from Norway in the mid-1920s used it as a drip catcher for a tea pot. The family believes that it was new at around the turn of the twentieth century. I have seen a similar piece offered for sale as a pincushion half-doll. Stamped "Germany" in black. 0.75"

Fig 14.34 These two dwarves have incised numbers that show they are part of a set. Molding is not well detailed. **a.** Kneels on one knee. Stamped "Germany" in black. #5148; 1.0" **b.** Squats, hands on knees. #5150; 1.0"

Fig 14.35 Four Japanese dwarves, three of which were meant to hang as Christmas ornaments. All are stamped "Japan" in red. They could have been made after 1950. **a.** On hands and knees. 1.62" **b.** Hanging dwarf with star. 3.0" **c.** Hanging dwarf holds a stack of wrapped packages. 3.0" **d.** Hanging dwarf with a wreath. 3.0"

Fig 14.36 Dwarf sits with his knees up, legs apart and hands together. He has lost most of his face paint. 1.25"

Fig 14.37 This pair of unusual figures, a dwarf and an elf, have long, bendable wire legs attached to large, heavy shoes. These look like wooden Dutch shoes. It has been suggested that these may have been made to straddle a branch of a Christmas tree, their shoes acting as counterweights. Examples of these two and two other slightly different poses were purchased new between 1924 and 1934. **a.** Dwarf stamped "Germany" in purple. 2.12" **b.** Elf incised "Germany". #7294; 2.25"

Chapter 15
Elves

Fig 15.1 An elf hides from a witch beside the witch's house. The roof and the base are snowed. At the back of the house there is a hole to hold a tiny tree. Stamped "Germany" in black. #8398; 2.25″

If bisque dwarves are workers, then bisque elves are definitely pleasure-seekers. Not one piece photographed for this book shows an elf involved in any activity that even vaguely resembles work.

Description

The total absence of beards and mustaches distinguishes elves from dwarves. In addition, elves have youthful faces with impish expressions. Most have bodies shaped like babies, and all but a few are dressed in red. In fact they are occasionally difficult to distinguish from the red babies shown in chapter 10. However, most elves have tiny blue wings, like budding angel wings. Their hats, which are never attached hoods, often perch above large pointed ears. I have never seen an elf wearing snowed clothing.

A few elves (Figs 15.20 and 15.21) have slender, mature bodies and no wings. Each wears a tall, pointed cap that is adorned with a distinct widow's peak. Some collectors call these figures pixies.

Santa's Elves

In the United States, Santa's helpers are Christmas elves. Their work in Santa's workshop helps explain how he can make toys for so many children each year. However, bisque elves seem set more on enjoying toys than on making them. They play with a jack-in-the-box, ride a rocking horse and tug at either end of a concertina. But we never see them at any task that might help to produce a toy.

Two pieces show Santa and an elf riding together on a motorcycle (Fig 13.66) and on a train (Fig 13.67). They lend credibility to the idea of an early association between Santa Claus and elves. Children's books published near the turn of the century picture Santa with his "elves," but as often as not these "elves" are bearded. Although some collectors may insist that there is a difference between dwarves and elves, the illustrators of children's books have not always made the same distinction.

Fig 15.2 Two elves, apparently amused at the result, tug on either end of a concertina. Stamped "Germany" in purple. #732; 1.75″

Fig 15.4 Elf kneels inside the doorway of a snowed doghouse; a Scottie stands and waits outside. #516; 1.37″

Fig 15.3 Two elves ride back to back in a motorboat. One steers; something has startled the other. #7151; 1.5″

Fig 15.5 Three elf pieces; the first and third are a pair. **a.** Tiny elf lies on his back with his feet in the air. His right hand cradles his head. #9708; 1.12″ **b.** Three small elves link arms on a snowed base. Stamped "Germany" in purple. 1.5″ **c.** Tiny elf lies prone, feet up, hands under chin. Stamped "Germany" in black. #9707; 0.87″

Fig 15.6 Three elf pieces. The first two are identical except for the color. **a. & b.** Elf stands on a base, left hand cupped behind his ear. Incised number is in series with Figs 15.5a and 15.5c. #9706; 2.0″ **c.** Elf wearing green with large yellow wings sits on a mushroom with his knees up. #373; 1.75″

Fig 15.9 One elf sits on this donkey; the other has just slid off the back, and grabs the tail. A little black dog crouches in front of the donkey. #513; 2.0″

Fig 15.7 Unusual elf pushes a long sled down a low wedge. Sitting on the sled are two teddy bears of the style popular in the first decade of the twentieth century. Each has a molded bow at his neck. #5929; 1.5″

Fig 15.10 Three elves take a ride on a large turtle. #741; 2.25″

Fig 15.8 Three tiny elves sit on a log with a Pan figure playing a harmonica. The base is snowed. #314; 2.25″

Fig 15.11 This elf plays with a golliwog jack-in-the-box. The little elf clutches his throat in surprise. #1177; 1.5″

Fig 15.12 Two elf-katydid pieces on bases. **a.** Elf rides in a cart pulled by a katydid. 1.75" **b.** Elf rides on a katydid. #734; 2.25"

Fig 15.16 Elves on hobby horses. **a.** Two elves ride a horse on a very long, bow-shaped rocker. One elf has his arms around the waist of the other. #9703; 2.0" **b.** This single elf is rocking energetically on a smaller hobby horse. #735; 2.0"

Fig 15.13 Three Christmas fairy pieces, each on its own base. **a.** Fairy dressed in pink stands with an elf. #168; 2.25" **b.** Little girl fairy with tiny, budding wings. #9006; 1.87" **c.** Elegant fairy with yellow wings fully spread. 2.5"

Fig 15.15 Elf sits on a bench between two dressed-up children. The elf has a hand on one knee of each child. They appear to be watching a performance of some sort. #738; 1.75"

Fig 15.17 Elf plays a guitar. He sits on a spotted mushroom, whose stem is a smiling, winking face. Judging from his gleeful expression, the elf is having a wonderful time. #733; 2.37"

Fig 15.14 **a.** Elf sits atop a bell tower vigorously ringing a tiny hand bell. A robin sits next to the tower. The tower and base are snowed. Stamped "Germany" in purple. #1628; 2.5" **b.** Three elf musicians on a base. Two sing from books, and one plays a recorder. An example of this piece was purchased new in the 1930s. Stamped "Germany" in black. 1.62"

Fig 15.18 Two little elves fly in an open-cockpit airplane. Each has his hands on the controls. #9709; 1.5"

Fig 15.19 Unusual elf on a base strides along carrying a lantern. Stamped "Germany" in black. 1.62"

Fig 15.20 Tall, slender elf with a child's face, quite different from all other elves. He is playing his violin using a tricky bowing technique. Unlike most elves, he has no wings. #8427; 2.75"

Fig 15.21 Elf band, sometimes called the pixie band. All of the pieces have pedestal bases. The elves wear tall, pointed hats that cover their large ears. None of them has wings. An example of this band was purchased new between 1924 and 1934. From the top: **a.** Saxophone. 2.5" **b.** Violin. Stamped "Germany" in purple. 2.75" **c.** Clarinet. "Germany" stamped in purple. 2.75" **d.** Trumpet. "Germany" stamped in purple. 2.75" **e.** Elf conductor. 2.75"

Fig 15.22 Two pixie-type elves. **a.** This elf on a pedestal base glides confidently on silver skates. An example of this piece was purchased new in the 1930s. Stamped "Germany" in black. 1.75" **b.** Elf rides a broom and waves. 1.87"

Fig 15.23 Pixie-type elf sits on a sled with one leg folded under him and one knee up. 1.75"

Fig 15.24 Two English plaster elves. **a.** Elf lies prone on a sled. Stamped "Made in England". 1.12" **b.** Elf stands on a base carrying a lantern. Stamped "Made in England" in a circle. 1.5"

Chapter 16
Animals

Fig 16.1 This polar bear riding a scooter is sought-after as much for its whimsy as for its workmanship. Although bears in circuses ride all sorts of vehicles, including scooters, I wonder whether polar bears ever have. #369; 1.5"

Fig 16.2 A polar bear trying to learn to ski is a wonderful idea. By his expression, it looks as if he'd like to go back to fishing for salmon. His pinkish-brown nose is characteristic of many fine German bears; the color appears to wash off readily. This piece was from a large estate in Portland, Oregon, and was purchased new in the late 1920s or early 1930s. It has its original department store price tag marked "10¢". Stamped "Germany" in black. 1.5"

BEARS AND OTHER ANIMALS

Several facts suggest that most of these animals were created between the world wars. None of the pictures of snow baby scenes from before World War I include any bisque animals (see chapter 21). Some owners remember when their animal pieces were purchased in the 1920s and 1930s. Finally, in style these animals are like snow babies made between the wars.

Some pieces, such as the Scottie and Westie by a doghouse, show the animal in a natural pose. Others are whimsical; they give human qualities to realistic-looking animals. An example of this is the penguin band. These look like real penguins, but they are engaged in an activity usually pursued by people. A few pieces are caricatured, sometimes to the extent that it is difficult to know what animal was intended.

Bears

Polar bears are by far the most common snow baby animal found. They were popular zoo animals even before the era of heroic Arctic explorations. Polar bears had been captured for zoos by arctic fur traders, who did an even brisker trade in their hides. They were also occasionally found as far south as the Gulf of St. Lawrence. Still, until well into the 20th century very little was known about their habits and behavior. News about the exploration of the Arctic increased the public's interest in the habits of polar bears. This may help explain why so many were created in bisque during this era.

Bears with large, coarse snow like Fig 16.17a are easily identifiable as post-World War II pieces. But some earlier Japanese bears are difficult to distinguish from German examples. Some photographs (Figs 16.16 and 16.17) show German and Japanese bears side by side in similar poses to allow comparison. Sometimes subtle features, such as the care with which the ears and nose were molded, provide the key to making the distinction.

German bears usually look as if they have been modeled from nature, whereas the Japanese bears often look awkward. When you compare Fig 16.17b (German) with Fig 16.17c (Japanese), the difference is clear. However, not all German bears were molded with such care (Fig 16.4), and some Japanese bears were made with good detail (Fig 16.18). Until marked examples are found, some German and Japanese bears will remain too similar to distinguish reliably.

Penguins

Second to polar bears in popularity are the snow baby penguins. Of course, penguins are not found in the Arctic, just as polar bears are not found in Antarctica. During the late twenties and early thirties there was great interest in Admiral Bird's explorations of Antarctica. Penguins were the subject of children's stories, advertisements and magazine articles. This may help to explain the number and variety of bisque penguins available from that period. Even real penguins without props look comical. In bisque they are some of the most fanciful animal pieces.

Other Animals

Dogs, which are also seen on Santa pieces and with babies, were sometimes featured by themselves, snowed and unsnowed, comic and realistic. Some seem to be no identifiable breed, but the characteristic features of Scotties and Huskies can be distinguished on some pieces. Scotties were very popular domestic dogs during the twenties, which probably accounts in part for their appearance in bisque. Huskies were

Fig 16.3 Set of three small bears playing with large, colored balls. **a.** Bear on his back. 0.5" **b.** Standing bear. Stamped "Germany" in blue. 1.37" **c.** Seated bear has lost his pink nose coloring. 1.25"

Fig 16.4 This pink-nosed bear in an igloo can be found with either fine or coarse snow. Because the bear was molded separately, he may be positioned differently at the doorway of the igloo. This piece is incised, but only two digits were legible; snow obliterates the rest of the number on this example. On other examples it was not visible at all. #-40-; 1.5"

used in the Arctic, and later in Antarctica, because of their excellent performance in extreme cold as sled dogs.

Few cats that could be called snow baby pieces seem to have been created. The only naturalistic bisque cat is shown in Fig 7.33. The rest were made to look like cartoon cats or were shown engaged in human tasks.

Included in this chapter are some tiny no-snow bisque rabbits and sheep. Although it is not clear that they were intended to be used with snow babies, they provide useful detail in scenes.

Comic-Strip Animals

One bisque comic character is Bonzo the dog (Fig 16.37a), who appeared in the English magazine *Sketch* from 1920 to 1927. Because of his popularity, he continued to be featured in toys, figurines and advertising throughout the 1920s and 1930s. Pip, Squeak and Wilford (Fig 16.45) were featured in a slow-paced British comic strip that ran from 1919 to 1947. The mouse (or rabbit), Wilford, is shown again alone in Fig 16.46b. The other comic animals pictured (Fig 16.47) do not seem to represent any specific characters.

Fig 16.8 a. Polar bear stands on an orange sled. This is a commonly found bear that I have never seen marked Germany or Japan; it could be either. 1.87″ b. Bear squats on a snowball. 1.75″

Fig 16.5 This bear makes his way up the side of an igloo. His face paint has apparently fallen victim to over-zealous cleaning. 1.75″

Fig 16.7 Small bear stands on all fours atop a snowball. This piece is also found in a larger size measuring 2.25″ tall. He appears to be the same bear shown in Fig 16.4. 1.37″

Fig 16.9 This carefully painted polar bear cub is not a common piece. The pose is somewhat unusual: the back legs look like they are walking, but the front legs are together, at rest. It does not look like it was modeled from nature. 1.37″

Fig 16.6 A large, pink-nosed bear stands on a snowball. He has a carefully painted face with whisker marks and line-and-dot eyes. 3.25″

Fig 16.10 Two similarly posed, pink-nosed polar bears. a. This one has somewhat coarser snow. 0.87″ b. This is the polar bear shown in Fig 16.4. Here stamped "Germany" in blue. 0.5″

Fig 16.11 Three tiny, pink-nosed bear cubs. You could call them the "tumblers of the polar bear set." There is at least one additional pose, shown in Fig 16.12b. The poses of these bears seem quite naturalistic. **a.** Walks, head turned to the right. Stamped "Germany" in black. 0.62" **b.** Partly lying, propped up on front legs. Stamped "Germany" in blue. 0.87" **c.** Lies down at full stretch. 0.87"

Fig 16.12 Three highly unusual bears covered with brown snow. These bears are part of the same set as Fig 16.11. **a.** Walks, head turned to the right. 0.62" **b.** Stands with head down, as if he is sniffing. Stamped "Germany" in black. 0.75" **c.** Partly lying, propped up. 0.87"

Fig 16.13 These three polar bears seem to be having a good laugh together. Their origin is unclear. None of these is marked, and these are the only examples I have seen of them. **a.** Sits, with arms and legs outstretched. 1.12" **b.** Stands erect with arms crossed. 1.62" **c.** Sits with arms crossed. 1.25"

Fig 16.14 Bear stands with front paws on a sled. This solid, boxy sled is also seen with several German babies (chapter 10). Although he is unmarked, this bear closely resembles others that are marked Germany. 1.87"

Fig 16.15 Four bears stand on their hind legs. Only Fig 16.15c is marked. **a.** Tall, skinny bear with splayed toes. 2.25" **b.** Stands with left paw raised. 2.25" **c.** Fat bear stands with paws down. An example of this bear was purchased new between 1924 and 1934. Stamped "Germany" in black. 2.5" **d.** Large bear seems to be investigating something. Although he stands on his hind legs, his posture is unusual. He strongly resembles Fig 16.14. 2.12"

Fig 16.16 Three bears stand on their hind legs. **a.** An example of this piece was purchased new in the 1930s. Stamped "Japan" in black. 1.75" **b.** Unmarked, but not German, this bear has coarse snow and is crudely molded. 1.62" **c.** Fat bear with his paws crossed in front of him. An example of this bear was purchased new between 1924 and 1934. Stamped "Germany". 1.37"

Fig 16.20 Three no-snow polar bears, perhaps a mother and two cubs. They have nicely molded fur. **a.** Cub stands on all fours. 0.87" **b.** Cub lies down with head turned to right. 0.75" **c.** Adult bear on all fours. 1.12"

Fig 16.17 Three bears on all fours. **a.** (Top) Judging from the coarse snow that is glued on, this is a late production bear. It is not German. 1.62" **b.** This walking bear is stamped "Germany" in black. Notice his square head and nicely defined ears. 1.25" An example of this bear was purchased new between 1924 and 1934. This also exists in a smaller (0.62") version. **c.** He is posed awkwardly for walking. An example of this piece was purchased new in the 1930s. Stamped "Japan" in black under his chin. 1.12"

Fig 16.21 Large, seated bear with crystalline (translucent) snow. Unmarked, its origin is uncertain. Not commonly found. 2.37"

Fig 16.18 Bear slides on his back, head-first down a wedge. This well-executed piece is incised "Japan". #5900; 1.87"

Fig 16.22 This beautifully molded china polar bear was made by Heubach. It is incised with their sunburst mark. 3.37"

Fig 16.19 Bear lies on his back on a sled. His molding is so like that of the previous bear on the wedge that, although he is not marked, he is probably Japanese. 1.25"

Fig 16.23 The Teddy Bear Musicians. Two wear scarves and one wears a red vest as they carry their instruments on a snowed base. 2.12"

Fig 16.24 Four sports bears, possibly all incised and numbered, but they are tiny pieces and the snow obscures some of the writing. Each is 1.5″. a. Plays hockey. #3649 b. Wears boxing gloves. #3647 c. With a tennis racket and ball. Incised "Germany". d. Guides a soccer ball with his foot. Incised "Germany".

Fig 16.28 What could be more entertaining than a serenade by three penguin musicians? They stand on an icy, no-snow base. 2.0″

Fig 16.25 A small, standing, snowed teddy bear with a scarf around his neck. Also found in 2.5″ size. 1.75″

Fig 16.27 A tiny no-snow bear with his head lowered stands on a tall block of ice in this snow globe. The base of the globe is made of amber glass and is embossed "Germany". Although other snow globes I have seen are about 4″ high, this one is only 2.75″.

Fig 16.29 Proud mother penguin pushes blanket-covered twin babies in a buggy. Stamped "Germany" in black. 1.62″

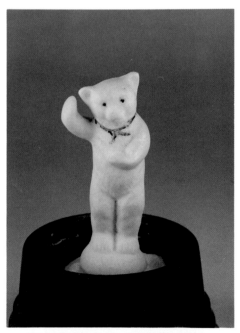

Fig 16.26 Nearly identical to Fig 16.25, this no-snow version was made as a snow dome insert. Stamped "Germany". 2.62″

Fig 16.30 Penguin pushes a wheelbarrow filled with Christmas ornaments over a no-snow base. Stamped "Germany" in black. 1.5″

Fig 16.31 Three penguin pieces. **a.** Set of three penguins walking in the usual bisque formation: single file, the shortest in front. 1.75″ **b.** Single, snowed, fat penguin with his head turned. 2.25″ **c.** Three penguins march single file down an icy wedge, the smallest in the lead. Stamped "Germany" in black. 2.12″

Fig 16.35 Snowed husky stands on all fours on a base. 1.12″

Fig 16.32 Single, fat penguin on short, yellow skis looks straight ahead. 2.0″

Fig 16.36 Snowed husky seated. 1.12″

Fig 16.33 Two snowed penguins stand on a wedge. This is unmarked, but it is not a German piece. Well-executed, but the snow is coarse and applied with a yellow glue. 2.5″

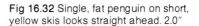

Fig 16.34 Scottie and Westie dogs sit outside on a snow-covered base, next to a snowed doghouse. Two robins perch on the doghouse. #382; 1.5″

Fig 16.37 Three snowed animals on skis. These three pieces were part of the Portland, Oregon, estate mentioned in the text. All three still have their original Meier and Frank department store price tags from the 1920s or 1930s. **a.** Bonzo, the comic dog created by GE Suddy and popular in England during the 1920s. Stamped "Germany" in purple. 2.0″ **b.** Pig clutches a blue scarf wrapped around his neck. Notice that the same shade of pink was used on the pig's feet and nose as was popular on bears' noses. This piece was glued to a cardboard round that may have been stamped. 2.0″ **c.** Skiing elephant wears a red scarf. This piece is more commonly found without the bisque skis. Stamped "Germany" in purple. 2.25″

Fig 16.38 Black mother cat in a ruffled dress pushes a kitten dressed in a red coat and a muff on a fancy sled. "Germany" in black. 1.75"

Fig 16.39 a. Bird sits on a no-snow mound next to a bird house built on a stump. Probably Japanese. 2.87" b. Two fat robins sit on a bisque fence. The base and part of the fence are snowed. #6003; 2.0"

Fig 16.40 Plaster piece shows a robin on an English letter box. 2.0"

Fig 16.41 These are not bisque pieces, but they are often displayed with snow babies. a. Two spring-mounted plaster robins on and near a twig fence. This fence seems to be made of real twigs. Glitter snow. Stamped "Germany US Zone". 2.25" b. Single robin on a spring attached to a stump. There is a small pond at the foot of the stump. Glitter finish. Stamped "Germany" in black. 2.37"

Fig 16.42 This type of early, carefully made sheep is sometimes displayed with snow babies. The sheep itself has a china finish. Similar sheep can be found in other positions. This could be German or English. 1.25"

Fig 16.43 Four tiny, bisque, no-snow rabbits. a. Sits up. Incised "Germany". 1.0" b. Sits down, with ears down. 0.75" c. Sits up, with light coloration. #966; 1.12" d. Sits down, with ears up. Incised "Germany". #489; 0.87"

Fig 16.47 Three snowed animal caricatures that show considerable similarity in the way they were molded. a. Comic dog. 1.12″ b. Tiny cat on all fours. 0.87″ c. Cat stretching, with tail up. An example of this cat was purchased new between 1924 and 1934. "Germany" in purple. 1.25″

Fig 16.44 Four no-snow sheep, all lying down. a. Large sheep with blue collar and red bell. Incised "Germany". #786; 1.25″ b. Tiny ram. #SP 786; 0.75″ c. Head turned to right; red collar and gold bell. #968; 0.75″ d. Lying down, with head turned to left. Incised "Germany". #SP 786; 0.75″

Fig 16.45 Pip, Squeak and Wilford, popular British cartoon characters drawn by A. B. Payne. The strip ran from 1919 to 1947. Here they maneuver a cart through the snow. Wilford rides. The snow is molded, rather than applied. 1.75″

Fig 16.48 This is not really a snow baby, but is sometimes collected or sold with them. This monkey is stamped "Japan" in red, and was probably meant to hang in a chain with other monkeys. 1.12″

Fig 16.46 a. A pig in a red jacket and black tie reclines on his back on a sled. He wears a very surprised expression. 1.25″ b. Wilford (from Fig 16.45) stands, painted red. I have read that he is a rabbit; other sources call him a mouse. Perhaps A. B. Payne wanted us to wonder. 2.0″

Fig 16.49 Seated comic bear with crystalline pink snow. Similar pieces have been found marked "1951 Styson". Stamped "Made in Japan" in red. There are several other poses. 2.0″

Chapter 17
Snowmen

Snow baby collectors sometimes ignore snowmen as unimportant pieces. They don't have the detailed molding that characterizes the babies, and they lack the more carefully executed facial features, but snowmen do have a charm of their own. Of all the types of figures captured in bisque and classed with snow babies, snowmen are the only figures that a child could actually make.

The bisque snowmen in this chapter show a considerable range of style. Some are composed of the traditional three round balls stacked on top of one another, with only the suggestion of molded arms. Others are creatures with distinct arms and legs that engage in human activities. They can be found snowed or unsnowed, German or Japanese. Because snowmen by nature lack detail, many of the Japanese examples compare favorably with the German pieces.

Some of the more elaborate examples were inspired by the popular notion of a snowman coming to life. In one case, snowmen have dressed up in overcoats and joined together to form a band. Although a snowman riding a sled seems almost expected, a snowman playing tennis represents a giant leap of the imagination.

Fig 17.3 See Fig 17.2. **a.** Sits with legs spread, winking and wearing a green top hat. This is a common piece. 1.25" **b.** Sits wearing a tasseled beanie. This snowman also appears in Figs 17.4 and 17.5. 1.25"

Fig 17.1 Snowman sits with his legs out and his hands folded across his stomach. Despite lack of detail, he has considerable personality. This piece has also been found on a cotton-covered snowball candy container, decorated with fabric holly. It has an incised number, but only the digits "69" are not covered with snow. Incised "Germany" in an arc on the bottom. 2.12"

Fig 17.5 Group of figures mounted on a bisque base. They include the snowman from Fig 17.3b, a standing snowman with a cane and top hat and a tiny bear on all fours. All the figures and the base are snowed. There is a hole in the base for the tree. An example of this piece was purchased new between 1924 and 1934. The piece is unmarked, but several of the individual pieces have been seen marked "Germany". 2.12"

Fig 17.2 This and Fig 17.3 show four German snowmen with well-defined arms and legs. The eyes of each tend to bulge out. Each is stamped "Germany" in purple. **a.** Wears yellow beret. Left hand is on his hip, and he carries a tennis racket under his arm. He has enormous feet. 1.75" **b.** Wears a yellow dunce cap, and lies propped up on one arm. 1.5"

Fig 17.4 Snowman from Fig 17.3b sits on a sled behind a seated bear cub. An example of this piece was purchased new between 1924 and 1934. "Germany" in black. 1.62"

Fig 17.6 One of the snowmen from Fig 17.5, this time winking, stands next to a tiny bisque rabbit. The base has a hole for a tree or other decoration. The entire piece is snowed, except for the snowman's hat and cane. Stamped "Germany" in purple. 2.0"

Fig 17.9 Set of three German snowmen in various states of repose, or perhaps, decomposition. All wear black top hats. Each is 1.5". a. Sits asleep, chin in one hand. b. Sits with arms back and legs raised. Is he exercising? c. Prone, he supports his torso by his hands. Maybe he is beginning to melt.

Fig 17.7 a. Commonly found Japanese version of the snowman in Fig 17.6. Notice that his hat is snowed, and his face is not. Some collectors call him the "WC Fields" snowman. Stamped "Japan". 1.62" b. Snowman smokes a cigar and carries a broom. He wears a tiny stovepipe hat. He is sometimes found with a blue or red scarf. "Germany" stamped in blue. 1.75"

Fig 17.10 Two no-snow snowmen (or perhaps snow women). a. Stands with a well-defined broom, top hat and black eyes and buttons. He is smiling. #7305; 2.12" b. Wears a tiny, pointed, red hat. He frowns and appears to have hands in pockets. #10295; 2.0"

Fig 17.8 Pair of Japanese snowmen with similar facial features. a. This snowman could be wearing a fireman's hat, or perhaps a London bobby's hat. He looks as if he might be directing traffic. An example of this piece was purchased new in the 1930s. Stamped "Japan" in black. 2.75" b. Notice the similarity to Fig 17.3b. This piece is larger, but is otherwise a fairly good copy. Stamped "Japan". 2.0"

Fig 17.11 Four glazed members of a no-snow snowman band. (Are there more?) Each wears a different type of hat. They even have defined ears. They have been owned by the same family since they were purchased new just after World War II and are the only examples I have seen of these wonderfully detailed pieces. They are priced on the bottom at 10¢ each. a. The conductor has a cigar in his mouth and wears a tuxedo, blue mittens and black bow tie. 2.37" b. Clarinetist. He and the other band members wear long coats and scarves around their necks. Stamped "Germany Western" in purple. 2.25" c. Plays the banjo and sings. Stamped "Germany" in purple. 2.25" d. Violinist, who also smokes a cigar. His eyes are shut (you can see his molded eyelids). 2.25"

129

Fig 17.12 This snowman is made of a composition material and painted with fluorescent paint. The whole piece glows brightly in the dark. I have not seen an example of this piece in bisque or china, contrary to my experience with most other fluorescent pieces. It is incised with a complicated mark I have been unable to identify. 2.75"

Fig 17.13 Disassembled snow dome shows the Japanese snow man that was inside. The snowman stands on two stubby legs and has two stubby arms. The figure was fired onto the type of base that has at times been misidentified as a bottle stopper. In front of the base is the rubber collar that fits around the narrow portion of the snowman's pedestal and holds the figure in the center of the globe. Snowman and pedestal are 2.5".

Fig 17.14 These two snowmen were meant to be snow dome inserts. a. This tiny unsnowed snowman holds a broom and wears a hat. He is so small that it is hard to imagine him in a snow dome, but it is harder to imagine any other use for him. 1.5" b. Holds up a pipe; snowed, except for his head. The top of his base is painted blue. Incised "Germany", unusual for a snow dome piece. 2.5"

Fig 17.15 Dancing snowman is made of a composition material. Everything but his hat, including the base, is snowed. Stamped "Germany" in purple. 1.75"

Fig 17.16 These pieces are made of a lightweight composition material such as papier mâché. They are hollow, and all are no-snow. They belong to the family of the original owner. Each is marked "5¢" in pencil. All were bought new in the 1930s. a. Snowman with a tiny child molded in low relief in front of him. 2.75" b. Santa at a chimney; only the rooftop shows. This and 17.16c are incised "Japan" and stamped "Japan" in black. 2.62" c. Molded child next to a molded snowman on a base. 2.25"

Chapter 18
Buildings

German snowed buildings are not common. For that reason, collectors who would like to use them in displays sometimes resort to unsnowed houses, Japanese bisque houses and small buildings made of other materials.

Of the few snowed German buildings shown in this chapter, most have regular snow. Two are coralene-covered and two have molded snow that is painted gold.

Collectors who mix contemporary pieces into their collections have an easier time finding buildings. In the past few years many types of small buildings have been produced that look much like the old ones. Some of these are modestly priced and work well in snow baby scenes.

Fig 18.1 Two snowed, red brick buildings, They are carefully molded, but only their fronts are painted. Undoubtedly German. **a.** Schoolhouse with a bell tower. 2.0″ **b.** Two-story house. 1.87″

Fig 18.2 Two-story snowed house with a fence and bushes out in front. Carefully molded, multi-paned windows and patterned front door. It originally may have been painted. #9779; 2.87″

Fig 18.4 Elaborate snowed inn with a woman in front and stagecoach pulled by two horses. Four people ride on the coach. Notice how similar this building is to Fig 18.3b. However, it is a completely different building, not simply the back view of that piece. 1.87″

Fig 18.5 Snowed church on a base, with molded shrubbery around it. #6003; 2.25″

Fig 18.3 Two carefully molded snowed buildings. **a.** Nearly identical to Fig 18.2 (but smaller), this one was made with two chimneys. Stamped ''Germany'' in purple. 2.37″ **b.** Very nicely molded, this looks like an inn with an arched drive-through. #9417; 2.37″

Fig 18.6 These two buildings are finished with coralene snow, not only on the roofs but also on the sides of the building and on the base. a. Two-story house with molded bushes. 1.62″ b. Church. #-6—; 2.5″

Fig 18.7 Standard two-story house with bushes and brick trim. The roof is snowed. 1.5″

Fig 18.8 Two variations of the house shown in Fig 18.7. Both roofs seem to have been painted after the snow was applied and have been sponged with a contrasting paint to highlight the snow. Notice the slightly different number and arrangement of windows on the two pieces. a. #5825; 1.5″ b. 1.5″

Fig 18.9 Two unsnowed, unmarked bisque buildings. These may be Japanese. a. 1.62″ b. 1.5″

Fig 18.10 Simple bisque church, incised "Made in Japan". 3.62″

Fig 18.11 Two buildings, both incised "Japan". a. Church. 2.25″ b. Two-story, half-timbered house. 2.12″

Fig 18.12 Two Japanese houses. **a.** Thatched roof, molded plants, no-snow. 1.75" **b.** No-snow, but with a molded snow roof. Incised "Japan". 1.75"

Fig 18.15 Composition Norman-style church. Stamped "Made in England". 1.25"

Fig 18.13 Three tiny houses. **a.** Unmarked and no-snow, but German. 1.12" **b.** More elaborate version of first house. It is unmarked, but German. 1.25" **c.** Mill with a water-wheel. Unmarked, but Japanese. 1.25"

Fig 18.16 Tiny composition Santa stands in front of a tinier two-story house, all on a base. The house and the base have applied glitter snow. Stamped "Germany" in black. 1.37"

Fig 18.14 This house is made of composition material and finished with glitter snow. It is sometimes seen without the robin on the spring or with a tiny snow baby sitting in front. Stamped "Germany" in black. 2.75"

Fig 18.17 Similar in style to Fig 18.16, this piece is Japanese. I have seen several examples of the church building alone. The base and roof have applied glitter snow. Stamped "Japan" in purple. 2.0"

Chapter 19
Newer Snow Babies — 1950s and Later

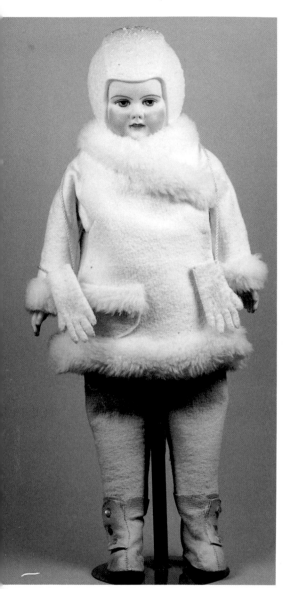

American

Snow baby manufacture steeply declined after the 1940s. However, a few pieces made during the 1960s were so well-executed that they are prized by doll collectors and snow baby collectors alike.

Four Patti-Jene shoulder head dolls, ranging in height from 14 to 16 inches, were advertised in the April 1962 issue of the *Toy Trader*. They appear to have applied snow, and were sold dressed in terry cloth suits or as doll kits. Patti-Jene also made a six-inch jointed no-snow baby with blond curls. It is incised "Patti-Jene".

Gerald LaMotte created a shoulder head doll that is as beautiful as any earlier snow baby (Fig 19.1). He also made a jointed no-snow polar bear that is elastic-strung and incised "LaMotte" on the bottom of one paw.

Japanese and Others

Snow babies were imported from Japan by Shackman and others during the 1960s, according to Daniel Jacoby (1987). Some of these pieces have coarse grout. In 1979 Shackman imported a boxed set of six babies from Taiwan.

The last half of the 1980s saw a renewed interest in vintage Christmas decorations. In response appeared reproductions of old glass ornaments, paper scraps and porcelain Christmas decorations. A part of this revival is the production of new snow babies. A few, such as the red huggers, are exact copies of earlier pieces, but most are new figures altogether.

The most widely available contemporary snow babies are the pieces made in Taiwan by Department 56. The creamy colored bisque babies are almost all about 3.5 inches tall and are sparsely snowed. Painting is limited to eyes, eyebrows and mouth. Some poses are reminiscent of earlier snow babies, but they have also been made in an assortment of new poses. Each year a few new pieces have been introduced and several pieces retired. Some limited edition figures have also been made. A booming secondary market for these pieces has spawned several newsletters.

In 1989 Department 56 began to release smaller versions of the original bisque poses. These figures are done in off-white enamel-covered pewter and are approximately 1.5 inches tall. Department 56 also produces miniature no-snow figures in many poses. These porcelain figures are also about 1.5 inches tall.

In Sri Lanka the George Z. Lefton Company makes no-snow figurines to about the same scale. Their faces are especially well-detailed for such small, inexpensive items. The figures may be incised on the bottom, but some have only paper labels. Because newer pieces show up in antique dealers' cases now and again, it pays the collector to keep up with the new pieces that are offered each Christmas season.

Fig 19.1 This large shoulder head snow baby doll has been dressed in an elegant winter snow suit. It is incised "LaMotte '61" on the back of the shoulder plate. Its snow has been sparsely applied. The hands are also bisque. 18.0"

Fig 19.3 See 19.2. Boy skier who carries his skis on a base. **a.** 4.0" **b.** 3.0"

Fig 19.2 The four pieces in Figs 19.2 and 19.3 are all glazed, and all are incised "Japan". They could have been made any time from the 1930s until the last few years. **a.** Girl with two poles skis down a wedge. 4.0" **b.** Smaller version. 3.0"

Fig 19.4 Boy plays leapfrog over a small snowman. Another china piece of unknown antiquity, it was purchased recently in an antique shop. However, it may be new. 5.5″

Fig 19.7 Three bisque snow babies that were sold as a group by Department 56, which called them "The Tiny Trio". They were first made in 1988 and retired in 1990. Each is 3.5″. **a.** Plays cymbals. **b.** Carries a base drum. **c.** Blows on a bugle.

Fig 19.5 Boxed set of six snow babies. The label on the box bottom states that it was made in Taiwan for Shackman in 1979. See also Figs 10.97d, 10.166b and 10.166c for comparison to pre-World War II pieces.

Fig 19.6 These huggers are currently being imported from Taiwan. They come dressed in a choice of several colors; some of the suits are covered with glitter snow. In addition, at least one snowed reproduction of this pose has been made in the United States. This piece is not marked. 1.75″

Fig 19.8 Large Department 56 music box. This baby wears a pale yellow snowsuit; only the scarf is snowed. It is among the earliest snow baby pieces made by this company, and is quite rare. It was retired in 1987. Incised "Department 56". 7.0″

Fig 19.9 Three Department 56 snow babies. The two larger are made of bisque; the miniature is pewter. Janet Middleton, a collector of snow babies and post cards, noticed the similarity of these babies to this set of four valentine cards. The cards were chromolithographed by International Art around 1907. She wonders whether the cards provided the original inspiration for the bisque pieces.

Fig 19.11 This is only part of a very large display that mixes mostly new buildings and no-snow pieces with a few old snow babies. The elaborate multilevel framework, including the train tunnel, is set up just for the Christmas season (and perhaps just a bit longer).

Fig 19.10 Group of bisque no-snow figures made by George Lefton and Company. Notice the detailed face painting. Some have stick-on labels, but most are incised "Lefton" and the year they were first made. Heights range from 1.25" to 2.75". From the top: **a.** Two children in a horse-drawn carriage. The horse's reins are string. **b.** Newsboy hawks his papers. **c.** Boy and girl carry a wreath and sled full of packages. **d.** Mustached gentleman drags home a Christmas tree, accompanied by dog. He has secured the tree with a string rope. **e.** Small boy peeks from behind a well-clad snowman. **f.** Little girl gives smaller sister a ride on a tiny sleigh. **g.** Ice-skating boy takes a tumble. **h.** Accomplished girl ice skater.

Fig 19.12 For this bookcase scene, one of nine on this wall, Department 56 miniature pewter babies are mixed with plastic figures and some earlier Christmas decorations to make an effective winter landscape.

Chapter 20
Christmas Scenes

The Christmas snow scene, as we know it today, has evolved from the tradition of displaying a nativity scene during the Christmas season. This custom is centuries old in many European countries, and most of the early pieces that have survived are museum treasures.

Phillip Snyder (1977) vividly described elaborate Christmas displays made by families of German descent in Pennsylvania more than one hundred years ago. These displays were called Putz, German for ornaments or adornment. Although the focus was the nativity, in some homes these scenes were extended and embellished year after year. Eventually some came to include Noah's Ark, farm or village scenes, and even areas for jungle animals. Although the custom was to construct the Putz under the Christmas tree, sometimes these scenes grew to occupy entire rooms. Enthusiastic families spent months gathering rocks, moss and twigs and hand-crafting additional tiny figures and props for each Christmas season. Ardent handymen constructed elaborate mechanical props, such as running streams, waterfalls and clockwork see-saws.

As artificial moss, commercially made wooden animals, tin skaters and toy soldiers began to appear on the market, they were incorporated into the Putz. When snow babies became available, they found an ideal setting in these scenes. The relative simplicity of putting together a display using ready-made figures meant that a Christmas scene, in one form or another, was adopted as a tradition by many families in this country.

During the first decades of the twentieth century, the United States and much of Europe followed with great interest the stories of polar exploration, both at the North and South Poles. What better way to celebrate the achievements of the great explorers like Admirals Peary and Bird than to create a miniature polar scene at home? In a Christmas issue in 1916, *Good Housekeeping* magazine offered to tell readers how to construct such a scene "...on receipt of 7 cents in stamps" (Fig 21.4).

A photograph album belonging to the family of Robert Peary shows the faded picture of such a scene constructed on a dining table in one Peary home. A tiny figure (it doesn't look like a snow baby) climbs a hummock of ice and snow to plant a flag at the top.

Today, families construct a great variety of Christmas scenes. Some display a nativity in one area and a Santa and reindeer made of ceramic, celluloid or plastic in another spot. Lighting and scenes have spread to the front of the house, the lawn and even the roof!

Although interest in snow babies declined during the period from 1950 to 1985, since the mid-1980s there has been a new generation of snow babies and a resurgence of interest in the earlier pieces. Although this book is primarily about the earlier pieces, Christmas snow baby scenes will undoubtedly continue to evolve and incorporate new pieces with the old.

Fig 20.2 Pond scene on a library table shows a nice mix of old and new snow baby pieces.

Fig 20.1 This is a part of a mantel piece scene that uses old snow babies. The pieces are held in place by adhesive. The ceramic tiles above are another collecting interest in this family.

Fig 20.3 This family mixes bisque-headed, cotton-bodied children with other antique Christmas decorations to create this mantel scene.

Chapter 21
Dating Snow Babies

Although many snow baby pieces can't be precisely dated, they do have features that will help collectors fit them into one of two broad periods, divided by World War I. The Great War is a natural dividing line because from 1914 to 1919 nothing was imported from Germany. German manufacturers concentrated on war production, and the United States enacted an embargo against German goods. If you compare the pieces for which there is absolute proof of manufacture before World War I with those for which there is proof of manufacture after the war, you will notice a number of substantial differences. From these observations we may assume the approximate date of manufacture of other pieces with similar characteristics.

Background

During the earlier period, snow baby figures emerged from two existing forms: figurines and dolls. The pink snows and the blue snow children are really figurines. Most of them have bases and no moving parts (such as articulated arms and legs). They were meant for display individually or in pairs on mantels or in cabinets. They were not intended to be used as toys or knick-knacks or to be arranged in scenes. Grout was used to represent snow (or possibly sand) on these pieces, and children were their subjects. They were an important element in the development of snow babies.

Doll history provides another lead for this story. Shoulder head dolls were in commercial production from about the 1840s; snow baby shoulder heads are just one type. Doll maker Emma Clear recalled seeing a snow-covered shoulder head doll when she was a young child in about 1880 or 1890 (Johl 1950). If this memory is accurate, shoulder head snow babies provide the second line in the evolution of snow baby figures. The union of these two forms was, strictly speaking, neither doll nor figurine.

BEFORE WORLD WAR I

The snow baby pieces we know to be pre-World War I were carefully painted and fired at the right temperature to bond paint to porcelain. Even on small pieces special attention was paid to the painting of the eyes. The eyebrows were typically a soft brown. The eyes themselves consisted of a pupil dot, sometimes placed on a circle of blue, that hung from a black eyelid line. In fine pieces a red line traced the crease in the upper eyelid, and tiny red dots were painted at the nostrils. Doll collectors view this treatment as a sign of quality or early workmanship.

All of the babies that definitely date from this period have black or brown shoes or no color to their feet at all. Any colors used on the rest of the piece were typically pastels —soft pinks, blues and yellows. The babies and children are often described as "lovely" or even "beautiful." Their poses were usually inactive, especially when compared to the later pieces. Far fewer poses, and probably fewer examples of each pose, were made during this period than after World War I.

Documentation

An excellent bit of good fortune is the label preserved with the three-inch baby (Fig 21.1). This piece was apparently sold as a souvenir of the 1909 Alaska Yukon Pacific Exhibition in Seattle. This is the earliest specific date that can definitely be assigned to any snow baby.

A rare photographic post card (Fig 21.2) showing an English Christmas cake must have been taken during the Christmas season of 1910 (or earlier), because it is postmarked in March of 1911. This document is the earliest definite date we have for any four-inch baby.

The Christmas 1911 *Ladies' Home Journal* showed a Mistletoe Cake decorated with three-inch babies. In 1912 *Ladies' Home Journal* showed a Christmas party table decorated with a mixture of three- and four-inch babies. Although the *Journal* offered to send readers information about purchasing the materials to construct these decorations, it no longer has copies of these instructions on file.

The 1916 Christmas issue of *Good Housekeeping* shows a gift-filled, homemade replica of the North Pole that a reader could make for a children's party table. Pictured are several all-white snow babies.

One tiny baby (Fig 10.168) was described in the 1914 Marshall Field catalog as an "Alaska Tot" (Foulke 1981).

Two beautiful pieces (Figs 7.11 and 7.13) are incised with the Limbach mark and numbered 8535 and 8550 respectively. According to Jurgen and Marianne Cieslik, Limbach registered the number 2780 in 1893 and the number 10,000 in 1913. The Ciesliks suggest that these dates can be used to help determine the age of Limbach pieces (Cieslik 1985). If production of new pieces was reasonably steady, these Limbach snowed pieces were made around 1909.

Fig 21.1 This baby is identical to Fig 9.7a, except that it bears a paper label identifying it as a souvenir of the 1909 Alaska Yukon Pacific Exposition in Seattle. See text.

Fig 21.2 This picture was probably taken at home and printed directly onto post card stock. It is postmarked in Arundel, England, on March 22, 1911, so it would have been taken no later than Christmas, 1910. The card shows five examples of Fig 8.4 and one example each of Figs 8.6, 9.3a, 9.8 and 9.11b. Fig 8.6 is usually shown on his side, but here he stands on skis. The combination of tumblers on the sled is also different from the one shown in 9.8. (How are the babies fastened to the sides of the steep slopes?)

All of the above pieces have fired paint in soft colors, simple, rather passive poses, and shoes of white, black or brown. I found no magazine, catalog illustration or post card from this period that included polor bears, snowmen or even bisque Santas, although composition Santas turned up with some frequency.

Jean Crowley Goodman, who found the *Ladies' Home Journal* articles, spent many hours in public libraries looking for other, earlier references. In doing research for this book, I also searched diligently in libraries. I did find the *Good Housekeeping* article, but failed to turn up any other pictures or articles. The *Good Housekeeping* picture has remained buried until now; surely there is other information in print that will help us date more pieces.

Ski Poles

The ski pole is a prop that can help determine the age of bisque skiers. Until sometime around 1910 skiers used one pole, a long, heavy shaft, to provide balance and leverage. In 1911 a book was published in Munich that described in detail a new technique for skiing with two poles (Bilgeri 1911). It is not clear whether the book followed the introduction of the technique or whether it inspired it. Such a changeover would have taken place over several years at least. The reflection of that change in photographs and porcelain figures would have taken several years, also.

LATER SNOW BABIES—POST-WORLD WAR I
Characteristics

After the war came a second wave of snow baby production. A few of the same babies reappeared, especially some of the three-inch tumblers. But most of the post-war snow babies were entirely new. They ranged from under one inch to nearly three inches. I have found no evidence that four-inch pieces were made during this later period, though some may have been.

As before, there were single babies, sledders and skiers, but now they appeared in many more positions. There were also polar bears, penguins, dogs, Santas, dwarves, elves, snowmen and buildings. They were made in an astonishing variety of poses. In many cases several figures were grouped together on one piece.

Many more colors were used to decorate these post-war pieces. Primary colors and bright, contrasting colors were common. Sometimes even shoes were brightly painted. In addition to the traditional black and brown shoes, red, blue or green shoes are not uncommon on a snow baby from this period. Alive with color and activity, these pieces were called "action snow babies" by Marie L. Johnson (1972), and some collectors continue to use that phrase.

Faces of this period were more quickly and less carefully painted. Highlight on the cheeks was sometimes garish, but more often it was absent. The eyes, so carefully drawn on the earlier pieces, were painted with less detail. If eyebrows were present at all, they were often painted in black, the same as the eye. The blue around the pupil had generally disappeared, and in some cases the entire eye was reduced to a simple black dot.

Very few of these pieces will withstand washing. After painting they were either not fired at all or they were not fired at a temperature high enough to bond paint to porcelain. Collectors handling these pieces should be extremely careful; even damp or oily fingers can remove paint or leave marks.

The Children Will be Delighted With a Mistletoe Cake on Which Snow Babies Coast

Fig 21.3 Mistletoe cake from the December 1911 issue of *Ladies' Home Journal* shows three-inch babies from Figs 9.7b and 9.11b.

DESIGNED BY WINNIFRED FALES
A Jolly Company of Coasters Adds to the Fun at the Christmas Party Table

Fig 21.4 Christmas table decoration from *Ladies' Home Journal,* December 1912 shows examples of Figs 5.14, 5.15, 5.16, 8.15a and 8.15b as well as some pieces I have never seen.

Documentation

A Butler Brothers Catalog reprint (Anderton 1974) for 1928 to 1935 shows a nodder Santa (Fig 6.14b) and three tumblers (Fig 9.2b, 9.3a and 9.4).

A wholesale trade list for 1924-1925 (L-W Book Sales 1985) shows a tiny baby on wooden skis (Fig 10.177) and two small babies on a bisque sled similar to Fig 10.87. It also lists and describes what seem to be the sledder nodder (Fig 6.11) and skier nodders (Fig 6.12a).

The *Ladies' Home Journal* in December of 1920 pictured a Christmas table. The caption states, the "Bonbon Boxes are Snow Babies on Cotton Boxes." However the photograph is not clear enough to distinguish that there is a snow baby, much less which specific one.

In December of 1922 *Ladies' Home Journal* pictured an igloo cake decorated with all-white snow babies, some examples of which were previously shown in the December 1916 *Good Housekeeping* article. The caption advises readers to substitute cotton batting or china dolls for the snow babies. This suggests that these snow babies were no longer available for purchase new in 1922.

A few fortunate collectors own pieces that have been in their families since they were children. They can therefore bracket the time of purchase of some pieces. When this type of documentation exists for a piece, its caption will state when it was bought.

A large estate in Portland, Oregon, also produced some snow baby documentation. This was the estate of a woman who was a persistent sale shopper in the late 1920s and early 1930s. Pieces from her estate are cited in several picture captions, including Figs 16.2 and 16.37. Many items in the estate had never been removed from their original wrappings.

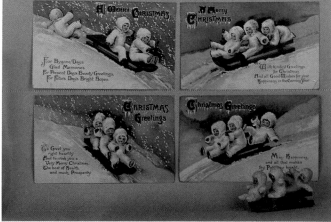

Fig 21.7 These embossed, chromolithographed post cards were issued by the International Art Publishing Company around 1910. They are signed by the artist, Ellen Clapsaddle. They have recently been reprinted. I photographed all four cards in the set with a small bisque piece (Fig 5.12) that shows three all-white snow babies in a pose remarkably similar to the babies on the cards.

Fig 21.5 North Pole decoration to be made for a children's party, published in *Good Housekeeping,* December 1916. Included are Figs 5.7b and 5.8a.

Fig 21.6 Christmas igloo cake, with snow babies. Reprinted from *Ladies' Home Journal* magazine. Copyright 1922, Meredith Corporation. All Rights Reserved. The picture shows examples of Figs 5.5, 5.7b and 5.8a.

Fig 21.8 This chromolithographed, fold-down valentine bears the same snow baby embossed scrap shown on one of the Clapsaddle post cards (Fig 21.7). The card is stamped "Printed in Germany".

Fig 21.9 Two Nimble Nick post cards, printed around 1916 to 1925 by the Whitney Company. They are not chromolithographed; they show tiny, red-suited babies in various active poses. Could they have been the inspiration for the red-suited snow babies?

Fig 21.10 This is an original 1930s advertisement for Clicquot Club Ginger Ale. I have included it here so you can judge for yourself whether this child is similar to the bisque container babies shown in Figs 7.23 through 7.28.

Chapter 22
Snow Baby Housekeeping

Cleaning Snow Babies

Caution is the most important instruction when cleaning any snow baby piece. One thoughtless act can result in irreversible damage.

Some snow babies can be cleaned more readily than others, and a few are completely washable. The problem lies in determining which pieces can be washed and which can't. China pieces can be gently washed. Large planters were intended to be used, and it would be quite unusual to find one that couldn't be washed. But I have seen some that have been badly damaged from overly vigorous cleaning. Candleholders, on the other hand, are usually not washable. The original paint on jointed babies with grout and on the bisque portions of shoulder heads was fired on, and is therefore washable. However, wires on the jointed babies can rust and the cloth bodies of shoulder heads need to be kept dry.

Until you have had a lot of experience, always assume that paint will come off if it becomes damp. A dirty piece is more valuable than a piece with no paint. Even completely washable pieces should be handled gently and, of course, washed by hand. Scrubbing can result in shiny noses and worn paint, even on pieces with fired paint.

Unless you are certain the paint has been fired on, follow these steps:

Step 1. Pick a safe place to work, such as on several layers of terry cloth toweling in a location with excellent light. Resist the temptation to work over a sink.

Step 2. Use an artist's soft brush to remove dust from the smooth and painted portions of the piece. A soft, dry toothbrush may be gently used to brush dust from the grout. But a toothbrush is abrasive, so avoid touching painted surfaces! If the grout has been painted—that is, if it appears to be colored snow—it is safer to use an artist's brush for this step.

Step 3. If Step 2 does not produce satisfactory results, the snowed and unpainted portions may be cleaned using a Q-Tip. Moisten the Q-Tip with a diluted liquid household cleaner such as Liquid Ajax and squeeze the cotton until it is nearly dry. Use the damp cotton to blot dirt from unpainted surfaces. *Do not* try to clean faces or any of the painted portion of the piece this way! You must work patiently and carefully, avoiding the painted area of the piece. If the snow becomes too wet, it will act like a wick and spread the liquid to the painted area. Frequently refresh your Q-Tip with clean liquid, and keep it as nearly dry as possible.

Step 4. When you have finished, let the piece dry completely. Then gently brush the snow with a toothbrush to remove any cotton fibers that have been snagged by the rough-edged bisque grout. Repeat steps 3 and 4 if necessary.

Making Skis

For one reason or another, many snow babies that were made to stand on wooden skis do not. It is very likely that most of the pieces attached to wooden skis today do not have factory made skis. Only a few pieces photographed for this book have "Germany" stamped on their wooden skis. Because babies who were meant to wear skis do not stand well without them, your collection may benefit from some homemade skis.

I do not advocate adding skis to every piece that stands. I have only made skis for my own pieces when I have seen a similar snow baby on skis, either in another collection or in an old photograph. This does not change the original design of the piece.

First collect some flat, broad pieces of soft wood. Coffee stirrers, ice cream bar sticks and tongue depressors all work nicely. Look at snow babies that have skis or study pictures in this book to judge what size seems appropriate for your piece. There is no "right" size. Babies of the same size have sometimes shorter, sometimes longer skis.

Next, cut the wood to the size you want with a razor blade knife. Cut the front ends to a point, then round them slightly with sandpaper. Sand all edges lightly, then soften your skis in water for a few days.

When the wood bends without breaking, clamp the skis into shape. Fig 22.1 shows a simple apparatus to hold and shape the skis. (If you are only going to make one or two pairs, you may want to improvise something even simpler.) To ensure that each ski of a pair will be bent at the same point, clamp a pair of skis, one on top of the other. Put a flat piece of wood between the skis and the clamp to prevent the metal clamp from leaving a dark stain (Fig 22.2).

The skis will dry in about 24 hours. Then they may be stained with brown shoe polish or coated with household wax. After they have dried, buff them so that none of the polish rubs off onto the snow baby.

Spread a thin film of white household glue, the type that dries clear, on the bottom of each foot. Blot on paper to remove any excess glue, and position the piece at the midpoint of each ski. It will take about half an hour to dry, so prop the piece up and lay some padding around it, in case it falls. Don't neglect to give your skier a pole if the hand is shaped for one. Bamboo skewers in various sizes are an easy solution to lost poles.

Displaying Snow Babies

Throughout this book are photographs of displays created by snow baby collectors. Some of these are permanent, year-round arrangements; others are put up for the holiday season and packed away the rest of the year. Some collections are displayed in scenes with props, and others are arranged on shelves. A few collectors recreate the displays they remember from childhood, but most have no such memories to call upon. They use imagination and perhaps a few ideas from magazines to plan their arrangements. Even a few pieces arranged with bottle brush trees, Japanese houses and doll house miniatures make an impressive show.

The base for an arrangement can be a mirror, a piece of plywood, a shelf or a piece of furniture. Cotton or polyester batting, a white cloth or flakes of artificial snow will simulate a wintery landscape. Aluminum foil becomes a fine pond for ice skaters. Tiny white lights hidden in the snow or around the edge of the display make it seem almost magical at night.

Some displays are constructed over a base of styrofoam that has been contoured to look like hills. Toothpicks inserted into the drain holes of your bisque pieces will secure them to the styrofoam. Those pieces without drain holes can often be secured by staples bent from paper clips. This system permits freedom to place pieces on slanted surfaces, and protects them from tumbling into other pieces—a bonus if you live in earthquake country.

Another method that works well is to secure the pieces to a flat, hard surface with a moldable adhesive such as Duco Stik-Tak. Several other adhesives on the market work less well. Wax-based products leave a residue that is difficult to remove, especially from a grouted piece.

Many other methods will work as well. If you aren't concerned about earthquakes, children or curious adults, you may want to arrange the pieces more simply on a scarf, doily or mirror plateau.

Any scene will benefit from the addition of a few props. These can be old or new bottlebrush trees, bisque or cardboard houses, and snowmen or angels made of wax—or mica-covered cardboard. Container pieces, especially the larger ones, may not fit into a snow baby scene. However, they often work well as part of a table centerpiece or mantel piece decoration. A bit of evergreen or even a base of cotton batting is sometimes all you need to complete an arrangement.

If you leave your display out all year long, you should enclose it in something to keep the pieces clean. Dust can accumulate to the point where it is impossible to remove without refiring the piece. One collector displays her babies all year long in a covered brandy snifter.

Here is a bit of snow baby trivia: What recent movie, set in the 1930s, showed a Christmas snow baby scene? Answer: *Mr. and Mrs. Bridge.* It is available on video tape.

Fig 22.1 These simple materials and tools are all you need to press thin wood such as coffee stirrers into skis for your snow babies. Here, the stirrers have already been sanded into rounded, ski-shaped points.

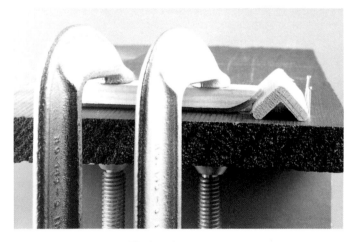

Fig 22.2 A pair of skis clamped to a press. The clamps don't actually touch the skis; they apply pressure to the thicker piece of molding. You can barely see the two skis between the molding and the plank. Drying time is about 24 hours. See text for details.

Fig 22.3 The simplest mantel display uses just four snow baby pieces and a few props.

Fig 22.4 Here a collection of old bisque Santas is arranged on an alcove shelf with a composition house and bottle brush trees.

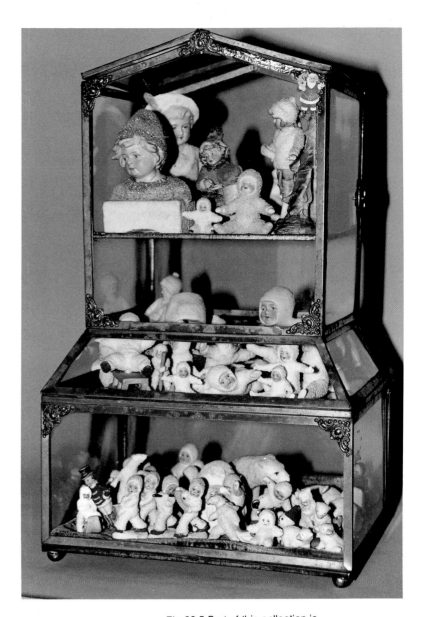

Fig 22.5 Part of this collection is displayed all year round in this elegant glassed-in case.

Fig 22.6 A close up view of part of a large Christmas display using all old snow babies. Some of the props are new.

Chapter 23
Marks, Rarity and Evaluation

This information is gathered from looking closely at pieces, comparing them and keeping records about them. Not all collectors are interested in this aspect of collecting, but for those who are, there are puzzles to solve, notes to compare and exciting discoveries to make.

INCISED MARKS

Incised markings are those that were in the mold or were pressed into the porcelain before firing. They cannot easily be altered after the piece is finished, so they are more reliable to use for identification.

Some snow baby pieces have incised the country of origin, either Germany or Japan. This marking is nearly indisputable; I have heard no reports of questionable incised markings.

Many pieces have incised numbers, which can help identify the piece as a part of a series. In some cases they can even help identify the manufacturer.

For a variety of reasons these numbers are sometimes difficult to read. They may not have been incised deeply enough, or applied snow may have drifted over part of the number. In some cases the digits have filled up with paint. Although a magnifying glass may allow you to read extremely small print, enlargement alone won't help much with numbers that are indistinct. Instead, examine the piece, with a magnifying glass if necessary, in strong sunlight. Hold the surface you are trying to read nearly parallel to the sun's rays. This will cause portions of the number to be thrown into shadow. Rotate the piece so the sun strikes the number from different directions. These shadows can often help you identify even shallow or poorly formed digits.

However, for several reasons I have become skeptical about the reliability of incised numbers as indisputable identification: 1. Two people reading the same poorly incised number often interpret it differently. Keep this in mind when you use the incised numbers in this book as identification. 2. I have seen identical pieces with and without an incised number. The four-inch snow babies in Fig 8.9 and the fancy dwarf band in Fig 14.10 are examples of this. 3. I have also seen identical pieces, such as the snow baby pulled by huskies in Fig 10.28, that bear two entirely different numbers. Incised numbers are only a limited tool for identification, and should be used with some caution.

Fig 23.1 Heubach sunburst. This mark can also be found printed onto snow baby pieces. Gebrüder Heubach (Heubach Brothers) made knick-knacks, dolls and doll-heads from before 1880 to 1938. Heubach sometimes used a square mark, but I have not seen it on any snow baby pieces. Some collectors also believe that pieces stamped "Made in Germany+" or "Made in Germany" inside a donut were made by Heubach. These donuts are often seen with the Heubach sunburst.

Factory Logos

Few snow baby pieces are incised with actual factory logo marks. Of the 1000 pieces photographed for this book, only eight have incised logos. Of those, two bear the Heubach sunburst, three have the Limbach cloverleaf, two have a Carl Schneider mark and one has a Fritz Pfeffer mark (see chapter 23). All of these are large pieces. Undoubtedly many other factories made snow babies, large and small, and sold them unmarked. I have seen no small snow baby pieces incised with a recognizable factory logo.

PRINTED MARKS
Country of Origin

Many snow baby pieces have been stamped with the country of origin, usually on the underside. The color most often used was black, but purple, blue, aqua and orange-red were also used. Sometimes this information is printed in a circle, in an arc or between two concentric circles that look like a donut.

About half the pieces in this book bear no stamp at all. In some cases the stamp may have washed or worn off. In others the piece was probably not stamped in the first place. Since 1891 the United States has had a tariff act that requires identification of the country of origin on new imported goods. But often this requirement was fulfilled by stamping not the item itself but the box that it was shipped in.

It is also important that England apparently had no such law. I have been told by collectors living there that imported pieces did not have to be stamped, though some pieces bought in the 1940s in England were marked "Foreign". Ann Wyatt, a British collector, has told me that none of her 60 "new" store stock items preserved from the 1930s (Wyatt 1982) was marked with a country of origin.

What is the significance of this? Many of the snow babies currently found for sale in the United States were originally exported to England from Germany. Later they were brought to the United States by collectors or dealers. Others are imported as antiques from Germany; of course, they bear no country of origin stamp. So a snow baby piece that is unmarked may have been packed in stamped boxes, or it may have been washed to remove cake icing. But it could instead have been produced originally for the British or German market.

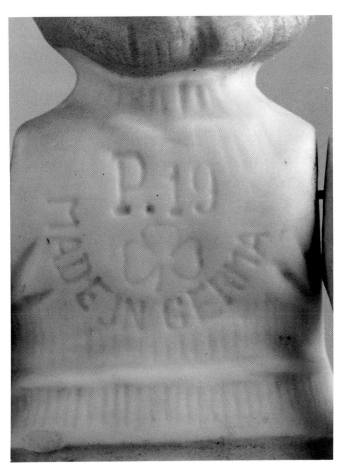

Fig 23.2 Limbach cloverleaf. Incised mark of the Limbach Company, active in making dolls and other figurines from about 1883 to 1930.

Fig 23.3 Drawing of the insignia of the Carl Schneider Company mark, found incised on a few large pieces. Active from 1861 to 1970.

Factory Logo

A very few pieces are stamped with the manufacturer's insignia. Two in this book are imprinted with the Galluba and Hoffman shield, one has the Heber and Company shield, four bear a printed Heubach sunburst and seven have the Erphila logo. (Erphila is actually the logo of an importer, not a manufacturer.) All of these except the Erphila are large or blue snow pieces.

EVALUATING

How does a collector decide that "the price is right" for a snow baby piece? How should a dealer determine a fair price? There are many factors to consider in arriving at a fair evaluation of snow baby piece.

Age

Because porcelain is fragile, older pieces are scarcer and often command higher prices. In addition, some older snow babies were manufactured more carefully and in smaller numbers. These are priced higher for their quality as well as for their rarity.

Subject Matter

Certain types of pieces are in great demand. Babies and Santas receive more attention than carolers. Pieces that depict cats, teddy bears or golliwogs can command higher prices, in part because they appeal to eclectic collectors of cats, black memorabilia and the like.

Whimsy

Each collector must evaluate the special appeal that some pieces seem to have. Some collectors value especially imaginative, fanciful or whimsical pieces.

Workmanship

The care that is exercised when a piece is manufactured contributes substantially to its value. Here are some considerations that fall under this heading: Was the piece carefully painted? (In some cases it may have even been artistically painted.) Was it fired? (Will it be washable?) Was the piece molded carefully so that features such as the nose or fingers are distinct?

Fig 23.4 Incised mark of the Fritz Pfeffer Company, manufacturers from 1892 to 1930.

Fig 23.5 Galluba and Hoffman shield on the bottom of a blue snow piece. This photo also shows the block numeral style consistently used on these pieces. This company was active from 1891 to 1930, but apparently this mark has not been verified on pieces made before 1905 (Roentgen 1981).

Condition

Here, condition refers to what has happened to the piece after it left the factory.

Breaks. Missing parts considerably decrease the value to most collectors. Some will accept a broken piece if it has been carefully mended, or if the piece is rare. Certainly the location of the break is important. A broken sled runner is less important than a broken arm. It may take an experienced eye to tell a break from a firing flaw. Firing flaws occur while the porcelain is still in the kiln. They usually don't substantially reduce the value of a piece.

Dirt. If a piece has dirty snow, try to determine whether it is a fired piece. If so, it can be cleaned. To some extent an unfired piece may be carefully cleaned (see cleaning tips in chapter 22), but it will probably never look pristine.

Paint problems. Paint loss is also a serious consideration. A figure whose paint has faded or has been rubbed off evenly is generally more acceptable than one that is missing paint over large areas. Some collectors are especially fussy about the condition of the face paint.

Rarity

Rarity alone does not make an item desirable. However, you may have few opportunities to buy a truly rare piece, so be sure that you evaluate it carefully. Some pieces are much more common in certain regions of the country. For example, glazed Santas are found principally in Wisconsin and Minnesota. The baby hugging a teddy bear (Fig 10.145) is more common on the West Coast. Fig 10.141, the fallen baby on wooden skis, is more common in New England.

It is likely that this regional rarity developed when importers sent quantities of the same piece to a single geographic area, or even to one retail store. This would have simplified the task of the wholesaler, who could then ship lots as they were received without sorting and dividing them. Also, this procedure would have allowed a retailer to offer and advertise specific snow baby pieces. As pieces are bought and sold nationally, this pattern of regional rarity will undoubtedly change. But for now it does have an effect upon the pricing of snow baby pieces and on any rarity scale.

Fig 23.6 Shield of Heber & Company, which made porcelain figures only from 1900 to 1922. "Ges. gesch." is an abbreviation for "Gesetzlich geschützt", German for "protected by law" (copyright or patent).

Fig 23.7 Elaborate stamped logo of Erphila includes the phrase "Made in Germany". This is one of several marks used by the import firm Erphila, located in Philadelphia.

Bibliography

Books

Anderton, Johana Gast. *More Twentieth Century Dolls, Volume 1.* Lombard, IL: Wallace Homestead, 1974.

Angione, Genevieve. *All Bisque and Half-Bisque Dolls, 5th Edition.* Exton, PA: Schiffer Publishing, 1981.

Bilgeri, Georg. *Der Alpine Skilauf.* Munich: Verlag der Deutschen Alpenzeitung, 1911.

Borger, Mona. *Chinas: Dolls for Study and Admiration.* San Francisco: Borger Publications, 1983.

Cieslik, Jürgen and Marianne. *German Doll Encyclopedia 1800-1939.* Cumberland, MD: Hobby House Press, 1985.

Crichton, Robin. *Who is Santa Claus?* Edinburgh: Canongate Publishing, 1987.

Early, Ray and Eilene. *Snow Babies.* Westerville, OH.: Ray and Eilene Early, 1983.

Favors and Novelties. Gas City, IN: L-W Book Sales, 1985.

Feazel, Charles T. *White Bear.* New York: Henry Holt and Company, 1990.

Foulke, Jan. *Focusing on Gebrüder Heubach Dolls.* Cumberland, MD: Hobby House Press, 1980.

Johl, Janet Pagter. *Still More About Dolls.* New York: H.L. Lindquest Publications, 1950.

Leuzzi, Marlene and Kershner, Robert. *Antique Doll Price Guide: Third Edition.* Corte Madera, CA: Marlene Leuzzi and Robert Kershner, 1975.

Peary, Marie Ahnighito. *The Snowbaby's Own Story.* New York: Frederick A.Stokes, 1934.

Roentgen, Robert E. *Marks on German Bohemian and Austrian Porcelain 1710 to the Present.* Exton, PA: Schiffer Publishing, 1981.

Schiffer, Margaret. *Christmas Ornaments: A Festive Study.* Exton, PA, Schiffer Publishing, 1984.

Snyder, Phillip V. *The Christmas Tree Book.* New York: Penguin Books, 1977.

Stanton, Carol Ann. *Heubach's Little Characters.* Middlesex, England: Living Doll's Publications Ltd., 1978.

Articles

Cieslik, Jürgen and Marianne. "Schneebabies." *Puppenmagazin,* April 1987.

Crowley, Jean H. "More About Snow Babies." *Spinning Wheel,* December 1971.

Crowley, Jean H. "Continuing Research of ... Snow Babies." *Spinning Wheel,* October 1978.

Fairchild, June. "The Zucker Puppen of Germany." *Toy Trader,* February 1970.

Foulke, Jan. "Those Adorable Snow Babies." *Doll Reader,* February/March 1981.

Garcia, Beth. "Four Rare Dolls." *Toy Trader,* June 1962.

Good Housekeeping, December 1916.

Jacoby, Daniel Shackman. "B.Shackman & Co.: Snow Babies and Related Figurines." *Antique Trader Weekly,* January 25, 1987.

Johnson, Marie L. "Snow Babies." *United Federation of Doll Clubs Convention Book,* 1972.

Ladies' Home Journal, December 1911.

Ladies' Home Journal, December 1912.

Ladies' Home Journal, December 1922.

Shuart, Harry Wilson. "Snow Babies." *Spinning Wheel,* January-February 1970.

Wyatt, Ann. "The Instant Collection." *Nutshell News,* December 1982.

Table 1

Table 1: Data, Rarity Scale and Price Guide

This table is intended to give you a quick look at the important features of the pieces in this book. It does not include the new snow babies, because that information is readily available elsewhere.
The rarity scale and price guide were compiled with the help of nine other collectors and dealers who buy or sell in widely dispersed geographic areas. The price guide is not intended to set prices. It is a reflection of actual prices paid throughout the United States in the early 1990s.
The prices stated are for pieces in the size shown and in excellent condition, regardless of the condition of the piece shown. Any damage or missing paint will reduce the value of the piece (see the section on pricing in chapter 23).

Key to symbols used for marks indicating country of origin:
I = incised
M = Made in
Germ = Germany
O = in a circle
bk = black
bl = blue
p = purple
g = green
r = red
W = Western
US Z = Germany, US Zone
I-bk = stamped in black and incised

G&H = Galluba & Hoffman
Heubach = Heubach sunburst
H&C = Heber & Company
FP = Fritz Pfeffer

Rarity Scale:
1 = Very rare
2 = Rare
3 = Average
4 = Common
5 = Very common (as snow babies go)

FIG #	BRIEF DESCRIPTION	HT IN	SNOW	BASE	COUNTRY	INCISED	RARE	PRICE
1.1a	Large Cook and Peary	4.37	regular	no	Germ MI-O-g	9439	1	500-750
1.1b	Small Cook and Peary	3.5	regular	no	Germ MI-O-g	9447	2	325-600
1.2	No-snow Cook and Peary	3.5	no	no	H&C-aqua	9439	1	300-575
1.3	Peary inkwell	3.0	no	no	Germ-I	no	1	250-450
1.4	Peary mug	4.37	no	no	Germ-I	5569	1	175-275
2.1	Children carrying milk	4.87	multi	yes	no	4614	1	550-800
2.2	3 school children	6.0	blue	yes	no	4603	1	1000+
2.3	5 school children	7.0	regular	yes	no	4563	1	1000+
2.5	3 children on sled	3.5	blue	yes	G&H	4714	1	450-700
2.6	Boy and girl with sled	3.62	blue	yes	no	4705	1	450-700
2.7	Girl with muff	4.0	blue	yes	no	4194	1	400-650
2.8	Girl with dulcimer	3.5	regular	yes	no	4194	1	175-325
2.9	Children and snowball	6.5	blue	yes	no	4653	1	450-750
2.10	Bust of boy	4.0	blue	yes	no	4479	1	350-575
2.11	Girl & coins, sitting	3.5	blue	yes	G&H	4647	1	400-650
2.12	Girl & coins, standing	7.5	blue	yes	no	4584	1	450-750
2.13	Girl & coins, standing	7.5	multi	yes	no	4584	1	375-475
2.14a	Boy & umbrella	3.75	blue	yes	no	4664	1	300-450
2.14b	Girl & umbrella	3.62	blue	yes	no	4664	1	300-450
2.15	Girl on skis	4.87	blue	yes	no	4656	1	325-450
2.16	Boy on skis	5.0	blue	yes	no	4656	1	325-450
2.17	Girl on skis	4.87	regular	yes	no	4656	1	200-400
2.18	Boy carrying sled	5.25	multi	yes	no	4657	1	200-400
2.19	Girl with cape, dog	4.25	regular	yes	no	4837	1	200-400
2.20	Boy holding beer stein	4.25	regular	yes	no	4645	1	200-400
2.21	Child pulling wagon	5.0	regular	no	no	no	1	200-450
2.22	Girl lying on sled	2.5	regular	no	no	no	1	200-400
3.1	Girl in ermine	3.12	pink	no	no	32	1	250-375
3.2	Girl in hat, muff	3.87	multi	no	no	no	1	250-375
3.3	Girl in feather hat	3.87	pink	no	no	no	1	250-375
3.4	Girl sitting	3.12	multi	no	no	52	1	250-375
3.5	Girl in shawl	4.0	pink	yes	no	42	1	250-375
3.6	Boy in coat, top hat	5.25	multi	yes	no	43	1	250-375
3.7	Child kneeling	3.87	multi	no	no	no	1	250-375
3.8	Child, cornucopia	4.62	pink	no	no	28	1	250-375
3.9	Child in kilt	4.75	multi	no	no	no	1	250-375
3.10	Girl kneeling	3.87	regular	no	no	no	1	250-375
3.11	Boy with boat	3.5	multi	no	no	10	1	250-375
3.12	Boy sweeping	4.12	grey	no	no	no	1	250-375
3.13	Boy & girl swingers	6.0	multi	no	no	67	1	250-450
3.14	Girl with purse	3.62	grey	no	no	no	1	250-375
3.15	Boy with hat	4.12	multi	no	no	no	1	250-375
3.16	Girl with hat, muff	4.0	multi	no	no	no	1	250-375
4.1	Doll, blue coat	11.0	regular	no	no	no	1	400-650
4.2	Doll, shoulder head	11.0	regular	no	no	no	1	400-650
4.3	Doll, head turned	11.5	regular	no	no	no	1	400-650
4.4	Doll, black shoes	9.0	regular	no	no	no	2	400-600
4.5	Doll, ruffled bonnet	8.5	regular	no	no	no	1	400-700
4.6	Doll, cloth body	6.75	regular	no	no	no	2	225-400
4.7	Doll, furry body	4.25	regular	no	no	no	1	300-400
4.8	Doll, shoulderhead only	0.87	regular	no	no	no	1	150-300
5.1	Baby prone	1.5	regular	no	no	no	1	175-300
5.2	Baby prone	1.75	regular	no	no	no	1	175-300
5.3	Seated fat baby	3.12	regular	no	no	no	1	200-325
5.4	Standing fat baby	3.25	regular	no	no	no	1	200-325
5.5	Chubby early baby	2.87	regular	no	no	no	1	175-250
5.6a	All-white fat baby	1.12	regular	no	no	no	1	70-125
5.6b	All-white fat baby	2.0	regular	no	no	no	2	170-250
5.6c	All-white fat baby	1.25	regular	no	no	no	2	70-150
5.7a	Baby in peaked hood	1.75	regular	no	no	no	2	110-185
5.7b	Seated fat baby	1.75	regular	no	no	no	2	110-160
5.7c	Seated fat baby	1.0	regular	no	no	no	3	75-115
5.8a	Baby with snowball	2.5	regular	no	no	no	3	185-275
5.8b	Baby prone, head up	0.87	regular	no	no	no	2	70-110
5.9	Baby prone, arm up	1.0	regular	no	no	no	1	80-110
5.10	Winged angel baby	1.62	regular	no	no	no	2	200-450
5.11a	Baby lying on side	2.0	regular	no	no	no	1	275-400
5.11b	Skiing baby	3.5	regular	no	no	no	1	275-400
5.12	3 babies on sled	1.5	regular	no	no	no	1	185-325
5.13	Baby on sled	1.75	regular	no	no	no	1	110-175
5.14	Helmeted girl on sled	2.37	regular	no	no	8268	1	350-500
5.15	Girl sitting on sled	3.0	regular	no	no	8263	1	350-500
5.16	Baby sitting on sled	2.12	regular	no	no	no	1	160-225
5.17	Standing baby	3.5	regular	no	no	no	1	185-260
5.18	Baby card holder	1.87	regular	yes	no	506N	1	200-275
5.19	Baby on bisque skis	1.62	regular	no	no	no	1	145-225
5.20a	Standing thin baby	1.62	regular	no	no	no	2	60-110
5.20b	Baby on bisque skis	1.62	regular	no	no	no	1	80-140
5.21a	Baby seated, stiff	2.25	regular	no	no	no	1	170-260
5.21b	Baby seated, stiff	1.87	regular	no	no	no	2	135-195
5.21c	Baby seated, stiff	1.12	regular	no	no	no	2	70-120
5.22a	Baby leaning back	1.5	regular	no	no	no	1	70-120
5.22b	Thin baby sitting	1.5	regular	no	no	no	2	70-120
6.1a	Jointed baby	2.87	regular	no	no	2	2	225-350
6.1b	Jointed baby	5.25	regular	no	no	4	2	475-550
6.2a	Elastic jointed baby	4.0	regular	no	no	2	2	350-450
6.2b	Jointed baby	4.0	regular	no	no	2	2	350-450
6.3	Jointed baby	4.75	regular	no	no	3	2	350-500
6.4	Jointed boy	6.0	no	no	no	no	1	250-325
6.5a	Boy with jointed arms	4.25	no	no	Limbach-I	19	3	175-250
6.5b	Boy with jointed arms	6.0	no	no	no	no	4	225-275
6.6	Jointed boy skier	5.37	no	no	no	1456	2	250-375
6.7a	Girl pegged to sled	2.0	no	no	no	no	1	145-250
6.7b	Boy pegged to sled	2.12	no	no	no	no	1	145-250
6.8	Angione jointed bear	6.0	no	no	no	5	1	425-650
6.9	Angione jointed bear	3.37	no	no	no	no	2	250-445
6.10	Jointed bear	3.25	no	no	no	0	3	125-200
6.11	Boy nodder on sled	2.75	glitter	no	no	no	1	150-240
6.12a	Nodders on skis	3.5	glitter	yes	no	1456	1	200-325
6.12b	Boy nodder waving	3.0	glitter	no	no	no	1	120-200
6.13a	Angel nodder	3.5	no	no	Germ	no	3	75-125
6.13b	Angel nodder	3.25	no	no	Germ	no	3	75-125
6.14a	Santa nodder	2.5	no	no	Germ-I	no	4	135-185
6.14b	Santa nodder	3.5	no	no	Germ-I	748	3	175-240
6.15	Elf nodder	2.62	no	yes	Germ-I	741	3	35-65
6.16	Santa nodder	3.37	no	yes	no	no	1	185-275
7.1	3 children on sled	4.25	Heubach	no	no	no	1	500-800
7.2	3 children on sled	6.25	no	no	no	4628	1	500-800
7.3	Boy on sled	8.0	no	no	no	4612	1	500-800
7.4	Boy on sled	3.62	no	yes	no	no	1	175-300
7.5	Whistling boy	6.0	Heubach	no	no	6969	1	500-700
7.6a	Child-faced snowman	4.5	Heubach	no	Germ MI-O-g	--38	2	400-600
7.6b	Child-faced snowman	4.37	no	no	no	no	1	375-500
7.7	Child-faced snowman	8.0	no	no	no	no	1	400-660
7.8	Child-faced snowman	11.0	no	no	Heubach-I	6627	1	400-700
7.9	Girl on sled	6.5	no	no	Heubach-b	4013	1	300-450
7.10	Girl on egg	7.0	no	no	Heubach-I	no	1	450-550
7.11	Boy carrying sled	4.5	regular	yes	Limbach-I	8535	1	375-500
7.13	Girl on skis	5.0	multi	yes	Limbach-I	8550	1	375-500
7.14	Boy on skis	4.25	regular	no	no	3204	1	375-475
7.16	Girl on skis	4.75	regular	yes	no	3197	1	375-475
7.17	Girl on sled	3.75	regular	yes	no	3200	1	350-450
7.18	Baby on sled	1.75	regular	no	Germ-I	no	1	95-175
7.19	Boy on short skis	5.75	no	yes	no	16	1	375-450
7.20	Girl on short skis	6.0	no	yes	no	16	1	375-450
7.21	Girl on skis	7.75	no	yes	Schneider-I	11796	1	300-425
7.22	Boy on skis	7.75	no	yes	Schneider-I	11796	1	300-425
7.23a	Googly with skis	3.75	regular	no	no	no	1	350-475
7.23b	Googly with skis	3.5	regular	no	no	no	1	350-475
7.24a	Googly with skates	3.75	regular	no	no	no	1	350-475
7.24b	Black googly	3.75	regular	no	no	no	1	450-575
7.25a	Black googly prone	2.25	regular	no	no	no	1	450-575
7.25b	Googly lying prone	2.0	regular	no	no	no	1	350-475
7.26a	Googly lying prone	3.0	regular	no	no	no	1	350-475
7.26b	Googly standing	4.0	regular	no	no	no	1	350-475
7.27	Black googly standing	4.12	regular	no	no	no	1	450-575
7.28	Googly sitting	1.62	regular	no	no	no	1	175-275
7.29	Couple on sled	8.0	no	no	no	2266	1	425-700
7.31	Father Xmas in blue	5.0	no	no	no	no	2	175-250
7.32	Santa in sleigh	3.5	no	no	Japan MI-r	no	1	40-85
7.33	Kitten in cart	1.62	no	no	no	no	1	85-145
7.34	Bear pulling cart	1.75	no	no	Germ-I	5855	2	50-140
7.35	Bunny pulling cart	2.5	no	no	no	no	1	85-145
7.36	Girl on sled	2.25	no	no	CD KINNEY-I	no	5	25-50
7.37	Boy skier	5.0	no	yes	Japan-I	no	3	5-15
7.38	Skier squatting	5.0	no	yes	Japan-bk	MK943	3	5-15
7.39	Baby sitting on box	2.12	regular	yes	no	no	2	120-175
7.40	Baby on skis	2.5	regular	yes	Germ-p	no	2	120-175
7.41	Santa and snowman	3.5	coralene	yes	GermUS Z-p	no	1	80-135
7.42	Santa on scooter	3.5	no	yes	GermUS Z-p	no	2	125-185
7.43	Birds on springs	5.0	coralene	yes	Germ-bl	no	2	45-85
7.44	Dwarf driving truck	1.87	no	no	no	no	2	40-120
7.45a	Dwarf by tree stump	1.75	no	yes	no	no	2	45-85
7.45b	Dwarf on bud vase	2.62	no	no	no	no	5	20-45
7.46a	Dwarf with mushroom	1.25	no	yes	Germ-I-bk	no	1	35-50
7.46b	Dwarf with mushroom	1.37	no	yes	no	no	1	35-50
7.47	Dwarf candleholder	1.0	no	no	Germ-I	3482	5	30-40
7.48a	Dwarf, hands on knees	1.25	no	no	no	3483	4	15-25
7.48b	Dwarf standing	1.37	no	no	no	3484	4	15-25
7.48c	Dwarf with legs apart	1.25	no	no	no	3485	4	15-25

Table 1

FIG #	BRIEF DESCRIPTION	HT IN	SNOW	BASE	COUNTRY	INCISED	RARE	PRICE
7.48d	Dwarf sitting	1.25	no	yes	Germ-bk	no	4	15-25
7.49a	Dwarf on one knee	1.12	no	no	Japan-bk	5803	3	10-15
7.49b	Dwarf sitting	1.12	no	no	Japan-bk	no	3	10-15
7.49c	Dwarf lying down	0.75	no	no	Japan-bk	5806	3	10-15
7.50	Dwarf holding urn	1.75	no	no	no	no	1	25-40
7.51a	Long-nosed dwarf	1.37	no	no	Germ-bk	no	2	30-60
7.51b	Long-nosed dwarf	1.0	no	no	Germ-bk	no	2	30-60
7.51c	Long-nosed dwarf	1.25	no	no	Germ-bk	no	2	30-60
7.52a	Baby standing	1.25	regular	no	no	no	3	65-120
7.52b	Baby sitting	1.0	regular	no	no	no	3	65-120
7.53a	Baby lying on side	1.12	regular	no	Germ-bk	no	3	65-120
7.53b	Baby sitting on 1 leg	1.25	regular	no	Germ-bk	no	3	65-120
7.54	Baby with orange cap	1.25	regular	no	no	no	2	65-120
7.55	Baby with both arms up	1.75	regular	no	Germ-bk	no	1	65-120
7.56	Baby with skis	1.5	no	no	no	no	1	40-85
7.57a	Santa sitting	1.0	no	yes	Germ-p	657	2	35-65
7.57b	Snowman sitting	1.25	no	no	Germ-p	11963	1	30-85
7.58a	Angel standing	1.5	no	yes	Germ-I	4640	3	10-20
7.58b	Angel sitting	1.0	no	yes	Germ-I	4642	3	10-20
7.58c	Angel lying	0.87	no	yes	Germ-I	4646	3	10-20
7.58d	Angel sitting	1.12	no	yes	Germ-I	4639	3	10-20
8.1	Boy with metal sled	4.25	regular	yes	no	9224	2	375-475
8.2	Girl with metal sled	4.0	regular	yes	no	no	2	375-475
8.3	Baby learning to ski	4.25	regular	no	no	no	3	350-450
8.4	Baby holding pole	4.25	regular	no	no	no	2	350-450
8.5	Boy without pole	3.75	regular	no	no	no	2	275-375
8.6	Baby lying on side	2.5	regular	no	no	no	2	350-450
8.8a	Baby sitting	3.12	grey	no	no	9916	2	350-450
8.8b	Baby sitting	3.12	regular	no	no	9916	2	350-450
8.9b	Baby sitting	3.12	regular	no	no	no	2	350-450
8.10	Boy skater on base	4.0	regular	yes	no	no	1	350-450
8.11	Girl skater on base	4.0	regular	no	no	no	1	350-450
8.12	Girl skier	4.0	regular	no	no	no	3	350-435
8.13	Boy skier	4.5	regular	no	no	no	3	350-435
8.14	Boy skier	4.12	flocked	no	no	no	1	300-400
8.15a	Girl skier	4.25	regular	no	no	no	1	375-525
8.15b	Boy skier	4.12	regular	no	no	no	1	375-525
8.16a	Girl on sled	3.25	china	no	no	no	1	350-465
8.16b	Boy on sled	3.5	china	no	no	no	1	350-465
8.17	Girl roller skater	4.75	regular	no	no	no	1	500-800+
8.18	Girl carrying basket	3.87	regular	no	no	no	1	375-500
8.19	Boy prone on sled	2.62	Heubach	no	Heubach-g	no	1	500-800
8.20	Child in bear suit	3.0	Heubach	no	Heubach-g	no	1	500-800
8.21a	Striped cuff skier	5.5	regular	no	no	no	2	300-400
8.21b	Striped cuff skier	5.5	regular	no	no	no	2	300-400
8.22	Striped cuff skier	4.5	regular	no	no	no	2	150-250
8.23	Boy on sled	3.62	crystal	yes	FP-I	3978	1	350-475
8.24	Boy in white clothes	3.25	no	yes	no	no	1	250-350
8.25a	Child in bear suit	4.12	no	no	no	4925	1	375-500+
8.25b	Child in bear suit	7.0	no	no	no	4924	1	375-500+
8.26	Girl skiing	5.75	no	yes	no	8912	1	200-275
8.27	Bear carrying skis	7.75	no	no	no	9885	1	100-185
8.28	Boy piano baby	2.5	regular	no	no	no	1	350-475
8.29	Girl piano baby	2.75	regular	no	no	no	1	350-475
9.1a	Baby skier crouching	2.75	regular	no	no	no	2	165-225
9.1b	Baby pegged for sled	2.5	regular	no	no	no	3	165-225
9.2a	Baby pegged for sled	2.12	regular	no	no	no	3	165-225
9.2b	Baby sitting	2.25	regular	no	no	no	4	110-160
9.3a	Baby lying on side	2.0	regular	no	no	no	2	165-225
9.3b	Baby crouching	2.75	regular	no	no	no	2	165-225
9.4	Baby prone	1.12	regular	no	no	no	2	165-225
9.5a	Baby prone	1.25	regular	no	no	no	3	120-185
9.5b	Baby lying	1.12	regular	no	no	no	3	110-160
9.6	Baby prone on sled	1.75	regular	no	Germ-I	no	1	225-325
9.7a	Baby on sled	2.87	regular	no	Germ-I	no	2	225-300
9.7b	2 babies on sled	3.0	regular	no	Germ-I	no	2	350-450
9.8	3 babies on sled	3.0	regular	no	Germ-I	no	1	425-500
9.9	3 babies on sled	3.0	regular	no	no	no	1	450-600
9.10	Baby sitting on sled	2.5	gold	no	no	no	1	175-250
9.11a	Baby with tassel cap	2.12	regular	no	no	no	1	135-185
9.11b	Baby standing	2.87	regular	no	no	no	2	175-245
9.12a	Girl sitting	2.0	regular	no	no	no	2	185-265
9.12b	Boy sitting	2.0	regular	no	no	no	2	185-265
9.13	Baby sitting on sled	2.25	regular	no	no	8195	1	185-275
9.14	Boy lying on back	1.12	regular	no	no	no	2	90-155
9.15a	Fallen girl skater	1.25	regular	no	no	8516	1	275-375
9.15b	Fallen boy skater	1.75	regular	no	no	no	1	275-375
9.16a	Girl sitting on sled	2.87	no	no	no	no	1	275-375
9.16b	Girl lying on sled	2.5	no	no	no	no	1	275-375
9.17	Baby on back	1.37	Heubach	no	no	no	1	160-220
9.18	2 children on sled	3.0	no	no	no	457-I	1	175-230
9.19	Baby prone	1.25	no	no	no	no	2	55-95
9.20a	Child skater	3.5	no	yes	Japan Occ-r	no	1	20-35
9.20b	Child skater	3.25	no	yes	Japan Occ-r	no	1	20-35
10.1	Baby on ice house	2.0	regular	yes	Germ-bl	2702	1	175-260
10.2	Baby hugging bear	2.0	regular	yes	Germ-bl	no	2	155-230
10.3	2 babies carrying bear	1.87	regular	yes	no	1649	1	200-275
10.4a	Baby carrying torch	2.0	regular	yes	Germ-bl	no	2	155-230
10.4b	Baby holding skis	1.75	regular	yes	France MI	1180	2	155-235
10.5	Baby and bear	1.87	regular	yes	no	378	3	185-265
10.6	Baby leading bear	1.5	regular	no	no	no	1	165-230
10.7	Baby in igloo	2.37	regular	yes	Germ-bk	no	3	125-165
10.8a	2 babies with bear	1.62	regular	yes	no	371	3	165-230
10.8b	Bear pulling baby	1.62	regular	no	Germ	370	4	150-225
10.9	Baby with bear	2.0	regular	no	Germ-bl	no	2	140-200
10.10	Baby on bear	2.0	regular	yes	Germ-p	no	2	165-220
10.11a	Baby on bear	2.25	glitter	no	Germ-bk	no	1	140-200
10.11b	Baby on bear	2.25	regular	no	no	no	4	145-175
10.12	Baby on bear	2.25	regular	no	no	no	2	145-210
10.13a	2 babies on bear	1.75	no	yes	--an--	no	2	85-155
10.13b	Baby on bear	1.5	regular	no	Germ-bl	no	3	125-160
10.14a	Child on bear	4.12	no	yes	no	2938	2	95-140
10.14b	Child on bear	4.12	no	yes	no	2938	2	95-140
10.15	Baby on bear	2.75	coarse	no	no	no	4	40-90
10.16	3 babies on bear	1.75	regular	yes	Germ-p	367	1	155-215
10.17	Baby on reindeer	2.62	regular	yes	Germ-r	347	2	165-225
10.18	Baby on reindeer	2.25	regular	yes	no	no	3	135-190
10.19	Baby on walrus	2.0	no	no	no	no	1	175-240
10.20	Dog licking baby	2.0	regular	yes	Germ-bk	2865	2	145-235
10.21	Baby feeding seal	2.0	regular	yes	Germ	2364	2	145-235
10.22a	Baby with seal and ball	2.0	regular	yes	Germ	2366	4	135-195
10.22b	Baby with seal and ball	2.5	no	yes	no	no	3	15-50
10.23	Baby with seal and ball	2.0	coarse	yes	no	no	4	20-45
10.24	Baby with seal and ball	1.5	glitter	yes	no	no	2	25-50
10.25a	Baby hugging penguin	2.0	regular	yes	Germ-bk	2365	3	145-225
10.25b	Baby hugging penguin	1.87	no	yes	no	no	1	45-60
10.26	Baby pulling penguins	1.37	regular	no	Germ-bk	no	3	125-185
10.27	Penguin pushing	1.62	regular	yes	no	515	2	155-225
10.28	2 huskies pulling baby	1.37	regular	yes	no	7153	4	160-230
10.29	2 huskies pulling baby	1.25	regular	yes	Japan	no	4	55-90
10.30	Dog pulling baby	1.75	regular	yes	no	no	1	135-200
10.31	Reindeer pulling baby	1.5	regular	yes	no	no	3	125-200
10.32	Reindeer pulling baby	1.37	regular	yes	no	no	2	125-200
10.33a	Baby playing soccer	1.75	regular	no	Germ-bk	no	1	135-175
10.33b	Baby playing hockey	1.87	regular	yes	no	1188	1	175-245
10.34a	Baby holding ball	1.62	regular	yes	Germ-bk	2718	2	125-195
10.34b	Baby kicking ball	2.25	regular	yes	Germ-bk	2293	1	175-245
10.35a	Baby paddling kayak	1.12	regular	no	no	no	2	130-195
10.35b	Baby rowing boat	1.37	regular	no	no	no	1	145-220
10.35c	Baby at canoe	2.0	regular	no	no	2867	1	165-235
10.35d	Baby on raft	2.5	regular	no	Germ-bl	1636	1	175-255
10.36a	Baby fishing in boat	1.12	regular	no	Germ-bk	no	1	110-175
10.36b	Baby carrying kayak	1.25	regular	no	Germ-bk	no	2	110-165
10.37a	Baby holding skis	1.62	regular	no	no	no	3	100-155
10.37b	Baby with hockey stick	1.87	regular	no	no	no	2	100-155
10.38	Baby with tennis racket	1.62	regular	no	Germ-bl	no	3	100-155
10.39a	2 babies dancing	2.0	regular	yes	Germ-bl	2714	3	135-195
10.39b	2 babies fighting	1.5	regular	yes	Germ-bl	no	2	175-260
10.40	2 babies, igloo	2.25	regular	no	no	no	2	165-265
10.41	2 babies, igloo	3.25	regular	no	no	no	2	165-265
10.42	2 babies, ice ledge	3.12	regular	yes	no	no	1	185-230
10.43	Baby and bear	2.75	regular	yes	Germ-O-r	no	2	185-230
10.44	2 babies on globe	3.25	no	no	Germ-I	5617	2	200-275
10.45	Baby on ladder	2.62	regular	no	no	no	1	125-210
10.46	Baby on ladder	3.5	regular	no	no	no	1	125-210
10.47	Baby on swing	3.12	regular	no	no	no	1	140-235
10.48a	Baby on airplane	1.75	regular	no	no	1699	3	165-225
10.48b	Baby on airplane	1.5	no	no	no	no	1	145-205
10.48c	Baby on airplane	1.5	crystal	no	Germ-bk	no	1	145-205
10.49	2 babies on tank	2.25	regular	yes	no	514	2	195-265
10.50	2 babies on wall	1.5	regular	no	no	6602	3	145-200
10.51	2 babies on wedge	1.5	regular	no	Germ-bk	no	1	145-200
10.52	2 babies on wall	2.25	regular	no	no	no	2	145-200
10.53	2 children on wall	2.25	glitter	no	Germ-bk	no	5	140-180
10.54	2 babies skiing	2.37	regular	no	no	338	2	200-275
10.55a	Baby on sled	1.62	regular	no	Germ-bl	1221	4	100-160
10.55b	Baby pushing another	1.25	regular	no	no	no	1	120-170
10.56	Baby on sled	2.12	regular	no	Japan-I	no	3	45-80
10.57a	Baby lying on wedge	1.5	coarse	no	no	no	3	20-40
10.57b	Baby standing on wedge	1.87	coarse	no	no	no	3	20-40
10.58	3 children with snowman	2.25	regular	yes	Germ-p	no	2	155-235
10.60	2 babies, igloo	2.0	coralene	yes	no	no	1	50-85
10.61	Girl carrying tree	2.37	no	yes	no	no	1	10-35
10.62a	Baby with club	1.5	regular	no	Germ-bk	no	1	100-130
10.62b	Baby with club	1.5	regular	no	no	no	1	100-130
10.62c	Baby with noose	1.5	regular	no	Germ-bk	no	1	100-130
10.63a	Baby with rifle	1.5	regular	no	Germ-bk	no	1	100-130
10.63b	Baby with rifle	1.5	regular	no	Germ-bk	no	1	100-130
10.63c	Baby with rope	1.5	regular	no	Germ-bk	no	1	100-130
10.64a	Baby band conductor	2.0	regular	yes	Germ-bl	1180	4	125-185
10.64b	Baby playing fife	2.0	regular	yes	Germ-bl	1182	3	125-185
10.64c	Baby playing drum	2.0	regular	yes	Germ-bl	1181	3	125-185
10.65a	Baby playing tuba	2.0	regular	yes	Germ-bl	1184	4	125-185
10.65b	Baby playing concertina	2.0	regular	yes	Germ-bl	1185	4	125-185
10.65c	Baby playing saxophone	2.0	regular	yes	Germ-bl	1183	4	125-185
10.66a	Baby playing drum	1.62	coralene	yes	no	no	2	25-80
10.66b	Baby with baton	1.62	coralene	yes	no	no	2	25-80
10.67a	Baby playing banjo	1.75	regular	no	Germ-bk	no	5	125-185
10.67b	Baby playing tuba	1.62	regular	no	Germ-bk	no	5	125-185
10.67c	Baby playing trumpet	1.75	regular	no	Germ-bk	no	5	125-185
10.68a	Baby playing saxophone	1.75	regular	no	Germ-bk	no	5	125-185
10.68b	Baby playing concertina	1.75	regular	no	Germ-bk	no	5	125-185
10.68c	Baby playing drum	2.0	regular	no	Germ-bk	no	4	125-185
10.69a	Baby playing concertina	1.75	no	no	Germ-p	no	2	25-95
10.69b	Baby playing saxophone	2.0	no	no	Germ-p	no	2	25-95
10.69c	Baby playing banjo	1.87	no	no	Foreign-p	no	2	25-95
10.69d	Baby playing trumpet	2.12	no	no	Foreign-p	no	2	25-95
10.69e	Baby playing drum	2.37	no	no	no	no	2	25-95
10.69f	Baby playing tuba	1.87	no	no	no	no	2	25-95
10.70	Baby playing drum	2.0	coralene	no	GermUS Z-bk	no	2	95-135
10.71	Girl on snowball	2.5	regular	no	no	no	2	135-200
10.72a	Girl pushing snowball	2.0	regular	no	no	no	2	135-200
10.72b	Boy pushing snowball	2.0	regular	no	no	no	2	135-200
10.73	Baby pushing snowball	1.87	regular	no	no	no	1	155-220
10.74	Child near snowball	1.87	no	yes	no	no	3	10-30
10.75	Girl pushing snowball	1.5	no	yes	Eng MI-O	no	2	10-25
10.76	Mother pushing twins	2.5	regular	no	Germ	7156	3	225-300
10.77	Baby sitting on baby	2.62	regular	no	no	no	1	175-225
10.78	3 babies form tower	2.0	regular	yes	no	2773	1	175-225
10.79a	3 babies form tower	2.25	no	yes	no	no	2	30-55
10.79b	Girl skater	2.87	no	yes	no	no	4	15-35
10.80	Boy skier	1.5	no	yes	no	no	1	85-165
10.81	Boy on brown sled	1.75	no	yes	no	no	1	85-165
10.82	Boy carrying sled	2.62	no	yes	Japan-bk	no	3	15-40
10.83a	Boy skater	2.62	regular	yes	Japan-bk	no	3	30-50
10.83b	Girl skater	2.62	regular	yes	no	no	3	15-35
10.84	3 babies on sled	1.5	regular	no	Germ-p	no	2	155-240
10.85a	3 babies on sled	1.62	no	no	no	5106	3	125-170
10.85b	3 babies on sled	1.75	regular	no	no	no	3	145-200
10.86a	Baby lying on side	1.5	coralene	no	no	no	3	25-35
10.86b	3 babies on sled	2.0	coralene	no	no	no	2	25-80
10.87	2 babies on sled	1.62	regular	no	no	no	1	125-185
10.88	2 babies on sled	1.75	regular	no	Germ-r	5107	3	100-150
10.89a	Baby pushing baby	1.62	regular	no	Germ-p	5299	3	145-185
10.89b	Baby pulling baby	1.62	regular	no	Japan-p	no	3	45-90
10.90	Baby pushing baby	2.25	regular	no	Germ	5010	3	140-185
10.91	Baby pushing baby	2.25	regular	no	Germ-bk	5010	1	140-185
10.92a	Baby on baby on sled	1.87	regular	no	Germ-bk	no	1	140-190
10.92b	Baby with soccer ball	1.37	regular	no	no	no	3	100-145
10.93a	Children on toboggan	1.62	no	no	Germ-bk	no	4	65-110
10.93b	3 children on sled	1.5	no	no	Germ-I	no	3	85-150
10.94a	2 children on sled	1.62	regular	no	Germ-p	2236	2	85-160
10.94b	Boy and girl on sled	1.5	no	no	no	no	2	30-50
10.95	Baby on sled	1.75	coarse	no	no	no	2	75-110
10.96	Baby on sled	1.25	gold	no	no	no	1	110-140

Table 1

FIG #	BRIEF DESCRIPTION	HT IN	SNOW	BASE	COUNTRY	INCISED	RARE	PRICE
10.97a	Baby falling on sled	1.37	regular	no	no	no	4	50-85
10.97b	Baby sitting on sled	1.37	regular	no	Germ-bk	no	4	50-85
10.97c	Baby standing on sled	1.62	regular	no	Germ-bk	no	4	50-85
10.97d	Baby standing on sled	1.62	regular	no	no	no	4	20-40
10.98	Baby on sled	1.5	coralene	no	no	no	3	20-35
10.99a	Baby lying on sled	2.0	regular	no	no	5130	3	110-155
10.99b	Baby lying on sled	1.5	no	no	no	no	3	75-120
10.100a	Baby lying on sled	1.62	regular	no	no	no	4	25-40
10.100b	Baby lying on sled	1.62	no	no	no	no	4	20-30
10.101a	Girl on sled	2.25	regular	no	Germ-l	8721	2	125-160
10.101b	Boy on sled	2.25	regular	no	Germ-l	8721	2	125-160
10.102a	Girl on sled	1.5	regular	no	no	no	4	50-90
10.102b	Boy on sled	1.62	regular	no	Germ-bk	no	4	50-90
10.103	Girl lying on sled	1.5	regular	no	Germ	no	5	50-105
10.104a	Girl kneeling on sled	1.75	coralene	no	no	4882	2	135-190
10.104b	Girl standing on sled	2.25	coralene	no	no	4883	1	135-190
10.104c	Girl astride sled	1.5	coralene	no	Germ	7	2	135-190
10.105	Child on sled	1.87	regular	no	no	8113	1	145-190
10.106a	Boy sitting on sled	2.5	no	no	no	5891	1	125-165
10.106b	Girl sitting on sled	2.5	no	no	Germ-bk	5891	1	125-165
10.107	Boy pulling sled	2.37	no	yes	Germ-l	5714/6/0	1	120-165
10.108a	Boy on back on sled	1.62	regular	no	Germ-l	4642	1	80-160
10.108b	Girl sitting on sled	1.75	regular	no	Germ-l	4641	1	80-160
10.109a	Baby crawling onto sled	1.5	regular	no	Germ-l	5119	3	85-140
10.109b	Baby sitting on sled	1.75	regular	no	Germ-l	5121	3	85-140
10.109c	Baby sitting on sled	1.75	regular	no	Germ-r	5120	3	85-140
10.110a	Baby waving from sled	1.37	crystal	no	Germ-r	no	3	90-130
10.110b	Baby standing on sled	1.62	regular	no	no	no	2	90-125
10.110c	Baby lying on sled	1.62	regular	no	no	no	1	85-135
10.111a	Baby pulling sled	2.25	no	no	no	no	3	110-165
10.111b	Baby pulling sled	1.87	regular	no	Germ-p	no	4	110-160
10.112	Baby pulling sled	1.87	regular	no	no	no	1	110-160
10.113	Baby lying on sled	1.75	regular	no	no	no	3	110-160
10.114	Baby on sled	2.25	regular	no	Germ-bk	no	3	110-160
10.115a	Girl lying on sled	1.62	regular	no	Germ	8447	5	65-110
10.115b	Girl sitting on sled	1.25	regular	no	Germ-bl	8446	3	65-125
10.115c	Girl prone on sled	1.62	no	no	Germ-bl	8448	3	65-125
10.116a	Girl lying on sled	1.75	regular	no	Japan-l	no	4	20-35
10.116b	Girl lying on sled	1.5	regular	no	Japan-bk	no	5	20-35
10.117	Baby sitting on sled	1.5	glitter	no	no	no	2	30-45
10.118a	Baby on sled	1.75	regular	no	Japan-l	no	4	20-35
10.118b	Baby stands, waving	2.37	regular	no	no	no	3	40-60
10.119	Girl on sled	3.0	no	no	Germ	no	5	75-125
10.120a	Child skating	2.0	regular	yes	Germ-bk	no	2	110-130
10.120b	Child skating	1.87	regular	yes	Germ-bk	no	2	110-130
10.120c	Girl skating	2.0	regular	yes	Germ-bk	no	2	110-130
10.121a	Girl skating	2.0	no	yes	Germ-bk	no	4	40-75
10.121b	Girl skating	2.25	no	yes	no	11905	2	30-50
10.121c	Boy sitting on sled	1.75	no	no	no	no	3	40-70
10.122a	Boy throwing snowball	2.37	no	no	no	no	3	40-70
10.122b	Girl on tiny skis	2.25	no	no	Germ	no	3	40-70
10.122c	Girl throwing snowball	2.25	no	no	no	no	3	40-70
10.123a	Boy on gold skates	2.12	regular	yes	Germ-p	461	3	85-130
10.123b	Girl on gold skates	2.0	regular	yes	Germ-p	460	3	85-130
10.124a	Boy on gold skates	2.0	no	yes	no	460	3	55-90
10.124b	Girl on gold skates	2.0	no	yes	Germ-p	460	3	55-90
10.125a	Girl on gold skates	2.0	regular	yes	Germ-bl	461	3	85-130
10.125b	2 children skating	2.12	no	yes	no	2711	1	40-60
10.125c	Boy throwing snowball	1.87	no	yes	Germ-bl	5012	2	40-80
10.126	Girl skating	2.0	no	yes	no	no	4	20-35
10.127	Boy skating	2.87	no	yes	Japan-r	no	1	20-40
10.128	Baby, silver skates	1.25	regular	yes	Germ-l	5117	2	100-155
10.129a	Baby skating	1.62	regular	yes	Germ-r	5115	2	100-155
10.129b	Baby skier	1.75	regular	no	Germ-l	5114	3	100-145
10.130	Baby skier	1.62	regular	no	Germ-bk	no	3	100-145
10.131a	Boy skier	2.12	coralene	no	Germ-l	no	4	135-180
10.131b	Boy skier waving	1.75	coralene	yes	Germ-l	4881	2	135-180
10.132a	Baby sledder	2.75	no	no	Germ-O-bk	no	2	85-135
10.132b	Baby skiing, red shoes	2.87	no	no	Germ-O-bk	3488	2	85-135
10.132c	Baby sledder	3.0	no	no	Germ-O-bk	3516	2	85-135
10.133	Boy skier on wedge	2.25	no	yes	Germ-l	5714/4/0	1	120-165
10.134a	Boy skier on mound	2.75	no	no	Germ-r	12056	1	45-145
10.134b	Girl skier	2.87	no	no	Germ-r	12057	1	45-125
10.135a	Boy skier	1.87	regular	no	no	no	1	90-120
10.135b	Baby skier waving	1.37	crystal	no	Germ-r	no	3	90-120
10.136a	Baby skier with pole	2.0	regular	no	no	no	4	20-40
10.136b	Baby skier	1.5	regular	no	Japan-bk	no	4	20-40
10.137	Baby carrying baby	2.62	regular	no	no	no	3	175-250
10.138a	Striped cuff skier	2.5	regular	no	no	763	3	125-165
10.138b	Girl skier	2.5	regular	no	no	763	3	125-165
10.139a	Striped cuff skier	2.75	regular	no	no	9470	4	125-165
10.139b	Striped cuff skier	2.75	regular	no	Germ-bk	9469	3	125-165
10.140a	Boy fallen on skates	1.5	glitter	no	no	no	1	85-135
10.140b	Boy carrying skis	2.75	glitter	no	no	no	1	85-135
10.141a	Child lying prone	0.87	regular	no	no	no	2	125-180
10.141b	Child standing on skis	2.25	regular	no	no	no	2	125-180
10.142	3 singing babies	1.75	regular	yes	no	6712	2	145-195
10.143	3 babies on sled	1.75	no	no	no	no	2	110-160
10.144	3 babies walking	1.87	regular	no	no	no	1	165-230
10.145	Baby with teddy bear	2.25	regular	no	Germ-p	no	2	175-250
10.146	Baby with teddy bear	2.25	no	no	Germ-bk	no	3	150-200
10.147a	2 baby huggers	1.75	regular	no	Germ-bk	no	4	115-175
10.147b	2 baby huggers	1.75	no	no	no	no	4	90-135
10.148	Baby balancing	2.5	regular	no	no	no	1	145-180
10.149	Baby hugging self	2.25	regular	no	no	no	1	145-180
10.150	Baby standing	2.25	regular	no	no	no	3	95-155
10.151	Baby waving hand	2.0	regular	no	Germ-bl	no	1	85-140
10.152	Boy prone	1.12	regular	no	no	8187	2	100-170
10.153a	Fallen baby skater	1.5	regular	no	no	no	1	110-160
10.153b	Baby sitting	1.37	regular	no	Germ-bl	no	3	85-120
10.154a	Baby sitting, red hood	2.0	regular	no	Germ-p	no	4	75-120
10.154b	Baby stands, laughing	2.5	regular	no	Germ-p	no	5	75-120
10.155	Baby lying on side	1.5	regular	no	no	no	3	75-120
10.156	Baby with snowballs	2.0	regular	no	no	no	2	75-120
10.157a	Baby with gold ring	1.5	regular	no	no	no	1	90-140
10.157b	Baby sitting, arms back	1.0	regular	no	no	no	1	90-120
10.158	Baby with umbrella	1.75	regular	no	Germ-bk	no	1	90-140
10.159	Baby carrying bag	1.75	regular	no	no	no	1	100-165
10.160a	Round-headed baby	2.75	regular	no	no	no	3	100-145
10.160b	Round-headed baby	1.5	regular	no	no	no	3	100-145
10.160c	Round-headed baby	2.5	no	no	Germ-bk	9774	2	90-130
10.161a	Baby in bunny suit	2.5	regular	no	Germ-p	no	1	125-185
10.161b	Baby in bunny suit	2.62	no	no	no	no	1	115-145
10.162a	Baby in bunny suit	2.37	regular	no	Germ	no	1	125-185
10.162b	Baby in bunny suit	1.87	regular	no	Germ-bk	no	1	125-185
10.162c	Baby in bunny suit	2.12	regular	no	no	no	1	125-185
10.163a	Baby crawling	1.0	regular	no	no	no	1	65-110
10.163b	Baby sitting, arms up	1.12	regular	no	no	no	1	65-110
10.164	Baby sits, leaning	1.62	coarse	no	no	no	1	65-95
10.165	Baby sitting	1.25	regular	no	Japan-bk	no	3	35-50
10.166a	Baby on snowball	2.0	regular	no	Japan MI-bk	no	4	35-50
10.166b	Baby on snowball	2.25	regular	no	no	no	5	25-35
10.166c	Baby on snowball	2.12	regular	no	no	no	5	25-35
10.167	Baby on snowball	1.75	crystal	no	no	no	4	30-50
10.168a	Baby, Alaska tot	1.12	regular	no	no	no	1	75-120
10.168b	Baby, Alaska tot	1.12	regular	no	no	no	4	75-110
10.169	Baby, tot on sled	1.62	regular	no	no	no	2	110-155
10.170a	Baby holding skis	1.62	regular	no	Germ-bk	no	5	65-115
10.170b	Baby on one knee	1.5	regular	no	no	no	5	65-95
10.171a	Tiny baby sitting	1.12	regular	no	no	no	4	45-75
10.171b	Tiny baby standing	1.37	regular	no	no	no	4	45-75
10.171c	Tiny baby standing	1.25	regular	no	no	no	3	45-75
10.171d	Tiny baby lying	1.0	regular	no	no	no	4	45-75
10.172	Tiny baby prone	0.75	regular	no	no	no	3	55-85
10.173a	Tiny baby sitting	1.12	regular	no	Germ-bl	no	5	65-95
10.173b	Tiny baby standing	1.12	regular	no	Germ-bl	no	4	40-60
10.173c	Tiny baby lying	1.0	regular	no	Germ-bl	no	4	45-75
10.174a	Tiny baby standing	1.37	regular	no	no	no	3	30-40
10.174b	Tiny baby sitting	1.12	regular	no	Japan-bk	no	4	30-40
10.174c	Tiny baby standing	1.37	regular	no	no	no	4	30-40
10.175a	Tiny baby sitting	0.87	regular	no	Germ-p	no	3	40-60
10.175b	Tiny baby sitting	0.87	regular	no	Germ-bl	no	3	40-60
10.175c	Tiny baby standing	1.0	regular	no	Germ-bl	no	2	40-60
10.175d	Tiny baby lying	0.87	regular	no	Germ-bl	no	3	40-60
10.176a	Tiny baby in red cap	0.87	regular	no	Germ-p	no	2	45-75
10.176b	Tiny baby in red cap	0.87	regular	no	Germ-p	no	2	45-75
10.176c	Tiny baby in red cap	0.87	regular	no	Germ-p	no	2	45-75
10.176d	Tiny baby in red cap	1.12	regular	no	Germ-p	no	2	45-75
10.177	Tiny baby skier	1.5	regular	no	Germ-bk	no	2	55-85
10.178a	2 children, penguin	1.75	no	no	Germ-bk	no	3	100-145
10.178b	2 children, penguin	1.75	no	no	no	no	2	20-55
10.179a	2 children with bell	2.0	regular	yes	Germ-bk	no	3	80-120
10.179b	2 children with bell	2.0	no	yes	Germ-bk	no	4	60-100
10.180a	Tiny baby with snowman	1.5	no	yes	Germ-bk	no	3	135-155
10.180b	3 children on hill	2.0	no	yes	Germ-bk	no	4	125-155
10.180c	2 children on hill	2.0	regular	yes	no	no	2	110-135
10.181a	Baby in ornament	2.0	regular	no	no	no	1	30-45
10.181b	Celluloid baby	1.37	no	no	Japan-l	no	1	20-30
10.182a	Eskimo father	1.87	no	no	Germ-l	17682	1	20-30
10.182b	Eskimo girl with dog	1.25	no	no	Germ-l	no	1	20-30
10.182c	Eskimo boy with hatchet	1.37	no	no	Germ-l	no	1	20-30
10.182d	Eskimo mother	1.75	no	no	Germ-l	17682	1	20-30
10.182e	Eskimo summer home	2.87	no	no	Germ-l	17682	1	20-30
11.1a	3 child carolers	2.25	no	no	Germ-l	7476	1	60-140
11.1b	3 child carolers	2.12	no	no	no	no	1	60-140
11.2a	3 Italian carolers	2.0	no	yes	no	8461	1	60-130
11.2b	3 musicians	1.75	no	no	Germ-bk	no	1	60-135
11.3a	Single girl caroler	2.5	no	no	no	no	1	25-55
11.3b	3 carolers	2.25	regular	yes	Germ-bk	9700	5	75-125
11.4	3 child carolers	2.0	china	yes	Japan-bk	no	5	25-45
11.5a	3 male carolers	1.87	regular	yes	no	9699	2	60-120
11.5b	3 male carolers	2.25	regular	no	no	381	5	60-115
11.6	3 child carolers	2.25	coarse	yes	no	no	5	25-55
11.7	3 male carolers	2.25	no	yes	Germ-bk	no	2	60-135
11.8	3 child carolers	1.75	no	no	Germ-bk	no	5	25-50
12.1a	Red woman skier	2.25	no	no	Germ-bk	no	5	35-70
12.1b	Red man skier	2.25	no	yes	Germ-bk	no	5	35-70
12.1c	Red man skier	1.87	no	no	Germ-bk	no	4	35-70
12.2a	Glitter woman skier	2.25	glitter	yes	Germ MI-r	no	4	40-75
12.2b	Glitter man skier	2.25	glitter	yes	Germ-bk	no	4	40-75
12.3	Woman carrying skis	2.5	glitter	yes	Germ-bk	no	1	55-100
12.4a	Red man skater	2.5	no	yes	Germ-bk	no	5	35-70
12.4b	Red woman skater	2.5	no	yes	Germ-bk	no	5	35-70
12.5a	Glitter man skater	2.62	glitter	yes	Germ-bk	no	3	40-90
12.5b	Glitter woman skater	2.5	glitter	yes	Germ-bk	no	3	40-90
12.6a	Glazed man skater	2.5	no	yes	Germ-p	no	4	12-40
12.6b	Glazed woman skater	2.5	no	yes	Germ-p	no	4	12-40
12.7	Woman sledder	2.12	glitter	no	Germ-bk	no	2	65-120
12.8	Fluorescent skier	2.87	no	yes	no	no	2	10-35
12.9a	Woman skier	3.25	no	yes	Erph-Germ-l	K95	2	30-55
12.9b	Woman holding skis	3.5	no	yes	Erph-Germ-l	K93	2	30-55
12.9c	Kneeling woman skier	2.0	no	yes	Erph-Germ-l	K94	2	30-55
12.9d	Woman on skis	3.0	no	yes	Erph-Germ-l	no	2	30-55
12.10a	Woman sledder	3.0	no	no	Erph-Germ-l	K92	2	40-80
12.10b	Woman sledder	2.75	no	no	Erph-Germ-l	K89	2	40-80
12.11	Woman sledder	2.87	no	yes	Erph-Germ-l	K90	1	40-80
12.12a	Woman sledder winking	1.75	no	no	Germ-bk	no	4	35-55
12.12b	Woman sledder winking	1.75	no	no	Japan	no	4	20-35
12.13a	Plaid shirt skier	3.0	no	no	Japan-p	no	2	20-35
12.13b	Woman skier	1.75	no	no	Japan-p	no	3	20-35
12.14	Plaid shirt skier	3.25	no	no	Germ-bl	F0656	2	40-65
12.15	Woman skater, white	2.87	no	yes	Germ-r	no	1	80-135
12.16	Woman skater	2.12	no	yes	Germ-bk	no	2	70-125
12.17a	Woman skater	2.12	no	yes	Germ-bl	5866	1	60-110
12.17b	Man skater	2.12	no	yes	Germ-bl	5866	1	60-110
12.18	2 adults on toboggan	2.0	no	no	Germ MI-l	14824	3	45-90
12.19	Competition skier	2.75	no	yes	Germ-r	8607	1	45-85
12.20	Sonja Henie skater	2.5	no	yes	Germ-l	no	1	70-135
12.21	Woman on skates	2.5	no	yes	Japan Occ-r	no	3	20-40
12.22	Couple in snowball	3.5	regular	no	no	no	1	400-600
12.23	Man, horse & wagon	1.75	regular	yes	Germ-bk	no	2	145-195
13.1	Santa on skis	3.5	regular	no	no	no	1	375-600
13.2	Santa holding signboard	3.75	no	yes	no	89	1	70-125
13.3a	Santa, braid on coat	3.25	no	no	no	no	3	100-160
13.3b	Santa, braid on coat	2.25	no	no	no	no	4	85-125
13.3c	Small plain Santa	2.25	no	no	Germ	6080	4	45-85
13.3d	Small plain Santa	1.5	no	no	no	4284	5	40-55
13.4a	Santa with tree	2.0	no	no	Germ-l	5136	4	40-75
13.4b	Santa with white cane	2.37	no	no	Germ-l	8434	3	60-120
13.4c	Santa with cane	2.5	no	no	no	no	3	95-125
13.4d	Santa in short coat	2.75	no	no	Germ-bk	no	5	60-110
13.5a	Santa with basket	2.5	no	no	no	LH 376	2	85-135
13.5b	Santa, doll in pouch	2.75	no	no	Germ-p	no	2	110-160
13.6	Santa, doll in pouch	2.75	coralene	no	Germ-l	no	1	120-185
13.7a	Santa with lantern	1.87	no	no	no	no	4	60-100
13.7b	Santa with lantern	2.12	no	no	no	no	4	60-100
13.7c	Santa with lantern	2.5	regular	no	no	no	1	120-175
13.7d	Santa with lantern	3.0	no	no	no	8433	3	90-140

Table 1

FIG #	BRIEF DESCRIPTION	HT IN	SNOW	BASE	COUNTRY	INCISED	RARE	PRICE
13.8	Santa carrying stick	2.5	no	no	no	no	2	120-210
13.9	Santa on swing	3.0	regular	yes	Germ-I	5401	2	185-250
13.10	Santa, gold bell	2.37	regular	yes	no	379	3	125-160
13.11	Santa talking on phone	1.5	no	no	Germ-bk	no	2	135-185
13.12	Santa climbing fence	1.75	no	yes	Germ-bk	no	4	120-155
13.13a	Santa on sled	1.5	no	yes	Germ-bk	no	3	50-90
13.13b	Santa on skis	1.5	no	yes	Germ-bk	no	3	50-90
13.13c	Santa near fence	1.5	no	yes	Germ-bk	no	3	50-90
13.13d	Santa pulling sled	1.5	no	yes	Germ-bk	no	3	50-90
13.13e	Santa with stick	1.5	no	yes	Germ-bk	no	3	50-90
13.14a	Santa on skis	1.87	no	no	Japan	no	5	35-50
13.14b	Santa on ice skates	1.5	no	no	Japan-I-bk	no	5	20-35
13.14c	Santa waving on sled	1.75	no	no	no	no	3	50-90
13.14d	Santa on skis, wedge	1.75	no	yes	no	no	2	85-120
13.15	Santa waving on sled	2.25	regular	no	no	no	3	185-225
13.16a	Santa, braid on coat	3.5	no	no	Japan-bk	S/095	5	30-40
13.16b	Santa, green pack	4.0	no	no	Japan-I	no	5	30-40
13.16c	Santa, green bag	2.5	no	yes	Japan-I	no	5	20-30
13.17	Santa on ice ledge	2.37	regular	yes	Germ-bk	no	1	145-210
13.18	Santa on sled	2.25	regular	no	no	6698	4	145-190
13.19	Santa on sled	2.5	regular	no	Japan MI-I	no	4	85-110
13.20a	Reindeer pulling Santa	1.25	no	yes	Germ-bk	no	2	85-125
13.20b	Santa on sled	1.5	no	no	Germ-bk	no	3	85-130
13.21	Reindeer pulling Santa	2.25	no	yes	Germ MI-p	8266	2	110-150
13.22a	Reindeer pulling Santa	2.0	no	yes	Germ-I-r	no	1	120-150
13.22b	Reindeer pulling Santa	1.25	no	no	no	no	2	120-160
13.23a	Reindeer pulling Santa	1.75	regular	yes	Germ-bk	6699	4	110-150
13.23b	Reindeer pulling Santa	2.25	regular	yes	Germ-I	8395	3	120-185
13.24	Reindeer pulling Santa	1.87	no	yes	no	no	2	95-130
13.25	Reindeer pulling Santa	2.0	no	yes	no	no	5	100-155
13.26	Reindeer pulling Santa	1.5	no	yes	Germ-p	no	5	100-155
13.27	Doe pulling Santa	2.5	regular	yes	Germ-bk	730	1	185-245
13.28	Santa, donkey cart	1.75	regular	no	no	9696	2	185-240
13.29	Huskies pulling Santa	1.62	regular	yes	no	7154	3	165-230
13.30	Horse pulling Santa	1.87	no	yes	no	508	3	165-210
13.31	Santa on cracker	1.75	no	no	no	7155	2	175-240
13.32	Santa on toboggan	1.5	no	no	Germ-p	no	4	155-185
13.33	Santa on sled	1.37	no	no	no	2294	2	135-175
13.34	Santa on sled	2.0	no	no	Germ	4513	1	135-175
13.35a	Santa on igloo	2.37	regular	yes	Germ-bk	no	4	155-210
13.35b	Santa with 2 babies	2.0	regular	yes	Germ	2724	2	165-230
13.36	Santa, baby on see-saw	2.0	regular	yes	Germ-I-p	no	2	185-240
13.37	Santa by cradle	3.0	no	no	Germ-I	no	1	140-210
13.38	Santa giving doll	2.12	no	yes	Germ-p	507	2	160-215
13.39	Santa by baby's bed	2.12	no	no	Germ-p	758	2	160-215
13.40a	Santa with girl	2.25	no	yes	Germ-p	511	3	140-195
13.40b	Santa giving doll	1.67	no	no	Germ-bk	no	2	135-175
13.41	Santa with girl	1.87	no	yes	Germ-bk	no	1	160-200
13.42	Santa with 2 children	2.25	no	yes	Germ-p	869	3	155-195
13.43	Santa standing by pack	2.12	regular	yes	Germ-I-p	365	3	130-175
13.44	Santa pushing buggy	1.75	no	no	no	5959	1	165-230
13.45	Santa pulling buggy	2.25	no	yes	no	no	1	165-230
13.46a	Santa pushing cart	1.5	no	no	Germ-bk	no	2	135-175
13.46b	Santa pulling cart	1.75	no	no	Germ-bk	no	2	160-200
13.47a	Santa pulling wagon	1.25	no	yes	Germ-bk	no	3	75-145
13.47b	Santa pulling angel	1.25	no	yes	Germ	no	5	85-145
13.48a	Santa with angel	1.87	no	yes	no	no	2	100-145
13.48b	Santa with angel	1.87	no	no	Germ-bk	no	5	85-140
13.49	Santa pulling sleigh	2.12	no	yes	Foreign	no	1	110-165
13.50a	Santa on camel	2.62	regular	yes	no	9650	2	190-245
13.50b	Santa on elephant	2.37	regular	no	no	9692	2	190-245
13.51	Santa with elephant	1.62	no	no	Germ-bk	no	2	190-245
13.52	Santa on donkey	1.87	no	yes	no	no	1	155-195
13.53	Santa on polar bear	2.37	regular	no	Germ-p	no	3	190-240
13.54	Santa on polar bear	1.5	regular	no	no	no	1	155-195
13.55a	Santa on reindeer	2.75	no	yes	Germ-bk	no	3	160-190
13.55b	Santa on reindeer	2.25	no	yes	no	no	4	140-180
13.55c	Santa, reindeer, cub	2.0	regular	yes	no	no	3	165-210
13.56	Santa on moose	3.12	no	yes	Germ-I	6142	2	165-220
13.57	Santa walking Westie	3.25	no	yes	Germ-I	6140	2	185-230
13.58	Santa on sled	3.0	no	no	Germ-I	6141	2	185-260
13.59	Santa with duck	1.5	no	yes	Germ-bk	no	2	130-165
13.60	Santa in race car	1.37	no	no	no	no	1	190-250
13.61	Santa on silver car	1.5	no	no	Germ-bk	no	1	170-230
13.62	Santa driving red car	1.12	no	no	no	no	2	125-175
13.63	Santa in yellow car	1.62	regular	no	no	4696	3	185-235
13.64a	Santa in silver car	1.37	no	yes	no	no	5	95-155
13.64b	Santa in silver car	1.5	no	yes	Germ-bk	no	4	95-155
13.65	Santa on motorcycle	2.12	no	yes	no	9056	2	185-235
13.66	Santa on motorcycle	2.12	no	yes	no	877	2	200-240
13.67	Santa in train	1.62	regular	no	Germ-p	9695	3	185-235
13.68	Santa in train	1.75	regular	no	Japan-bk	no	3	60-90
13.69	Santa in train	1.87	no	no	no	731	1	190-250
13.70	Santa in sailboat	2.0	no	no	no	506	3	155-225
13.71	Santa in sailboat	2.25	no	no	Japan-bk	no	4	55-80
13.72	Santa in motorboat	1.62	no	no	no	7152	2	145-115
13.73	Santa at lighthouse	2.5	regular	yes	Germ-bk	no	2	175-225
13.74	Santa on airplane	1.5	no	no	Germ-bk	6697	3	185-245
13.75	Santa in airplane	1.25	no	no	Germ-bk	no	1	185-245
13.76	Santa on stagecoach	1.5	no	no	no	no	3	145-190
13.77	Santa on stagecoach	1.62	no	no	Germ-bk	no	2	190-220
13.78	Santa on stagecoach	1.75	no	yes	no	377	1	145-190
13.79	Santa on stagecoach	1.62	regular	no	no	510	1	185-220
13.80a	Santa peeks into house	2.12	no	yes	no	no	3	135-180
13.80b	Santa on house	3.0	regular	no	no	no	4	140-175
13.81	Santa on roof	2.0	no	no	Germ-bk	no	1	160-200
13.82a	Santa on roof	2.25	regular	yes	no	6695	4	110-160
13.82b	Santa on roof	2.37	regular	yes	Japan	no	4	35-80
13.83a	Santa on roof	1.62	no	no	Germ-bk	no	2	45-110
13.83b	Santa on roof	2.0	no	yes	Germ-bk	no	2	120-155
13.84	Santa at door	1.75	no	yes	Germ-bk	no	3	135-170
13.85	Santa reading paper	2.37	no	no	no	9688	2	165-230
13.86	Santa at mantel	1.5	no	yes	Germ-bk	no	2	155-190
13.87a	Santa, girl on sled	2.25	no	no	no	no	1	120-170
13.87b	Santa at lamp post	2.25	no	yes	no	no	1	120-155
13.87c	Santa on chimney	3.0	no	no	Germ-bk	no	2	165-195
13.88	Santa in chimney	3.0	no	no	no	no	1	100-135
13.89	Santa with lantern	2.5	no	no	no	no	2	95-125
13.90	Santa at sign post	1.87	no	yes	GermUS Z-p	no	2	50-95
13.91a	Santa carrying tree	1.87	no	no	no	no	2	65-95
13.91b	Santa with lantern	1.87	no	no	no	no	3	65-95
13.91c	Santa with lantern	3.0	no	no	no	no	2	85-140
13.92a	Santa, girl at house	1.12	no	no	no	no	3	60-90
13.92b	Santa climbing house	1.25	no	no	no	no	3	50-80
13.93a	Santa dumping toys	1.62	no	yes	no	no	3	60-85
13.93b	Santa with golf clubs	2.0	no	no	GermUS Z-p	no	2	85-150
13.94	Santa feeding deer	1.37	no	yes	Germ W-p	no	1	50-70
13.95a	Santa on skis	1.62	no	yes	GermUS Z-p	no	2	40-65
13.95b	Santa on giraffe	1.5	no	yes	Germ-p	no	1	50-85
13.95c	Santa and dog	1.37	no	yes	GermW-p	no	1	50-70
13.95d	Santa with teddy	1.37	no	yes	GermW-p	no	2	50-80
13.96	Santa with donkey	1.75	no	yes	no	no	2	65-85
13.97a	Santa pushing cart	1.12	no	no	no	no	2	55-70
13.97b	Santa waving	2.25	no	no	no	no	3	65-90
13.98	Santa at toy shop	1.37	no	no	Japan-Occ-r	no	4	35-55
13.99	Santa with tree	2.87	no	no	no	no	1	85-130
13.100	Santa insert	2.5	no	yes	no	no	2	20-55
13.101a	Santa in rowboat	1.0	no	yes	Eng MI-O	no	1	10-25
13.101b	Santa on rocket	1.75	no	yes	no	no	1	10-25
13.102a	Santa at mailbox	1.5	no	yes	no	no	3	10-25
13.102b	Santa in red car	1.12	no	no	no	no	3	10-25
13.103a	Santa, hands on belt	3.0	no	yes	Japan-bk	no	5	40-65
13.103b	Santa pulling sled	2.0	no	yes	Japan MI-bk	no	4	40-65
14.1a	Dwarf stands, waving	2.87	no	no	no	no	4	45-65
14.1b	Dwarf playing leapfrog	2.62	no	no	Germ-I	no	4	45-65
14.2a	Dwarf stands, waving	3.5	regular	no	no	no	1	150-175
14.2b	Dwarf playing leapfrog	3.37	regular	no	no	no	1	150-175
14.3a	Dwarf holding snowball	1.0	regular	no	no	no	2	65-95
14.3b	Dwarf holding snowball	1.75	no	no	no	2769	4	45-60
14.4a	Dwarf sitting on stump	1.75	no	no	no	no	2	45-65
14.4b	Dwarf carrying bag	2.12	no	no	no	no	2	45-65
14.5	Dwarf lying on side	2.0	no	no	Germ-bk	2757	4	45-65
14.6a	Dwarf lying prone	1.5	no	no	Germ-p	2755	5	45-65
14.6b	Dwarf holding notebook	2.5	no	no	Germ	2766	2	45-65
14.7a	Dwarf sitting	2.25	regular	no	Germ-bk	no	1	85-140
14.7b	Dwarf falling prone	1.62	regular	no	Germ-bk	no	1	85-140
14.8a	Dwarf playing sousaphone	2.25	no	no	Germ-bk	no	4	20-40
14.8b	Dwarf playing saxophone	2.25	no	no	Germ-bk	no	4	20-40
14.8c	Dwarf playing banjo	2.25	no	no	Germ-bk	no	4	20-40
14.8d	Dwarf conductor	2.25	no	no	Germ-bk	no	4	20-40
14.8e	Dwarf playing horn	2.25	no	no	Germ-bk	no	4	20-40
14.8f	Dwarf playing bass	2.25	no	no	Germ-bk	no	4	20-40
14.9a	Dwarf playing violin	2.25	no	yes	no	no	3	20-40
14.9b	Dwarf playing drum	2.0	no	yes	no	no	3	20-40
14.9c	Dwarf playing horn	2.25	no	yes	Germ-p	no	3	20-40
14.9d	Dwarf playing horn	1.87	no	no	no	no	3	20-40
14.10a	Dwarf playing guitar	2.37	no	no	no	no	1	50-90
14.10b	Dwarf playing bass	1.87	no	no	Germ-bk	6023	1	50-90
14.10c	Dwarf playing cymbals	2.37	no	no	Germ-bk	6022	1	50-90
14.11a	Dwarf playing saxophone	1.5	no	no	Germ-bk	6020	1	50-90
14.11b	Dwarf with concertina	1.62	no	no	Germ-bk	6019	1	50-90
14.11c	Dwarf conductor	2.37	no	no	Germ-bk	6021	1	50-90
14.12a	Dwarf kneeling	1.25	no	no	no	6119	4	25-50
14.12b	Dwarf prone	0.75	no	no	Germ-bk	no	4	25-50
14.12c	Dwarf sitting	1.12	no	no	no	6118	4	25-50
14.12d	Dwarf standing	1.87	no	no	no	2635	4	25-50
14.13	Dwarf standing	1.62	regular	no	no	no	2	65-95
14.14	Dwarf with snow shovel	2.25	regular	no	no	13667	1	145-195
14.15a	Dwarf playing drum	1.87	regular	no	Germ-I	5129	2	50-80
14.15b	Dwarf playing bugle	2.0	regular	no	no	no	2	50-80
14.16	Dwarf in big hat	2.0	regular	no	no	6---	1	110-175
14.17	Dwarf in nodder hat	2.0	no	no	no	7658	1	100-175
14.18	2 dwarves dancing	2.12	no	yes	no	no	1	120-175
14.19	2 dwarves on wall	4.0	no	no	no	no	1	85-165
14.20	Dwarf on swing	1.25	no	no	no	no	1	50-85
14.21a	Dwarf lying prone	1.37	no	no	no	no	3	20-40
14.21b	Dwarf sits, waving	1.75	no	no	no	no	3	20-40
14.21c	Dwarf lying on hip	1.62	no	no	no	no	3	20-40
14.22	Dwarf sitting, arms up	1.62	no	no	Germ-bk	no	4	30-50
14.23a	Dwarf on sled	1.5	no	no	no	no	2	40-65
14.23b	Dwarf sitting, arms up	1.25	no	no	no	no	4	20-35
14.24	Dwarf, back arched	2.25	no	no	no	no	1	35-75
14.25a	Long-nosed dwarf	2.12	no	no	no	no	2	50-85
14.25b	Long-nosed dwarf	2.5	no	no	no	no	2	50-85
14.26	Dwarf, bird & egg	1.5	no	no	Germ-bk	4787	1	50-95
14.27	Dwarf with cat	1.87	regular	yes	no	no	1	85-170
14.28a	Dwarf on one elbow	1.37	no	yes	no	6006C	1	30-55
14.28b	Dwarf holding bouquet	1.62	no	yes	no	6006E	1	30-55
14.28c	Dwarf standing	2.37	no	yes	no	6006A	1	30-55
14.28d	Dwarf sitting	1.75	no	yes	no	6006-	1	30-55
14.28e	Dwarf on one foot	2.37	no	yes	no	6006B	1	30-55
14.29b	Dwarf stretching	1.75	no	no	no	no	3	25-45
14.29c	Dwarf sitting on rock	2.0	no	no	no	no	2	25-50
14.30a	Dwarf playing bass	2.12	no	no	Germ-I	18378	1	20-40
14.30b	Dwarf at anvil	1.5	no	yes	GermW-p	no	1	15-35
14.31	Dwarf carrying dwarf	2.37	no	yes	no	no	1	70-155
14.32	Dwarf painting	2.25	no	yes	no	1638	2	50-120
14.33	Dwarf lying on back	0.75	no	no	Germ-bk	no	2	45-155
14.34a	Dwarf on one knee	1.0	no	no	Germ-bk	5148	3	15-30
14.34b	Dwarf squatting	1.0	no	no	no	5150	3	15-30
14.35a	Dwarf on hands & knees	1.62	no	no	Japan-r	no	3	5-15
14.35b	Dwarf, hat hanger	3.0	no	no	Japan-r	no	3	5-15
14.35c	Dwarf, hat hanger	3.0	no	no	Japan-r	no	3	5-15
14.35d	Dwarf, hat hanger	3.0	no	no	Japan-r	no	3	5-15
14.36	Dwarf with knees up	1.25	no	no	no	no	4	20-30
14.37a	Dwarf with long legs	2.12	no	no	Germ-p	no	2	35-65
14.37b	Elf with long legs	2.25	no	no	Germ-I	7294	2	35-65
15.1	Elf & witch at house	2.25	regular	yes	Germ	8398	3	125-200
15.2	2 elves play concertina	1.75	no	yes	Germ-p	732	2	135-185
15.3	2 elves in boat	1.5	no	no	no	7151	2	125-165
15.4	Elf sitting in doghouse	1.37	regular	yes	no	516	1	100-155
15.5a	Elf lying on back	1.12	no	no	no	9708	5	30-55
15.5b	3 elves, arm in arm	1.5	regular	yes	Germ-p	no	4	75-120
15.5c	Elf lying prone	0.87	no	no	Germ-bk	9707	5	30-55
15.6a	Elf standing to listen	2.0	no	yes	no	9706	3	30-65
15.6b	Elf standing to listen	2.0	no	yes	no	9706	2	30-65
15.6c	Elf on mushroom	1.75	no	yes	no	373	1	45-110
15.7	Elf pushing 2 teddies	1.5	no	no	no	5929	1	145-195
15.8	3 elves with Pan figure	2.25	regular	yes	no	314	1	145-195
15.9	2 elves with donkey	2.0	no	yes	no	513	1	135-185
15.10	3 elves on turtle	2.25	no	no	no	741	1	135-185
15.11	Elf with golliwog	1.5	no	yes	no	1177	2	150-210
15.12a	Elf in chariot	1.75	no	yes	no	no	1	125-185
15.12b	Elf riding katydid	2.25	no	yes	no	734	3	125-170
15.13a	Elf with fairy	2.25	no	yes	no	168	1	125-170
15.13b	Little girl fairy	1.87	no	yes	no	9006	2	65-80
15.13c	Fairy in yellow dress	2.5	no	yes	no	no	2	85-145
15.14a	Elf on bell arch	2.5	regular	yes	Germ-p	1628	3	45-90

Table 1

FIG #	BRIEF DESCRIPTION	HT IN	SNOW	BASE	COUNTRY	INCISED	RARE	PRICE
15.14b	2 elf musicians	1.62	no	yes	Germ-bk	no	5	40-65
15.15	Elf sitting with girls	1.75	no	no	no	738	3	65-155
15.16a	2 elves riding horse	2.0	no	no	no	9703	2	135-175
15.16b	Elf riding horse	2.0	no	no	no	735	3	100-150
15.17	Elf playing guitar	2.37	no	yes	no	733	2	110-175
15.18	2 elves in plane	1.5	no	no	no	9709	1	145-210
15.19	Elf with lantern	1.62	no	no	Germ-bk	no	3	20-30
15.20	Elf playing violin	2.75	no	no	no	8427	1	20-45
15.21a	Elf playing saxophone	2.5	no	yes	no	no	4	20-40
15.21b	Elf playing violin	2.75	no	yes	Germ-p	no	4	20-40
15.21c	Elf playing clarinet	2.75	no	yes	Germ-p	no	4	20-40
15.21d	Elf playing trumpet	2.75	no	yes	Germ-p	no	4	20-40
15.21e	Elf conductor	2.75	no	yes	no	no	4	20-40
15.22a	Elf on silver skates	1.75	no	no	Germ-bk	no	2	35-65
15.22b	Elf riding broom	1.87	no	no	no	no	1	35-75
15.23	Elf on sled	1.75	no	no	no	no	2	30-70
15.24a	Elf prone on sled	1.12	no	no	Eng MI	no	2	10-20
15.24b	Elf carrying lantern	1.5	no	yes	Eng MI-O	no	2	10-20
16.1	Bear riding scooter	1.5	regular	no	no	369	2	155-195
16.2	Bear learning to ski	1.5	regular	no	Germ-bk	no	1	155-195
16.3a	Bear with ball	0.5	regular	no	no	no	3	85-135
16.3b	Bear with ball	1.37	regular	no	Germ-bl	no	3	85-135
16.3c	Bear with ball	1.25	regular	no	no	no	3	85-135
16.4	Bear in igloo	1.5	coarse	yes	no	-40-	3	110-140
16.5	Bear climbing igloo	1.75	regular	yes	no	no	1	120-150
16.6	Bear on snowball	3.25	regular	no	no	no	1	105-165
16.7	Bear on snowball	1.37	regular	no	no	no	3	85-120
16.8a	Bear standing on sled	1.87	regular	no	no	no	4	25-45
16.8b	Bear on snowball	1.75	regular	no	no	no	2	65-120
16.9	Bear walking	1.37	regular	no	no	no	1	100-155
16.10a	Bear standing	0.87	regular	no	no	no	4	45-75
16.10b	Bear standing	0.5	regular	no	Germ-bl	no	4	45-75
16.11a	Bear walking	0.62	regular	no	Germ-bk	no	4	50-95
16.11b	Bear sitting	0.87	regular	no	Germ-bl	no	4	50-95
16.11c	Bear lying, stretched	0.87	regular	no	no	no	4	50-95
16.12a	Bear walking	0.62	brown	no	no	no	1	80-135
16.12b	Bear standing	0.75	brown	no	Germ-bk	no	1	80-135
16.12c	Bear sitting	0.87	brown	no	no	no	1	80-135
16.13a	Bear laughing	1.12	regular	no	no	no	1	50-90
16.13b	Bear laughing	1.62	regular	no	no	no	1	50-90
16.13c	Bear laughing	1.25	regular	no	no	no	1	50-90
16.14	Bear, paws on sled	1.87	regular	no	no	no	1	100-145
16.15a	Bear standing	2.25	regular	no	no	no	3	40-85
16.15b	Bear standing	2.25	regular	no	no	no	3	40-85
16.15c	Bear standing	2.5	regular	no	Germ-bk	no	2	75-115
16.15d	Bear walking	2.12	regular	no	no	no	1	75-110
16.16a	Bear standing	1.75	regular	no	Japan	no	4	60-75
16.16b	Bear stands, begging	1.62	regular	no	no	no	4	25-40
16.16c	Bear standing	1.37	regular	no	Germ-bk	no	5	75-95
16.17a	Bear walking	1.62	coarse	no	no	no	4	20-30
16.17b	Bear walking	1.25	regular	no	Germ	no	3	75-110
16.17c	Bear walking	1.12	regular	no	Japan-bk	no	5	45-65
16.18	Bear sliding on back	1.87	regular	no	Japan-l	5900	4	60-95
16.19	Bear on sled	1.25	regular	no	no	no	3	45-60
16.20a	Bear standing	0.87	no	no	no	no	1	25-35
16.20b	Bear lying down	0.75	no	no	no	no	1	25-35
16.20c	Mother bear	1.12	no	no	no	no	1	35-45
16.21	Bear sitting	2.37	crystal	no	no	no	1	40-70
16.22	China bear	3.37	no	no	Heubach-b	no	1	150-225
16.23	3 bear musicians	2.12	regular	yes	no	no	1	185-270
16.24a	Bear playing hockey	1.5	regular	no	no	3649	1	55-85
16.24b	Bear boxing	1.5	regular	no	no	3647	1	55-85
16.24c	Bear playing tennis	1.5	regular	no	Germ-l	no	1	55-85
16.24d	Bear playing soccer	1.5	regular	no	Germ-l	no	1	55-85
16.25	Bear with blue scarf	1.75	regular	no	no	no	2	85-145
16.26	Bear with blue tie	2.62	no	yes	Germ	no	2	85-145
16.27	Bear in snow dome	2.75	no	yes	Germ-l	no	1	125-175
16.28	3 penguin musicians	2.0	no	yes	no	no	1	140-190
16.29	Penguin pushing twins	1.62	no	yes	Germ-bk	no	1	110-155
16.30	Penguin pushing cart	1.5	no	yes	Germ-bk	no	1	100-135
16.31a	3 penguins walking	1.75	no	no	no	no	3	30-45
16.31b	Fat penguin standing	2.25	regular	no	no	no	3	65-95
16.31c	3 penguins on slope	2.12	no	no	Germ-bk	no	3	35-65
16.32	Penguin on skis	2.0	regular	no	no	no	2	100-135
16.33	2 penguins on wedge	2.5	coarse	no	no	no	5	20-35
16.34	2 dogs at doghouse	1.5	regular	yes	no	382	3	75-115
16.35	Husky on base	1.12	regular	yes	no	no	2	60-90
16.36	Husky sitting	1.12	regular	no	no	no	3	55-80
16.37a	Bonzo on skis	2.0	regular	no	Germ-p	no	2	175-195
16.37b	Pig on skis	2.0	regular	no	no	no	2	175-195
16.37c	Elephant on skis	2.25	regular	no	Germ-p	no	2	175-195
16.38	Cat pushing sled	1.75	no	no	Germ-bk	no	1	140-180
16.39a	Bird on stump	2.87	no	yes	no	no	3	8-15
16.39b	2 robins on fence	2.0	regular	yes	no	6003	3	60-115
16.40	English letter box	2.0	no	no	no	no	2	5-15
16.41a	Robins on springs	2.25	no	yes	GermUS Z-bk	no	4	20-35
16.41b	Robin on spring	2.37	glitter	yes	Germ-bk	no	2	25-35
16.42	Chelsea sheep	1.25	regular	no	no	no	4	60-110
16.43a	Rabbit sitting up	1.0	no	no	Germ-l	no	2	10-20
16.43b	Rabbit sitting down	0.75	no	no	no	no	2	10-20
16.43c	Rabbit sitting up	1.12	no	no	no	966	2	10-20
16.43d	Rabbit sitting down	0.87	no	no	Germ-l	489	2	10-20
16.44a	Sheep lying down	1.25	no	no	Germ-l	786	4	25-35
16.44b	Ram lying down	0.75	no	no	Germ-l	SP 786	4	10-20
16.44c	Sheep lying down	0.75	no	no	no	968	4	10-20
16.44d	Sheep lying down	0.75	no	no	Germ-l	SP 786	4	10-20
16.45	Pip, Squeak, Wilford	1.75	no	yes	no	no	2	125-185
16.46a	Pig on sled	1.25	no	no	no	no	1	45-85
16.46b	Wilford	2.0	no	no	no	no	2	30-45
16.47a	Cartoon dog	1.12	regular	no	no	no	4	40-55
16.47b	Cat on four feet	0.87	regular	no	no	no	4	40-55
16.47c	Cartoon cat	1.25	regular	no	Germ-p	no	4	40-55
16.48	Monkey	1.12	no	no	Japan-r	no	5	5-20
16.49	Comic bear sitting	2.0	crystal	no	Japan MI-r	no	5	10-35
17.1	Snowman sitting	2.12	regular	no	Germ-l	69--	3	100-155
17.2a	Snowman, tennis racket	1.75	regular	no	Germ-p	no	2	110-140
17.2b	Snowman lying on side	1.5	regular	no	Germ-p	no	3	75-110
17.3a	Snowman sits, winking	1.25	regular	no	Germ-bk	no	5	30-60
17.3b	Snowman sitting	1.25	regular	no	no	no	4	30-60
17.4	Snowman & bear cub	1.62	regular	no	Germ-bk	no	2	90-155
17.5	2 snowmen and bear	2.12	regular	yes	no	no	2	120-160
17.6	Snowman and rabbit	2.0	regular	yes	Germ-p	no	1	120-160
17.7a	Snowman, WC Fields	1.62	regular	no	Japan	no	5	25-40
17.7b	Snowman with cigar	1.75	regular	no	Germ-bk	no	5	30-55
17.8a	Snowman traffic cop	2.75	regular	no	Japan-bk	no	4	30-55
17.8b	Snowman sitting	2.0	regular	no	Japan-bk	no	4	30-55
17.9a	Snowman sitting asleep	1.5	regular	no	no	no	3	55-85
17.9b	Snowman sitting	1.5	regular	no	no	no	3	55-85
17.9c	Snowman lying down	1.5	regular	no	no	no	3	55-85
17.10a	Snowman with broom	2.12	no	no	no	7305	2	45-60
17.10b	Snowman with red hat	2.0	no	no	no	10295	2	45-60
17.11a	Snowman conductor	2.37	no	no	no	no	1	45-80
17.11b	Snowman clarinet	2.25	no	no	GermW-p	no	1	45-80
17.11c	Snowman playing banjo	2.25	no	no	Germ-p	no	1	45-80
17.11d	Snowman playing violin	2.25	no	no	no	no	1	45-80
17.12	Fluorescent snowman	2.75	no	no	no	no	1	20-40
17.13	Snow dome snowman	2.5	regular	yes	no	no	3	20-55
17.14a	Snow dome snowman	1.5	no	yes	no	no	3	15-35
17.14b	Snowman holding pipe	2.5	regular	yes	Germ-l	no	1	85-130
17.15	Snowman dancing	1.75	glitter	yes	Germ-p	no	4	5-10
17.16a	Snowman with boy	2.75	no	no	no	no	3	15-30
17.16b	Santa on roof	2.62	no	no	Japan-l	no	3	15-30
17.16c	Snowman with child	2.25	no	yes	Japan-l	no	3	15-30
18.1a	School house	2.0	regular	no	no	no	2	50-70
18.1b	Red brick house	1.87	regular	no	no	no	2	50-70
18.2	2 story house	2.87	regular	no	no	9779	2	50-65
18.3a	House	2.37	regular	no	Germ-p	no	2	50-65
18.3b	Long house with arch	2.37	regular	no	no	9417	1	60-80
18.4	Inn with stagecoach	1.87	regular	yes	no	no	1	60-130
18.5	Church	2.25	regular	yes	no	6003	1	70-90
18.6a	House with trees	1.62	coralene	no	no	no	2	55-65
18.6b	Church	2.5	coralene	no	no	-6--	2	60-70
18.7	House with trees	1.5	regular	no	no	no	1	55-65
18.8a	House with gold snow	1.5	gold	yes	no	5825	3	50-65
18.8b	House with gold trees	1.5	gold	yes	no	no	3	50-65
18.9a	House with gold windows	1.62	no	no	no	no	3	30-45
18.9b	House with red roof	1.5	no	no	no	no	3	30-45
18.10	Church	3.62	no	no	Japan MI-l	no	3	10-15
18.11a	Church	2.25	no	no	Japan-l	no	3	5-12
18.11b	2 story house	2.12	no	no	Japan-l	no	2	5-12
18.12a	Pink house	1.75	no	no	no	no	2	5-12
18.12b	Yellow house	1.75	no	no	Japan	no	2	10-15
18.13a	Orange house	1.12	no	no	no	no	2	35-45
18.13b	Orange house	1.25	no	no	no	no	2	45-60
18.13c	Mill with waterwheel	1.25	no	no	no	no	2	5-10
18.14	House with bird	2.75	glitter	yes	Germ-bk	no	4	45-65
18.15	Church, white	1.25	no	no	Eng MI-bk	no	2	5-15
18.16	House with Santa	1.37	glitter	yes	Germ-bk	no	1	35-65
18.17	Church with Santa	2.0	glitter	yes	Japan-p	no	3	10-30
19.2a	Girl skier	4.0	no	yes	Japan-l	no	3	5-15
19.2b	Girl skier	3.0	no	yes	Japan-l	no	3	5-15
19.3a	Boy skier	4.0	no	yes	Japan-l	no	3	5-15
19.3b	Boy skier	3.0	no	yes	Japan-l	no	3	5-15
19.4	Boy plays leapfrog	5.5	no	yes	no	no	3	5-15
19.6	2 baby huggers	1.75	no	no	no	no	5	8-12
19.8	Music box baby	7.0	no	no	Dept 56-l	no	1	700-900

Table 2: Incised numbers

Table 2

INCISED NUMBERS

This table includes only the bisque snow baby pieces with incised numbers. It is sorted to present the pieces in ascending order of their numbers. If you have pieces with incised numbers that are not shown in the book, they may fit into sequence with some that do appear in this table.

NUMBER	BRIEF DESCRIPTION	HEIGHT	FIG #	NUMBER	BRIEF DESCRIPTION	HEIGHT	FIG #
0	Jointed bear	3.25	6.10	1181	Baby playing drum	2.0	10.64c
2	Jointed baby	2.87	6.1a	1182	Baby playing fife	2.0	10.64b
2	Elastic jointed baby	4.0	6.2a	1183	Baby playing saxophone	2.0	10.65c
2	Jointed baby	4.0	6.2b	1184	Baby playing tuba	2.0	10.65a
3	Jointed baby	4.75	6.3	1185	Baby playing concertina	2.0	10.65b
4	Jointed baby	5.25	6.1b	1188	Baby playing hockey	1.87	10.33b
5	Angione jointed bear	6.0	6.8	1221	Baby on sled	1.62	10.55a
7	Girl astride sled	1.5	10.104c	1456	Nodders on skis	3.5	6.12a
10	Boy with boat	3.5	3.11	1456	Jointed boy skier	5.37	6.6
16	Girl on short skis	6.0	7.20	1628	Elf on bell arch	2.5	15.14a
16	Boy on short skis	5.75	7.19	1636	Baby on raft	2.5	10.35d
19	Boy with jointed arms	4.25	6.5a	1638	Dwarf painting	2.25	14.32
28	Child, cornucopia	4.62	3.8	1649	2 babies carrying bear	1.87	10.3
32	Girl in ermine	3.12	3.1	1699	Baby on airplane	1.75	10.48a
42	Girl in shawl	4.0	3.5	2236	2 children on sled	1.62	10.94a
43	Boy in coat, top hat	5.25	3.6	2266	Couple on sled	8.0	7.29
52	Girl sitting	3.12	3.4	2293	Baby kicking ball	2.25	10.34b
67	Boy & girl swingers	6.0	3.13	2294	Santa on sled	1.37	13.33
89	Santa holding signboard	3.75	13.2	2364	Baby feeding seal	2.0	10.21
168	Elf with fairy	2.25	15.13a	2365	Baby hugging penguin	2.0	10.25a
314	3 elves with Pan figure	2.25	15.8	2366	Baby with seal and ball	2.0	10.22a
338	2 babies skiing	2.37	10.54	2635	Dwarf standing	1.87	14.12d
347	Baby on reindeer	2.62	10.17	2702	Baby on ice house	2.0	10.1
365	Santa standing by pack	2.12	13.43	2711	2 children skating	2.12	10.125b
367	3 babies on bear	1.75	10.16	2714	2 babies dancing	2.0	10.39a
369	Bear riding scooter	1.5	16.1	2718	Baby holding ball	1.62	10.34a
370	Bear pulling baby	1.62	10.8b	2724	Santa with 2 babies	2.0	13.35b
371	2 babies with bear	1.62	10.8a	2755	Dwarf lying prone	1.5	14.6a
373	Elf on mushroom	1.75	15.6c	2757	Dwarf lying on side	2.0	14.5
377	Santa on stagecoach	1.75	13.78	2766	Dwarf holding notebook	2.5	14.6b
378	Baby and bear	1.87	10.5	2769	Dwarf holding snowball	1.75	14.3b
379	Santa, gold bell	2.37	13.10	2773	3 babies form tower	2.0	10.78
381	3 male carolers	2.25	11.5b	2865	Dog licking baby	2.0	10.20
382	2 dogs at doghouse	1.5	16.34	2867	Baby at canoe	2.0	10.35c
457-I	2 children on sled	3.0	9.18	2938	Child on bear	4.12	10.14b
460	Boy on gold skates	2.0	10.124a	2938	Child on bear	4.12	10.14a
460	Girl on gold skates	2.0	10.123b	3197	Girl on skis	4.75	7.16
460	Girl on gold skates	2.0	10.124b	3200	Girl on sled	3.75	7.17
461	Boy on gold skates	2.12	10.123a	3204	Boy on skis	4.25	7.14
461	Girl on gold skates	2.0	10.125a	3482	Dwarf candleholder	1.0	7.47
489	Rabbit sitting down	0.87	16.43d	3483	Dwarf, hands on knees	1.25	7.48a
506	Santa in sailboat	2.0	13.70	3484	Dwarf standing	1.37	7.48b
506N	Baby card holder	1.87	5.18	3485	Dwarf with legs apart	1.25	7.48c
507	Santa giving doll	2.12	13.38	3488	Baby skiing, red shoes	2.87	10.132b
508	Horse pulling Santa	1.87	13.30	3516	Baby sledder	3.0	10.132c
510	Santa on stagecoach	1.62	13.79	3647	Bear boxing	1.5	16.24b
511	Santa with girl	2.25	13.40a	3649	Bear playing hockey	1.5	16.24a
513	2 elves with donkey	2.0	15.9	3978	Boy on sled	3.62	8.23
514	2 babies on tank	2.25	10.49	4013	Girl on sled	6.5	7.9
515	Penguin pushing	1.62	10.27	4194	Girl with dulcimer	3.5	2.8
516	Elf sitting in doghouse	1.37	15.4	4194	Girl with muff	4.0	2.7
657	Santa sitting	1.0	7.57a	4284	Small plain Santa	1.5	13.3d
730	Doe pulling Santa	2.5	13.27	4479	Bust of boy	4.0	2.10
731	Santa in train	1.87	13.69	4513	Santa on sled	2.0	13.34
732	2 elves play concertina	1.75	15.2	4563	5 school children	7.0	2.3
733	Elf playing guitar	2.37	15.17	4584	Girl & coins, standing	7.5	2.12
734	Elf riding katydid	2.25	15.12b	4584	Girl & coins, standing	7.5	2.13
735	Elf riding horse	2.0	15.16b	4603	3 school children	6.0	2.2
738	Elf sitting with girls	1.75	15.15	4612	Boy on sled	8.0	7.3
741	Elf nodder	2.62	6.15	4614	Children carrying milk	4.87	2.1
741	3 elves on turtle	2.25	15.10	4628	3 children on sled	6.25	7.2
748	Santa nodder	3.5	6.14b	4639	Angel sitting	1.12	7.58d
758	Santa by baby's bed	2.12	13.39	4640	Angel standing	1.5	7.58a
763	Striped cuff skier	2.5	10.138a	4641	Girl sitting on sled	1.75	10.108b
763	Girl skier	2.5	10.138b	4642	Boy on back on sled	1.62	10.108a
786	Sheep lying down	1.25	16.44a	4642	Angel sitting	1.0	7.58b
869	Santa with 2 children	2.25	13.42	4645	Boy holding beer stein	4.25	2.20
877	Santa on motorcycle	2.12	13.66	4646	Angel lying	0.87	7.58c
966	Rabbit sitting up	1.12	16.43c	4647	Girl & coins, sitting	3.5	2.11
968	Sheep lying down	0.75	16.44c	4653	Children and snowball	6.5	2.9
1177	Elf with golliwog	1.5	15.11	4656	Girl on skis	4.87	2.17
1180	Baby holding skis	1.75	10.4b	4656	Boy on skis	5.0	2.16
1180	Baby band conductor	2.0	10.64a	4656	Girl on skis	4.87	2.15

TABLE 2 INCISED NUMBERS

NUMBER	BRIEF DESCRIPTION	HEIGHT	FIG #	NUMBER	BRIEF DESCRIPTION	HEIGHT	FIG #
4657	Boy carrying sled	5.25	2.18	8266	Reindeer pulling Santa	2.25	13.21
4664	Boy & umbrella	3.75	2.14a	8268	Helmeted girl on sled	2.37	5.14
4664	Girl & umbrella	3.62	2.14b	8395	Reindeer pulling Santa	2.25	13.23b
4696	Santa in yellow car	1.62	13.63	8398	Elf & witch at house	2.25	15.1
4705	Boy and girl with sled	3.62	2.6	8427	Elf playing violin	2.75	15.20
4714	3 children on sled	3.5	2.5	8433	Santa with lantern	3.0	13.7d
4787	Dwarf, bird & egg	1.5	14.26	8434	Santa with white cane	2.37	13.4b
4837	Girl with cape, dog	4.25	2.19	8446	Girl sitting on sled	1.25	10.115b
4881	Boy skier waving	1.75	10.131b	8447	Girl lying on sled	1.62	10.115a
4882	Girl kneeling on sled	1.75	10.104a	8448	Girl prone on sled	1.62	10.115c
4883	Girl standing on sled	2.25	10.104b	8461	3 Italian carolers	2.0	11.2a
4924	Child in bear suit	7.0	8.25b	8516	Fallen girl skater	1.25	9.15a
4925	Child in bear suit	4.12	8.25a	8535	Boy carrying sled	4.5	7.11
5010	Baby pushing baby	2.25	10.90	8550	Girl on skis	5.0	7.13
5010	Baby pushing baby	2.25	10.91	8607	Competition skier	2.75	12.19
5012	Boy throwing snowball	1.87	10.125c	8721	Girl on sled	2.25	10.101a
5106	3 babies on sled	1.62	10.85a	8721	Boy on sled	2.25	10.101b
5107	2 babies on sled	1.75	10.88	8912	Girl skiing	5.75	8.26
5114	Baby skier	1.75	10.129b	9006	Little girl fairy	1.87	15.13b
5115	Baby skating	1.62	10.129a	9056	Santa on motorcycle	2.12	13.65
5117	Baby, silver skates	1.25	10.128	9224	Boy with metal sled	4.25	8.1
5119	Baby crawling onto sled	1.5	10.109a	9417	Long house with arch	2.37	18.3b
5120	Baby sitting on sled	1.75	10.109c	9439	Large Cook and Peary	4.37	1.1a
5121	Baby sitting on sled	1.75	10.109b	9439	No-snow Cook and Peary	3.5	1.2
5129	Dwarf playing drum	1.87	14.15a	9447	Small Cook and Peary	3.5	1.1b
5130	Baby lying on sled	2.0	10.99a	9469	Striped cuff skier	2.75	10.139b
5136	Santa with tree	2.0	13.4a	9470	Striped cuff skier	2.75	10.139a
5148	Dwarf on one knee	1.0	14.34a	9650	Santa on camel	2.62	13.50a
5150	Dwarf squatting	1.0	14.34b	9688	Santa reading paper	2.37	13.85
5299	Baby pushing baby	1.62	10.89a	9692	Santa on elephant	2.37	13.50b
5401	Santa on swing	3.0	13.9	9695	Santa in train	1.62	13.67
5569	Peary mug	4.37	1.4	9696	Santa, donkey cart	1.75	13.28
5617	2 babies on globe	3.25	10.44	9699	3 male carolers	1.87	11.5a
5714/4/0	Boy skier on wedge	2.25	10.133	9700	3 carolers	2.25	11.3b
5714/6/0	Boy pulling sled	2.37	10.107	9703	2 elves riding horse	2.0	15.16a
5803	Dwarf on one knee	1.12	7.49a	9706	Elf standing to listen	2.0	15.6b
5806	Dwarf lying down	0.75	7.49c	9706	Elf standing to listen	2.0	15.6a
5825	House with gold snow	1.5	18.8a	9707	Elf lying prone	0.87	15.5c
5855	Bear pulling cart	1.75	7.34	9708	Elf lying on back	1.12	15.5a
5866	Man skater	2.12	12.17b	9709	2 elves in plane	1.5	15.18
5866	Woman skater	2.12	12.17a	9774	Round-headed baby	2.5	10.160c
5891	Girl sitting on sled	2.5	10.106b	9779	2 story house	2.87	18.2
5891	Boy sitting on sled	2.5	10.106a	9885	Bear carrying skis	7.75	8.27
5900	Bear sliding on back	1.87	16.18	9916	Baby sitting	3.12	8.8a
5929	Elf pushing 2 teddies	1.5	15.7	9916	Baby sitting	3.12	8.8b
5959	Santa pushing buggy	1.75	13.44	10295	Snowman with red hat	2.0	17.10b
6003	2 robins on fence	2.0	16.39b	11796	Girl on skis	7.75	7.21
6003	Church	2.25	18.5	11796	Boy on skis	7.75	7.22
6006A	Dwarf standing	2.37	14.28c	11905	Girl skating	2.25	10.121b
6006B	Dwarf on one foot	2.37	14.28e	11963	Snowman sitting	1.25	7.57b
6006C	Dwarf on one elbow	1.37	14.28a	12056	Boy skier on mound	2.75	10.134a
6006E	Dwarf holding bouquet	1.62	14.28b	12057	Girl skier on mound	2.87	10.134b
6006-	Dwarf sitting	1.75	14.28d	13667	Dwarf with snow shovel	2.25	14.14
6019	Dwarf with concertina	1.62	14.11b	14824	2 adults on toboggan	2.0	12.18
6020	Dwarf playing saxophone	1.5	14.11a	17682	Eskimo father	1.87	10.182a
6021	Dwarf conductor	2.37	14.11c	17682	Eskimo summer home	2.87	10.182e
6022	Dwarf playing cymbals	2.37	14.10c	17682	Eskimo mother	1.75	10.182d
6023	Dwarf playing bass	1.87	14.10b	18378	Dwarf playing bass	2.12	14.30a
6080	Small plain Santa	2.25	13.3c	F0656	Plaid shirt skier	3.25	12.14
6118	Dwarf sitting	1.12	14.12c	K89	Woman sledder	2.75	12.10b
6119	Dwarf kneeling	1.25	14.12a	K90	Woman sledder	2.87	12.11
6140	Santa walking Westie	3.25	13.57	K92	Woman sledder	3.0	12.10a
6141	Santa on sled	3.0	13.58	K93	Woman holding skis	3.5	12.9b
6142	Santa on moose	3.12	13.56	K94	Kneeling woman skier	2.0	12.9c
6602	2 babies on wall	1.5	10.50	K95	Woman skier	3.25	12.9a
6627	Child-faced snowman	11.0	7.8	LH 376	Santa with basket	2.5	13.5a
6695	Santa on roof	2.25	13.82a	MK943	Skier squatting	5.0	7.38
6697	Santa on airplane	1.5	13.74	SP 786	Sheep lying down	0.75	16.44d
6698	Santa on sled	2.25	13.18	SP 786	Ram lying down	0.75	16.44b
6699	Reindeer pulling Santa	1.75	13.23a	S/095	Santa, braid on coat	3.5	13.16a
6712	3 singing babies	1.75	10.142	6---	Dwarf in big hat	2.0	14.16
6969	Whistling boy	6.0	7.5	69--	Snowman sitting	2.12	17.1
7151	2 elves in boat	1.5	15.3	-40-	Bear in igloo	1.5	16.4
7152	Santa in motorboat	1.62	13.72	-6--	Church	2.5	18.6b
7153	2 huskies pulling baby	1.37	10.28	--38	Child-faced snowman	4.5	7.6a
7154	Huskies pulling Santa	1.62	13.29				
7155	Santa on cracker	1.75	13.31				
7156	Mother pushing twins	2.5	10.76				
7294	Elf with long legs	2.25	14.37b				
7305	Snowman with broom	2.12	17.10a				
7476	3 child carolers	2.25	11.1a				
7658	Dwarf in nodder hat	2.0	14.17				
8113	Child on sled	1.87	10.105				
8187	Boy prone	1.12	10.152				
8195	Baby sitting on sled	2.25	9.13				
8263	Girl sitting on sled	3.0	5.15				